The Making of an Ethnic Middle Class

The Making of
an Ethnic Middle Class

PORTLAND JEWRY OVER FOUR GENERATIONS

William Toll

STATE UNIVERSITY OF NEW YORK PRESS

Albany

Published by
State University of New York Press, Albany

© 1982 State University of New York

Printed in the United States of America

For information, address State University of New York Press, State University Plaza, Albany, N.Y., 12246

Library of Congress Cataloging in Publication Data

Toll, William.
    The making of an ethnic middle class.

    1. Jews—Oregon—Portland—History. 2. Middle
classes—Oregon—Portland. 3. Portland (Or.)—Ethnic
relations. I. Title.
F884.P89J57   305.8'924'079549   82-655
ISBN 0-87395-609-5   AACR2
ISBN 0-87395-610-9 (pbk.)

To my grandmothers
Rivka Brodsky and Bessie Toll
who, from the Russian debris, made new lives in America

Contents

Figures

Illustrations

Tables

Acknowledgments

My initial venture into American Jewish History has had many rewards. First, I have had the assistance of many women and men at archives and libraries who have been as eager to understand the past as I have been to uncover its documentary clues. They include Nathan Kaganoff and especially Nehemiah Ben-Zev of the American Jewish Historical Society, who assisted me with the Stephen Wise and the Industrial Removal Office papers. At the Western Jewish Historical Society in Berkeley, Suzanne Nemiroff and Ruth Rafael helped locate and often sent material to me pertinent to Portland Jewry. At the American Jewish Archives in Cincinnati, Fanny Zelcer, in her customary cheery manner, assisted me; her staff was also most cooperative. Philip Zorich, formerly at the Oregon Collection of the University of Oregon, has helped locate manuscripts, made city directories available "after hours," and followed this study with unusual interest. I gratefully acknowledge the prodding of the late Martin Schmitt, former curator of manuscripts at the Oregon Collection, whose plea that material on the state's social history was not being utilized first led me to consider this study. Finally, to Shirley Tanzer and her colleagues—especially Eva Carr, Michelle Glazer, Mollie Blumenthal, and Ruth Semler—at the Oregon Jewish Historical Society in Portland, I owe a debt that can never be repaid. Not only did they make available the institutional records that provide much of the documentation for this study, but they collected, transcribed, and photocopied for my use dozens of oral histories, which add corroborative evidence and vital details. Without them I could not have integrated social patterns with individual lives. In this regard, a special debt is owed by all students of Jewish history in the West to a man who devoted so much of his time to gathering material and making it available to others, the late Robert Levinson of San Jose State University. Himself a native Portlander, he induced many organizations to place their records in the Oregon Collection and especially in the Magnes Museum in Berkeley, where scholars can now consult them. I wish also to thank Liisa Fagerlund, archivist of the City of Portland for guidance through

1

public documents. The staff at the Oregon Historical Society provided many of the photographs that are included. Karen Yoerger of Eugene has prepared the maps.

This study was made possible by a generous grant from the National Endowment for the Humanities under their program in State, Local and Regional History. Grant Number RS–32429–78–1529 has supported my research, and that of Mrs. Tanzer, from July 1979 through September 1980. I hope the results have fulfilled the promise that the directors of the Endowment saw in the initial proposal. During the research and writing of this book I have been able to cultivate a new circle of colleagues whose support has come to mean a great deal to me. They have given generously of their critical judgment to improve my understanding of this subject and of the craft of social history. I wish to thank particularly Moses Rischin, Marc Lee Raphael, Norris Hundley, and the late Robert Levinson for their patience and their excitement over the work we are doing together. I also wish to thank editors of journals for permission to use certain material, which, in somewhat different form, appeared there. Portions of Chapter 1 appeared in the *Pacific Historical Review*. Portions of Chapter 4 pertaining to the B'nai B'rith appeared in the *Western Historical Quarterly*. Portions of Chapters 2 and 4 appeared in *American Jewish History*, published by the American Jewish Historical Society, Waltham, Massachusetts.

For his hospitality and warm interest I owe a special debt to Herschal Tanzer of Portland, Oregon. For their general support, good humor, and fellowship I will always be grateful to Barbara and Daniel Pope, George Sheridan, Jonathan Sarna, and Val Lorwin. My mother, Mrs. Sylvia Toll of Philadelphia, must also understand the significance of this study to me.

William Toll

Eugene, Oregon

Introduction: Social Process and Ethnic Identity, A Complex Relationship

Until recently, studies of ethnic communities in America have been largely filio–pietistic in tone and antiquarian in method. However, the celebration of individual achievements and the growth of institutions that assured the second generation that they and their parents deserved the new freedoms of America, failed to explain to their more secure descendants why particular ethnic enclaves occupied their respective places in the American class structure. A new social history focusing on the relationship of groups to one another has required a more critical analysis of social organization and economic opportunity. A comparative method had to be devised to explain the relationship of groups to one another. The focus had to be shifted from extraordinary individuals to those patterns of social adjustment in the lives of ordinary people that shaped the community over the generations. Pioneering studies by Stephen Thernstrom, Howard Chudakoff, and others of occupational, residential, and property "mobility" for several ethnic groups in single cities were complemented by more intensive studies of groups like Italians, Poles, Croats, and Germans in cities as diverse as Chicago, Cleveland, Milwaukee, New York, San Francisco, and Steelton, Pennsylvania.[1] Since the mid-1960s a large body of specialized literature on specific ethnic groups and on the process of social change has accumulated.

Nevertheless, as several scholars have emphasized, social change can be a slow and complex process, with cultural *continuity* often making changes in occupation, living arrangements, and institutions possible. The studies of Herbert Gutman, Josef Barton, and Virginia Yans McLoughlin, especially, have demonstrated how work traditions and extended family networks have eased the transition of craftsman and peasant into industrial society.[2] However, no study of the modernization of an ethnic enclave with predominantly

3

mercantile and craft background has been undertaken, and no study has linked changes in the activities of women as well as of men to new patterns of institutional organization.[3] Furthermore, the Pacific Northwest as a region has received very little attention as an area of urban growth.[4] The Jewish community of Portland, Oregon, therefore, seemed an ideal ethnic enclave in which to examine the relationship between cultural continuity and social change for families of mercantile and craft traditions who migrated, over several generations, from very different cultural backgrounds. Though the enclave may have appeared to outsiders as a group held together by a distinctive religion, it consisted of several very different segments. Indeed, the changing relationship between these segments over several generations helps to illustrate how Portland Jewry converged toward a modern middle class.

This study suggests that several assumptions about the sources of social and cultural changes should be reexamined. Most studies of modernization have emphasized how men at work shifted their sense of time from a steady round regulated by nature to a new routine regulated by the tick of a rational clock, while family life seemed to proceed with much less innovation.[5] For Portland Jewry, however, virtually the reverse occurred. While men reconstructed mercantile roles in the sparsely settled region, their family life underwent dramatic change. Extended families of varying composition organized both migration and resettlement, but the lives of women and their roles in organizing the new community underwent much more dramatic change over several generations than did the lives of men. The implications for contemporary relations between men and women are not drawn out in this study, but the relationship between work, social activity, and family organization has over three or four generations worked a revolution in the way Jews as Americans perceive themselves.

In the literature examining social mobility and cultural modernization, there has also been an implicit conflict between those who have examined aggregate patterns of change and those who have studied the cultural traditions of labor. The application of a single measure of change, for example, has suggested that some groups have "succeeded" while others have stagnated. Scholars who have emphasized gradual cultural transition, however, indicate that many men and women have not desired occupations drastically different from those of their parents or friends.[6] In this case, scholars must determine the mechanisms by which initial types of labor were chosen and the way newcomers were directed to the same or similar work. Likewise, the means by which men, women, and families were sustained during crises or assisted to improve their position has not been very carefully examined in most "mobility" studies. For Portland Jewry, as for many other groups, the voluntary asssociations and kinship networks became crucial in explaining how and why mobility of various sorts occurred, and why other patterns did not emerge. Whereas traditional studies of Jewish and other ethnic communities have mentioned the roles of benevolent associations and lodges, efforts to utilize membership rolls in conjunction with patterns of individual mobility have generally not been undertaken.[7] Here, however, such patterns seemed crucial for explaining both economic and cultural change. Through an assessment of the changing composition and functions of these organizations, analyses of cultural continuity and social mobility have been more easily integrated.

In addition, voluntary associations have helped explain how ethnic enclaves were related to the evolution of the body politic. As Dean Esslinger, Peter Decker, and, especially, Don Doyle have recently shown, fraternal lodges, volunteer fire companies, and even vigilance committees have seen themselves as part of the civic order.[8] In an era when political parties were themselves considered private organizations, and when government performed relatively few functions, the ordering of society was considered a matter for scrutiny by one's colleagues, with government considered a last resort. Social order was preserved as much by fraternal lodges and benevolent societies as by the police. For Portland Jewry, the same was true for women as for men, although women, of course, were denied access to formal political procedures. Studies of "voting behavior," therefore, reveal very little about the political interests or consciousness of nineteenth-century ethnic groups, because most of their problems were defined and managed within the confines of their own institutions. Their organizations, in turn, contributed equally with the organizations of other groups to maintain social control and civic orderliness. Although many Portland Jewish men participated actively in politics and several were elected mayor, their daily contribution to civic order came by regulating one another's lives through voluntary associations. By tracing changes in the membership and functions of these associations, we can understand how Jews over several generations perceived changes in their relationship to the political system.

Portland, though remote from the major population centers, also demonstrated a remarkable similarity—in patterns of settlement, mobility, and institutional variation—to other Jewish communities that have recently been studied. The community, however, is not so much representative of Jewish settlement in America as simply another locus in a vast network of Jewish traders carrying out traditional functions. A Jewish community was founded in the remote reaches of the Pacific Northwest only shortly after communities of similar structure and sophistication developed in Eastern cities like Syracuse, New York; Columbus, Ohio; and even Boston.[9] The Jews of Portland had friends and relatives in those locales, as they did in the larger cities of the Pacific Slope and in New York. A mercantile people scattered in order to persist in its functions, just as miners and industrial workers clustered because their labor required intensive gathering rather than extensive communication. American farmers, in turn, followed trade routes to reestablish agricultural traditions.[10] German and Polish Jews in Portland were not so much encountering unusual opportunities—as was the case for the handful of Irish who arrived in San Jose in the 1850s compared with the Irish who remained in Boston.[11] Instead, the wandering young Jewish men were following to their logical geographic limits the desire to stake out traditional trading services. They moved back and forth between Portland, the Oregon and Washington hinterland, San Francisco, and New York to complete transactions. Only at a later stage in their life cycle would they settle permanently in one city or another.

The question of periodization or the establishment of appropriate chronological divisions and limits for this study also arose. A logical beginning seemed to be the moment when Jews began to arrive in Portland, or perhaps the moment at which records of such arrivals began to be kept. Many studies of ethnic communities have tried to determine when the first ancestor arrived, partially for accuracy and partially to establish proper credentials for claiming a place of honor in the hagiography of a city. Other studies have tried to bring the chronology as close to the present as possible or have selected a dramatic moment in the history of the nation or of the locale, which had an impact on the ethnic community. For immigrant communities this historic moment has often been World War I, when the nation as a whole faced momentous mobilization, which set patterns of internal migration in motion and which also ended massive foreign immigration. Other studies have ended with the onset of the Depression of the 1930s, though with no clear explanation of why that domestic catastrophe should have provided a logical termination date. Because I have been most concerned with setting Portland Jewry into the larger network of Jewish communal growth, and because I have been most interested in the process of change over generations rather than individual achievements, I have somewhat modified the periodization. I have not been concerned with the arrival in Portland of the first Jew—whoever he or she may have been—as with the emergence of a recognizable pattern of stability. This seems to have occured within ten years of the origins of Portland as a trading center. Because I have also tried to trace the changing place of Jews in Portland's class structure, I have tried to identify the moments when the class position of the Jews became clear, or when new elements created a new social mix. The emergence of a social elite in the 1880s, of an East European Orthodox element in the 1900s, and of a property-owning middle class in the 1930s, provided such important moments of social transition and have received most attention. The study ends with a major national event, the entry of the

United States into World War II. Entry into that war culminated a decade of changing political consciousness for Portland's new Jewish middle class, as well as a decade of major social and demographic transition. The Depression decade constitutes a moment when major changes in birth rates, neighborhood formation, and institutional innovation coincided with a changing political activism in response to the Nazi menace. It seemed an era that required detailed examination, and it marked a fitting end point for this study.

1. Ethnicity, Mobility, and Class: The Origins of a Jewish Social Structure, 1855–1900

In 1850, Judge William Strong later recalled, Portland, Oregon, had about thirty houses and 250 people, "principally men," on the west bank of the Willamette River about nine miles south of its confluence with the Columbia River. It lay four to eight months—depending on the weather and mode of transportation—across plains and over mountains, from the Mississippi Valley. Although the census of 1850 officially gave Portland a population of slightly over eight hundred, as a trading center it remained subordinate to the old Hudson Bay Company trading station at Fort Vancouver on the Columbia, and to Oregon City, a few miles to the south on the east bank of the Willamette at the falls.[1] Portland, however, grew steadily as an importing and transhipment point just below the rapids of the Willamette. Wheat had become a commercial crop in the French Prairie region south of Portland by 1850, but its expansion throughout the valley led by 1871 to direct steamship connections to London. In addition, timber harvesting and sheep and cattle ranching in eastern Oregon and the Willamette Valley led to saw-milling and leather-tanning industries in Portland and a woolens industry in Oregon City. By 1883, Portland was joined by rail with the East, although the predominant mode of transportation to San Francisco through the 1880s remained the steamboat.[2]

Though continually subordinate to San Francisco as a commercial, industrial, and cultural center, Portland by 1890 held over forty thousand people and had created its own social ambiance. A very self-confident banking and transportation elite of Protestant origins in New England and the Middle Atlantic states presided over the town.[3] Like most frontier trading communities, it had much ethnic diversity. From the 1870s through the end of the century, the Chinese were the largest and most conspicuous minority in Portland and in Oregon City, as well as in San Francisco. After their labor on the transcontinental railroads, thousands of Chinese men sought employment and shelter in the city. A small minority became servants in the houses of the rich, but most were settled in a virtually segregated rooming-house district along Second Street. There they shared living space with saloons, houses of prostitution, and second-hand stores in an urban district typical of many for transient working-class populations in nineteenth-century America.

The proprietors of many of the second-hand stores, as well as of liquor and tobacco shops within a block or two of the Chinese quarter, were members of perhaps the second most conspicuous ethnic minority in town, the German Jews. Like the Chinese, the Jews in the early years were predominantly young men seeking wider economic opportunity. Unlike the Chinese, however, the Jews found a growing demand for their entrepreneurial services, as well as the opportunity for citizenship, which they were still denied in most villages of their native German states. The Chinese community of aging males remained segregated from the city's expansion, was occasionally the victim of mob violence in Portland and Oregon City, and gradually disintegrated.[4] The Jewish men, however, brought wives and raised families, and many were to play conspicuous mercantile and political roles in the city.

The first Jewish men to arrive in Portland, as in so many other American cities between 1830 and 1860, came from southern Germany, primarily from Bavaria, with others from Hesse and Baden. Although Bavaria sent relatively few immigrants to the United States,[5] many Jews left because of restrictions placed on them by town governments. Local autonomy for most economic and social policies was part of the system of government through which most German states maintained order. Power in the towns was held largely by the masters of guilds, who through their control of town councils restricted competition by limiting the number of marriages and the right to permanent domicile and suffrage. Journeymen as well as Jews and gypsies were considered interlopers, or "groundrabbits," whose influence had to be controlled.[6] As competition from factory goods after 1830 combined with continuing legal proscriptions, Jews and others began to leave the towns. Most resettled in cities like Munich, Nuremburg, and Frankfort in southern Germany,[7] but more adventuresome young men continued the trek, some going to England and others to America. As Bernard Goldsmith recalled when interviewed in the late 1880s, his father had been a well-to-do merchant who furnished him with passage money and several hundred dollars to begin a business career in America. He left not because of poverty but because fresh opportunities seemed limited. "The inducement to come over was this; I was the oldest of eight boys and I did not like things over there. In

1848 there was a general revolution and general dissatisfaction . . . and I just made up my mind that I would come here; that was all."[8] Though Goldsmith came to be known as something of an agnostic, his exodus was spurred neither by ideological commitment nor by economic necessity. Instead, it typified the steady stream of young Jews leaving a peasant economy and seeking wider opportunities and the prospects of new freedoms.

Recent historians of German Jewish communities in the Northeast, the South, and the Midwest have emphasized how immigrant peddlers pursued expanding commercial opportunities. As young adventurers they followed the proliferating water, rail, and even pack mule routes across America from the 1840s through the 1870s, seeking opportunities that seemed to be drying up in Central Europe and even in the British Midlands.[9] In Portland, Oregon, in the 1850s—as in Syracuse, New York; Atlanta, Georgia; and Columbus, Ohio—young peddlers made the town their base as they traded through a mining and farming frontier that lacked established merchants. Indeed, many characteristics of Jewish migration to Oregon conform to patterns observed for other European immigrants to the United States in the nineteenth century, and even for native-born Americans who crossed the plains in search of new prospects. Middle-Western farmers seeking land in the Willamette Valley in the late 1840s and 1850s usually obtained information from young and adventuresome male relatives who had preceded them on the western trek. They then came in small family groups and settled near one another.[10] The initial Jewish immigrants of the early 1850s, more like the predecessors of the farm families, were young men travelling in the company of brothers or cousins. Their own opportunities had been created by the settlement of the farm families who needed supplies. Like the Middle Westerners before them—and like so many European immigrants to East Coast cities—they created a "chain" of migration through which contact was maintained with native villages and continual emigration encouraged.[11] Young Bernard Goldschmidt, for example, arrived in New York from a small Bavarian village in 1849 to be trained by his uncle in the wholesale jewelry business. After changing his name to Goldsmith to accomodate an English-speaking clientele, he headed West. By 1851 he was guiding pack mules to sell dry goods and sundries in the California goldfields. After several years of trading in southern Oregon, he again took pack mules to mining country, this time in eastern Oregon and Idaho, where he shared in business ventures and Indian encounters with the Loewenberg brothers.[12] Goldsmith then settled in Portland, where he assisted in the emigration of six of his seven brothers and several male cousins, each of whom spent some time in Portland.

The more succesful merchants, like Goldsmith, Julius Loewenberg, Moses Seller, Philip Selling, and the Ehrmans and Lowengarts, occasionally returned to their home villages in Germany and relied for advice on contacts with older relatives. In this they were similar to the gentile pioneer merchants William S. Ladd and Josiah Failing, both of whom relied on friends and relatives from their home towns to establish business partnerships in Portland. Failing arriving in 1851 with two sons "on a sort of adventure without knowing whether we would stay or not."[13] After seven years in a "shaky" general merchandising business, they prospered and eventually acquired the First National Bank. William Ladd came from New Hampshire with his friend Charles Tilton in 1851, and after clerking for a few years went into business with his brother. He brought a wife from his native village, and subsequently launched several businesses, including the Ladd and Tilton Bank.[14]

Work habits as well as patterns of social association for Portland's German Jews grew from European traditions. Much like the immigrant industrial workers that Herbert Gutman has studied, Portland's Jewish merchants and artisans "built on these strained but hardly broken familial and kin ties."[15] Men like Goldsmith, Seymour and Charles Friendly, and Charles Lauer completed school in Germany at age thirteen and then sought training in New York or Philadelphia with relatives who might initiate them in the "mysteries" of clerking and keeping books.[16] Others, like Louis and Jacob Fleischner, found similar work with Jewish merchants who were not relatives. By their late teens and early twenties these men typically took to peddling to learn the tastes of customers in the hinterland and to locate a site for a future store. This pattern of commercial apprenticeship was common for Jews in Germany; indeed, in Bavaria in the 1820s, when many of the early settlers in Portland were born, about 25 percent of Jewish men were peddlers.[17] Mark L. Gerstle, from a wealthy San Francisco Jewish merchant family which had dealings in Portland, related how his father took the family back to Bavaria in the mid-1870s and walked them over a route in the countryside on which he had peddled as a boy.[18] Peddling might remain a life long occupation for Jews in Europe, where they could not obtain licenses to establish sedentary businesses. On the West Coast of America, the young man in his late twenties or early thirties would probably become a partner in an established store or open a small retail outlet of his own.[19] The high rate of itinerancy which David Gerber has found for Jewish merchants in Buffalo, New York prior to the Civil War seems to have been a situation common primarily to the early stages of the life cycle.[20] Although partnerships were often short-lived, middle-aged merchants had relatively low rates of transiency from one city to another.

By 1860 the Jewish merchandising network stretched all along the Pacific slope and consisted of cousins and brothers, with the older usually more permanently established in the larger cities and the younger trading from general stores in the hinterland. Available accounts describe only the careers of the most successful merchants or those who might have become politically prominent, but the manuscript census confirms the existence of this pattern of retail apprenticeship. Men like Adolph Waldman, Moses Seller, Leopold Baum, Nathan Loeb, Herman Bories, and D. Jacobi settled in California or Nevada, where they married and their first children were born. By their mid-thirties they had decided to try their luck in Portland, where they established businesses, had still more children, and were able to maintain lengthy mercantile careers. After following this pattern, Aaron Meier from Hesse found a wife, Jeanette Hirsch, on a visit home, and two clerks of Hessian origin, Emil and Sigmund Frank, on a buying trip to San Francisco. Emil soon went into the drug wholesaling business with Louis Blumauer, the son of a Bavarian immigrant, while Sigmund became Aaron Meier's partner in what was to become the largest department store in the Northwest. In his quest for new clerks, Meier turned to his wife's family, and brought at least four Hirsch brothers over as apprentices. By the mid-1890s, after Aaron Meier's death, Sigmund Frank and the Hirsch brothers managed the expanding business under the watchful eye of the matriarchal Mrs. Meier.[21]

When economic opportunities declined, as in the California gold-mining country after the 1860s, Jewish merchants often left.[22] In many remote towns in the agricultural hinterland of eastern Oregon, however, Jews remained as the leading general merchants. Unlike in the mining districts, they found a more permanent population of families, but they also had to initiate credit policies which might ease the lack of specie and accommodate the annual growing cycles. As Sylvan Durkheimer recalled the experience of his father Julius in eastern Oregon in the late 1880s, "Of necessity store owners were constrained to grubstake their neighboring customers from one harvest to the next. Few if any of these merchants had the capital resources to extend such long deferred payment accommodations, and to deny acceptance would have produced no customers. . . . The retailer had to—because he was forced to—negotiate like annual settlement agreements with all of his wholesale suppliers."[23] When Julius opened a new store in Prairie City in 1887 and a branch in Canyon City in 1888, he called his three bachelor brothers from their clerking jobs in Portland to assist in the stores. By 1896, Julius, with his wife and three-year-old son, returned to Portland. He had accumulated enough capital to buy a one-third partnership in the city's largest wholesale grocery firm, Wadhams and Company. His brothers, however, stayed in eastern Oregon for many more years.

Occasionally, however, credit could become overextended and partnerships could end in bankruptcy. In the early 1880s Ben Selling, a prominent Portland general merchant, also operated a store in Prineville with Gus

Winckler, who managed operations on the scene. Winckler extended credit for over $25,000 and made infrequent reports to Selling. By the spring of 1883, Selling had to cut off supplies and continually to berate Winckler for failing to make collections. "In the Spring you say you will collect in summer. In the summer you say in the Fall, in Fall you say Spring. Do you wonder that I am disappointed," Selling concluded.[24] By August 1883, Selling sold the store at a small profit to Senders and Sternberg, two Jewish merchants then operating a general store in Albany, Oregon; but his partnership with Winckler was finally dissolved in a lawsuit.

The pattern of retail apprenticeship and supply was so well established by the 1880s that non-family members and even occasional non-Jews were being recruited as clerks. But the very success of some of the family businesses led young men with more independent inclinations to seek other outlets. Ben Selling's young cousin Alex Sinsheimer, for example, showed no interest in clerking. While living in Pendleton he was more attracted to the printing trade, accumulating debts and visiting saloons. After several years during which Sinsheimer ran up many unexplained debts, Selling ended his financial support and insisted that Sinsheimer "settle down" as a clerk. Selling's brother Jake also showed little business sense. Writing to his uncle in San Francisco, Selling complained that his brother preferred the excitement of New York or San Francisco to the drudgery of running a country store. "Jake, while good hearted and meaning well, is visionary and imagines himself a better businessman than he really is, and above all is too liberal," Selling complained. Other young men like Julius Lippitt and Simon Selling were moving continuously from the various small towns to Portland, seeking more lucrative openings.[25]

Nevertheless, men like Ben Selling through his Portland firm, Akin and Selling, and Louis Fleischner through the even larger firm of Fleischner-–Mayer and Company had built such large operations that they could control supplies to the general stores in eastern Oregon and the Washington Territory. They could spot potentially profitable retail locations and recommend them to investors, and they knew of opportunities for young men as far east as Boise. Selling felt that men with business experience could earn several thousand dollars annually running general stores in The Dalles, Prineville, Pendleton, and Baker. To one prospective merchant from California he wrote, "only those do not succeed who have no idea of business, having been farmers or sheep men all their lives."[26]

In manufacturing, however, even by 1880 the leading Jewish firms were quite small, having grown from craft skills which Jews had practiced in Europe. In the primitive industrial environment of frontier America, and especially in crafts where heavily capitalized technology was not needed, traditional skills could be used to build successful businesses well into the twentieth century. Most Jewish businesses were minimally capitalized and short-lived; none of the firms in 1870, for example, was listed in the manuscript census in 1880. Fishel and Roberts, clothing manufacturers, had by far the largest annual payroll in 1880—$14,000. They had been in business for nine years and employed twenty-one men and five women over age sixteen, some of whom were Jewish tailors. By 1882, however, Charles Fishel had dissolved the partnership and left the city with his family.[27] The general procedure for establishing a Jewish manufacturing enterprise was described by Ben Selling in a letter to a fellow merchant in San Francisco. Desiring to become more independent of suppliers from the West Coast metropolis, Selling had simply provided a man experienced in the manufacture of undergarments with sufficient capital to purchase the machinery with which to produce enough to meet local demands. Selling boasted, "We are now perfectly independent of your city and can tell Messrs H. K. & Company what we will do and what we won't."[28] Although other small-scale tailoring, hat manufacturing, and even tent and awning firms were subsequently established, only one grew into a major firm, and that not until World War II. The demand for skilled tailors expanded, as Fishel and Roberts was superceded, first by Marks and Rybke, and then, in 1890, by Haskell and Harris Brown. In 1908, Ben Selling informed the executive director of the Industrial Removal Office in New York that skilled tailors could always find work in Portland.[29] But a Jewish clothing industry did not develop until the 1920s, and it never rivalled in size even that of Milwaukee, Wisconsin, or Rochester, New York.[30]

The largest capital investment among Jewish manufacturers in 1880, $70,000, was made by Levi Hexter and Levi May, sheet metal and stove manufacturers, and their business survived much longer. They had sufficient skill and perhaps the political influence to obtain the contract for galvanizing the corners of the state capital building in Salem in 1879. In 1880, Hexter was a forty-four-year-old craftsman from Hesse; and May, who was thirty-seven years old, had been born in Pennsylvania to Issac and Caroline May, Bavarian immigrants, who had had him trained as a tinner. Though Hexter and May employed twenty-one men and five women, most of whom probably were not Jewish, they gradually absorbed their sons into the business as clerks and bookkeepers. Despite Hexter's death in the 1890s, the firm was expanded into a wholesale distribution outlet for a wide range of household appliances, and after 1910 it attracted a number of local Jewish investors.[31] Probably the largest Jewish manufacturing concern was the Oregon Woolen Mills, whose leading officers in 1880 were Ralph and Isaac Jacobs, immigrant brothers from western Poland. From their profits they built stone mansions next door to each other on West Park Street, the most fashionable address in the city, but their mills were located at Oregon City, where they employed over a hundred "hands." Like Charles Fishel, though, the Jacobs brothers were constantly seeking greener pastures, for by the 1890s Ralph and his family had left, and in 1903 Isaac sold his interest apparently to the Goodman brothers, and moved to Seattle.[32]

Though by 1890 several Jews were listed in the city directory as "capitalists" who invested in real estate and lent money at interest, Portland's small-scale economy did not produce a banker with the skill of I. W. Hellman of Los Angeles and San Francisco. Philip Wasserman, after a successful career in trade and many speculative ventures with his close friend Bernard Goldsmith, helped organize the First National Bank of Portland. By 1870, though, he had sold out to the Failing and Corbett interests, who had access to far more capital. Julius Loewenberg helped form the Willamette Savings Bank in 1883 and the Merchants National Bank in 1886, but he controlled neither. Benjamin I. Cohen, after a career in law, became president of the Portland Trust Company in the 1890s. Though he had a reputation as a "tight-fisted banker," he remained in the shadow of the leading gentile banks. Bernard Goldsmith invested—and lost—several hundred thousand dollars constructing locks to bypass the falls of the Willamette in the early 1870s, and then became a regional agent of the German Loan Association of California. Along with Loewenberg, Sol Hirsch and the lawyer–politician Joseph Simon, Goldsmith speculated in mining claims and stocks with gentile friends. Loewenberg and Goldsmith seemed willing to take risks, but Hirsch seemed to voice the mood of Jewish investors in the 1890s when he confided to a gentile friend, "I am such a thorough coward in everything which looks like share speculation that I naturally move very slow."[33] Much like the Jewish merchants in San Francisco, those in Portland preferred to reinvest in trade and in land, with occasional ventures into local produce like sheep, cattle, or wheat.

In later years, Portland's Jewish merchants would find clerks for their stores, occasionally spouses for their children, and doctors to care for their serious illnesses in San Francisco. But in Portland itself they established the economic, social and religious institutions to sustain a very self-confident community. Like Portland itself, the Jewish community grew steadily, but its rate of growth and internal organization differed from that of the total population. The city went through spurts of growth related to national events like the discovery of gold in California and the completion of the railroads, though the development of the timber industry and especially wheat farming in the Willamette Valley did bring some economic stability by the early 1870s. By then the Jewish community had achieved considerable stability and grew very slowly until the mid-1890s, when Russian Jews began to arrive. In 1860 slightly over one hundred Jews, almost half of whom were unmarried young men—like the Weil, Elfeld, and Rosenfeld brothers, and Aaron Meier and Nathan Meerholz—lived in Portland. Of the sixty men for whom occupations were listed in the federal manuscript census for 1860, only 23 percent remained through 1870. This percentage was somewhat lower than for frontier merchants in other towns that have been studied, but it was about average for young unmarried men. However, substantial new immigration boosted the Jewish population in 1870 to over four hundred. Some of the newcomers were the spouses and children of Bernard Goldsmith, Philip Wasserman, and Aaron Meier, who had returned to Germany for wives and started families in Portland. Others were simply arriving for the first time. By 1870 Jews were 5 percent of the city's total population, a proportion only slightly lower than their 7 percent in San Francisco.[34] By 1870, furthermore, the social organization of the Jewish population had dramatically changed, because only 10 percent were still single males residing in rooming houses. The rest were either married or residing with Jewish families. During the 1870s, a decade of depression and diminished immigration, the Jewish population grew by only about fifty persons and the proportion of Jews in the city fell to about 2 percent. However, the number of Jewish women over age sixteen increased more than did the number of men, and the community

Table 1. *Portland: Jewish Occupational Profile and Population, 1860–1880*

Males, 16 and over	1860		1870		1880	
	No.	%	No.	%	No.	%
Proprietor	46	76.6	81	62.8	79	47.6
Professional	0	0.0	1	0.8	5	3.0
Employee	5	8.3	31	24.0	52	31.3
Skilled work	7	11.7	14	10.9	24	14.6
Semi-skilled	0	0.0	0	0.0	2	1.1
Dairyman	1	1.7	0	0.0	0	0.0
No occupation	1	1.7	2	1.6	3	1.6
Student	0	0.0	0	0.0	1	0.8
Total	60	100.0	129	100.0	166	100.0
Females, 16 and over						
Keeping house	15		70		91	
Dtr/niece "at home"	2		13		19	
Teacher	0		0		1	
Clerk	0		1		0	
Brdng house	0		0		2	
Dressmaker	0		1		2	
Storekeeper	0		1		1	
Total	17		86		116	
Children, 15 and under						
Male	20		110		100	
Female	23		104		108	
Total Population	120		429		490	

came to consist primarily of stable families. In the 1880s, as Jewish wholesaling operations expanded, many young men came to town to serve as clerks, as traveling agents for San Francisco businesses, or as tailors, expressmen, and carpenters for the town's growing middle class. Most of those who remained eventually married, and by 1900 the sex ratio of German Jews and their adult children was virtually even, making them one of the most stable social elements in the city.

II

Precisely how Jewish merchants and manufacturers obtained credit for their ventures is somewhat difficult to document, but, because of the mercantile character of their activities, it is crucial for an understanding of the social infrastructure of the Jewish community. Reporters for Dun and Bradstreet, the credit rating service, felt that Jewish merchants did not comply with Protestant business ethics, and they often submitted reports replete with negative stereotypes. Local banks, presumably, would have been reluctant to lend money to men who seemed unusual risks. Most young Jewish peddlers presumably received goods on consignment from relatives and friends in larger cities or even through European connections, but despite the individual origins of credit, it grew steadily into a communal concern. Bernard Goldsmith expressly referred to funds provided by his father and later by his father's friend in San Francisco, on the basis of which he was able to make handsome profits on trading ventures. In addition, he maintained contact with the family business, which by the 1860s had been moved to Munich. Moses Seller, an importer and wholesaler of crockery, was supplied by the family business in Frankfort-am-Main, which also had branches in New York and Los Angeles.[35] By 1870, although only thirty-one Jewish merchants in Portland had accumulated real estate worth $1,000 or more, sixty-nine had accumulated at least that much in personal property, much of which must have been in inventory. Despite the anti-Semitic stereotypes, local friendships developed between Jewish merchants and gentile bankers. Aaron Meier, for example, in requesting a reassessment of his net worth for tax purposes in 1871, noted that he was indebted to D. P. Thompson, a local banker (and future mayor of Portland), and to a Whitney of Marion County, for a total of $7,000. His real estate, assessed at $17,500, had been given in mortgage.[36]

Once having settled in a frontier town, young Jewish men then had to be integrated into a network upon which they could rely for security. In frontier communities the problem of social integration has been the most crucial because the extraordinary flux of population created a continual struggle for power. Within such disorderly towns, men often found in common economic

Table 2. *Jewish Property Ownership, 1870, by Occupation and Sex*

Male	Real Property				Personal Property			
Occupation	I	II	III	IV	I	II	III	IV
Proprietor	5	15	7	9	11	44	10	15
Clerk	0	1	0	0	2	4	1	0
Other*	0	0	0	0	5	1	0	0
Female	1	1	0	0	2	1	0	0
Total	6	17	7	9	20	50	11	15

Note: I = less than $1,000; II = $1,000 to $5,000; III = $5,000 to $10,000; IV = $10,000 & up.

*Includes professionals, craftsmen, service

function and cultural background a dual basis for cohesiveness. Given the concentration of Jewish men in trade, they depended on civic orderliness and private credit for security. Unlike the Jewish enclaves in the cities of Germany and Poland, those in the United States were not legal corporations to which individual Jews were required to pay taxes and which in turn had to care for all members. Instead, American Jews as individuals had the choice of organizing into voluntary associations to meet specific needs. Indeed, as Don H. Doyle has emphasized, a voluntary association "integrated society as it defined social boundaries."[37] Led by Louis Fleischner, who no doubt knew of a similar organization founded in New York in 1854, Portland's Jewish merchants organized the First Hebrew Benevolent Association in the early 1870s. The members contributed three dollars a quarter to accumulate operating capital, which could be used for business loans as well as for private and communal emergencies. In older cities such voluntary associations collected small dues in weekly or monthly installments to further ethnic interests. Chicago's Poles, for example, accumulated capital in the late-nineteenth century through building and loan associations to purchase homes near the stockyards and steel mills where they were finding permanent jobs. They quite self-consciously translated the peasant desire for land into a worker's desire for the respectability they found in home ownership.[38] Portland's Jews likewise accumulated capital in steady installments, but they chose to base their social security on their tradition of proprietorship.

The records of the First Hebrew Benevolent Association are extant only from 1884, but by then it had accumulated over $17,000 in capital, most of which was lent out at interest. It had then 103 members, though over 170 memberships had been issued over the years. The largest loans, of $5,000 each, were to non-Jews willing to pay 10 percent annual interest for two to three years. Jewish members like Philip Wasserman, Lehman Blum, Moses and Sig Sichel, and Henry Ackerman, borrowed smaller amounts for slightly lower rates to finance their short-term partnerships. The interest from the loans, as well as some of the incoming dues, were entrusted to Louis

Fleischner (and after his death to Ben Selling) to dispense as charity. The synagogues were paid for the burial of the indigent, and physicians, nurses, and hospitals were paid for the care of the sick who lacked funds to pay for themselves. Occasionally, board for a poor Jew might be paid for several months, and Jewish men seeking work in other cities might apply to the association for transportation costs. In 1887, almost $1,400 was dispensed in charity, and by 1892 the amount so dispensed had grown to over $1,700. At the same time, loans were made to Congregation Beth Israel, to which many members belonged, and to individuals.[39]

In 1889, Benjamin I. Cohen became the salaried loan officer of the association, which in turn deposited some of its funds in his Portland Trust Company.[40] Cohen provided the association with information about secure and lucrative loans, while he utilized some of its assets in his own banking business. By 1895, the association had over $23,000 in active loans, ranging from $50 to Zachary Swett to $1,000 to Sig and Moses Sichel and $5,000 to a gentile couple for what appears to have been a property mortgage. In addition to the usual charity, small amounts of from $25 to $100 were lent for from one day to six months at no interest to Jewish non-members, some of which were simply noted as "charity notes."[41] The recipients, some of whom signed their notes in Hebrew script, seem to have been of Eastern European origin. By the turn of the century, several hundred dollars at a time were being donated to Jewish victims of natural disasters in Galveston and Oakland, to victims of pogroms in Rumania and in Kishineff, and to private and public charities. Capital accumulation, then, came to mean not merely a means to private gain, but a basis for social cohesiveness which might shield the community from public scrutiny and save all but the most desperate men from public asylums.

The benevolent association dealt largely with the welfare needs of an established community, but the earlier institutions founded by Portland's Jewish men illustrate how they utilized fragments of a tradition to foster social stability. The first institution seems to have been the Mt. Sinai Cemetary Association, founded sometime in the mid-1850s, which acquired a burial tract in the Caruthers Addition. The initial concern for ritual burial reflected both the high death rates from disease, accidents, and especially childhood illnesses, and the desire to rejuvenate a loyalty beyond the family.[42] The formation of such an organization was made easier because almost three-fourths of the heads of households and single unattached men in 1860 were from the villages of Southern Germany, which shared a simple orthodox Judaism. The young peddlers and traders had no elaborate tradition of ritual, but simply wished to have their lives marked by respect for the faith of their ancestors.[43]

In 1858, Portland Jewish men formed a more complex institution,

Table 3. Portland: Place of Birth, Jewish Male Heads of Household and Unattached Males

	1860		1870		1880	
	No.	%	No.	%	No.	%
South Germany	39	72.2	58	51.3	33	23.4
Prussia	6	11.2	33	29.2	35	24.8
Germany	0	0.0	0	0.0	18	12.8
Bohemia	0	0.0	1	0.9	3	2.1
Austria	0	0.0	4	3.5	1	0.8
Poland	1	1.8	0	0.0	16	11.3
Russia	1	1.8	7	6.3	4	2.8
United States	6	11.2	10	8.8	22	15.6
Other	1	1.8	0	0.0	9	6.4
Total	54	100.0	113	100.0	141	100.0

Congregation Beth Israel, which reflected their new status as both sedentary merchants and as heads of growing households. Indeed, some occupations—which men are more likely to hold at a particular stage in the life cycle—promote geographic persistence more than do others. German Jewish immigrants in their early thirties clustered in merchandising, which in turn required stability and contributed to family formation. Their need for a congregation indicates their dependence on tradition as a sanction for the passage from one stage of life to the next, and the synagogue in fact grew to meet their expanding social needs. Beth Israel held Sabbath as well as High Holiday services, and then engaged a rabbi, the first of whom, however, stayed only a short time. In 1862 it absorbed the Mt. Sinai Cemetary Association,[44] and in 1864 it erected a building for $4,500, which was considered a substantial sum for its day. Early in the 1860s, partially because there were no public schools, Beth Israel created a congregational school under the direction of Herman Bories, who made his living in part as a shoemaker and boot dealer. Bories was from Bohemia, where he apparently had absorbed more religious instruction than his Bavarian colleagues. In 1865, he also taught German and Hebrew. For reasons that remain unclear, the Hebrew and German departments of the school were discontinued in 1865, but some Hebrew continued to be taught in the Sunday school that was subsequently established.[45]

As Leon Jick has emphasized in his study of the "Americanization" of synagogues in the nineteenth century, the German immigrants had no strong intellectual tradition and very few of them had received a secular education as professionals. In Cincinnati, the center of German Jewry, for example, out of an estimated Jewish population of 15,000 in 1850, there were only three physicians, four lawyers, and ten teachers.[46] Portland certainly reflected this pattern; in 1870, with a Jewish population of about four hundred, only the rabbi could be classed as professional. In 1880, with a Jewish population of about five hundred, there were still only five professionals. Not surprisingly,

1. Meier & Frank, first location, Portland, ca. 1870 (Courtesy of the Oregon Historical Society)

2. J. Durkheimer & Co., Burns, Oregon, ca. 1890

3. Sylvan Durkheimer, son of Julius and
   Delia, 5 years old, 1898

4. Andelm Boskowitz, grandson of Henry
   & Adeline Bloch, 12 years old, 1893

5. Ignatz Lowengart and young S. Mason Ehrman, vacationing in Germany, ca. 1910 (Courtesy of the Oregon Historical Society)

6. Temple Beth Israel, second building, completed 1888

Beth Israel was not convulsed by disputes over theology, but vacillated over changes in ritual and deflected ideological disputes into personality conflicts. In 1865, for example, it affiliated with Isaac M. Wise's Board of Delegates of American Israelites, though it continued to follow orthodox ritual and resisted adoption of Wise's "Minhag America."[47]

In search of rabbis, Beth Israel's leaders like Bernard Goldsmith and Philip Wasserman turned to their German relatives for appropriately ordained young ministers to give respectability to their frontier synagogue. Rabbis Isaac Schwab and Mayer May were recruited from Bavaria,[48] though each saw his role as broader than providing ritual leadership and instruction for the young. In particular, Rabbi May, who arrived at age twenty-four with a young wife and quickly had four children, charged his commitment to ideological reform with the same youthful vigor that his pioneer congregants poured into their business ventures. He found his congregants both ignorant and nonobservant, yet unwilling to accept his arguments for reform in ritual and religious-school instruction. After holding the positions of rabbi, *chaz-zan*, and Hebrew-school teacher for over seven years, he was accused in January 1879 of outrageous personal conduct. Several congregants said he had visited houses of prostitution when in San Francisco, had slandered members of the congregation, and had accused the young women as well as the young men of immoral sexual conduct. A committee, including Bernard Goldsmith, Simon Blumauer, and Solomon Hirsch, investigated the charges and in April concluded only that May "did say some indiscrete things about the ignorance of the congregation."[49]

The tension between May and several members of his congregation was more than personal, however. A year after the committee had investigated May's conduct, Adolph Waldman accused him of failing to conduct the Sunday school properly; Waldman then resigned his position as chairman of the Sunday-school committee. May pressed the synagogue board for a replacement for Waldman, and the tension continued. In October the two men had a fight in front of Hexter and May's store, with the rabbi shooting Waldman in the leg. Rabbi May quickly became persona non grata, and within a month left town for a cash settlement of $1,200.[50] Reverend Alexander Rosenspitz took his place, but remained only a few years. In 1884, Jacob Bloch, a thirty-eight-year-old biblical scholar then officiating in Sacramento, was hired. He showed no desire to reform ritual, even though Sabbath services were poorly attended, membership grew very little, and the energies of the congregants were directed into building funds for a more elaborate temple and for the Concordia social club. The congregation retained membership in the Union of American Hebrew Congregations, the successor to the Board of Delegates, but only belatedly and with little discussion did it adopt the *Union Prayer Book*—at the suggestion of laymen rather than Rabbi Bloch—in 1895.[51] Bloch seems to have been forced to retire in 1900 at age fifty-four because he had outlived his usefulness to the congregation. Like so many in America at the time, Beth Israel was looking for an American-trained rabbi who could be their spokesman to the city's gentile elite. With great enthusiasm, in 1900, they recruited the most dynamic exemplar of rabbinic activism in America, Stephen S. Wise, whose rabbinate will be discussed later. Rabbi Bloch's efforts to participate in worship services in an emeritus capacity during Wise's stay were viewed by the trustees as an anachronistic embarrassment.[52]

The formation of a second congregation, Ahavai Shalom, in 1868 represented not an ideological withdrawal from Beth Israel by a disaffected orthodox contingent, but rather the arrival and permanent settlement of Prussian and Polish Jews who felt uncomfortable in the presence of a southern German contingent. By 1870, almost 30 percent of Jewish heads of household and unattached males in Portland were of Prussian birth, and by 1880 those of Prussian birth equalled in number those from southern Germany. Regrettably, the records of Ahavai Shalom for the nineteenth century are lost, but references to early members in minutes between 1912 and 1920 indicate that it absorbed some of the Polish Jews who began to arrive in the 1870s. Its rabbi during the late nineteenth and early twentieth centuries, Robert Abrahamson, as well as its *chazzan*, Mendel Cohen, were from Poland and showed no inclination toward reform. Abrahamson was also the local *mohel* (ritual circumciser), a skill he taught to the immigrant orthodox rabbi Isaac Faivusovitch by the early 1920s. Ahavai Shalom became the meeting ground for the new middle class in the second and third decades of the twentieth century, as the old German families diminished in size and retreated into an exclusive social enclave.[53]

The B'nai B'rith lodges rather early supplemented the synagogues and the benevolent Association as agents for community cohesion. The B'nai B'rith had been founded in New York in 1843 by German immigrants familiar with the mysteries and the enlightened philosophy of Masonry. Ironically, the Jews of Berlin and other German cities in the 1880s established B'nai B'rith lodges to compensate for their growing proscription from Masonic lodges, whereas the German founders of the B'nai B'rith in America adopted the gentile lodge format and secular philosophy to recreate Jewish fellowship in a new locale.[54] Like the Masons and Odd Fellows in most expanding American towns in the mid-nineteenth century, the B'nai B'rith lodges provided a meeting ground for young shopkeepers and clerks in search of sociability as well as mutual benefit insurance. Just as the Masons accepted men of most religious faiths—including Jews—so the B'nai B'rith accepted Jews of all synagogues. The gentile fraternal lodges in most communities contained a select mercantile and professional subgroup which helped formalize a local elite; but, because the German Jews were almost entirely within that subgroup, the B'nai B'rith, at least in its early stage, did not serve a socially selective function within the ethnic enclave.[55] Instead, it integrated young men rather than formalizing social boundaries. The first lodge, Oregon Lodge 65, was founded in 1866, only nine years after the first lodge on the Pacific Coast, Ophir Lodge in San Francisco, and eight years prior to the first lodge in Los Angeles.[56] Among the initial members were immigrants from Bavaria, Prussia, and Poland, thus indicating that whereas the synagogues might divide along regional lines, the members of the lodge overlooked those cleavages in their desire to join a modern organization with mutual insurance services. Over the next thirty years, however, three more lodges were founded, each containing a different social stratum. By 1897 the four lodges symbolized more than any other local institutions how complex an ethnic class structure had evolved.

Of the thirty-two original members of Lodge 65, twenty remained in Portland for at least fifteen years after joining, thus showing a far higher persistence rate than that of either most nineteenth-century ethnic enclaves or Portland's pioneer Jews of the 1850s and 1860s. No doubt the persistence rate was high because these men had accumulated capital to survive the early years. As with the founders of the original lodge in New York over two decades previously, most of the founders of Lodge 65 were merchants, though some skilled workers like glaziers, bartenders, and expressmen also joined. The high propensity of lodge members to remain in the city conforms to persistence patterns observed for members of gentile lodges in other small but growing towns,[57] but skilled workers did not persist for as many years as did merchants.

The purposes of the lodge can be further discerned by examining the age distribution of its members. According to the 1880 manuscript census, in which twenty-seven members of Lodge 65 could be located, the mean age of the members at that time was forty-two years. Most lodges nationally were founded by men in their late twenties and early thirties who were beginning small business, starting families, and seeking stable social ties and insurance services commensurate with their new household positions. By 1880, Lodge 65 had been in existence for fourteen years. All of its members listed in the 1880 census, except for two recent inductees still in their twenties, were married, and all but five owned their own businesses. One member in his late forties had owned a clothing store, but was then a clerk for another member. These men expected to stay in Portland and they needed health and life insurance for their families. Younger men would generally have been reluctant to join such a lodge and watch their premiums paid out in benefits to the families of older members.

The members of Lodge 65 found housing among the general population.

Table 4. *Occupational Profiles, Portland B'nai B'rith Lodges*

Occupational category*	Lodge 65 (1866–78)		Lodge 65 (1885)		Lodge 314 (1879–96)		Lodge 416 (1891–96)		Lodge 464 (1897–1904)	
	No.	%	No.	%	No.	%	No.	%	No.	%
Owner	39	50.6	14	45.2	34	28.3	33	42.8	79	55.6
Clerk, agent	16	20.7	5	16.1	37	30.8	34	44.2	22	15.5
Skilled, semi-skilled	9	11.7	3	9.7	29	24.1	0	0.0	22	15.5
Professional	5	6.5	3	9.7	1	0.8	8	10.4	3	2.1
No occupation	1	1.3	0	0.0	4	3.2	0	0.0	6	4.2
Not listed in city directory	7	9.1	6	19.3	16	12.8	2	2.6	10	7.0
Totals	77	100.0	31	100.0	121	100.0	77	100.0	142	100.0

*When joining lodge

In the 1860s and early 1870s most lived near their place of business in mixed commercial and residential areas near the city's center. A few lived in residential blocks near 5th and Salmon Streets, while a wealthy manufacturer like Levi Hexter and a commission broker like Charles Friendly lived in a still more exclusive area—for the 1870s—on North 6th Street. Like most urban populations of the late nineteenth century, members of Lodge 65 changed residence often; though, once having built homes, merchants like the Hexters, Fleischners, and Friedlanders remained in them for a decade or more. Nevertheless, because Portland remained through the 1880s a city where most people walked to work, changes of residence were usually not more than a few blocks.[58] Of the thirty-six members of Lodge 65 for whom addresses could be found in 1880, eight still resided at the same address that they had occupied during the year in which they joined. By 1885, only four of the eight remained at the same address, and one had left town. By the mid-1880s most of those who remained in Portland had moved to newer blocks adjacent to Park Avenue and as far west from the Willamette River as 13th Street.

The founding of Portland's second B'nai B'rith Lodge, North Pacific Lodge 314, in 1879, illustrates how a second generation was being recruited to supplement the pioneers. The members of Lodge 314 went into the same line of work as the members of Lodge 65, and by 1880 differed in specific occupations primarily because of their relative youth. According to the 1880 census, the mean age of the thirty members listed was thirty-two years. These men solidified the hold of Jews on the clothing and general merchandise trade of Portland because those in their early twenties were primarily clerks and travelling agents, while those in their late twenties and early thirties were retail merchants. Age is also correlated with differences in place of birth. Of the thirty members, eleven had been born in the United States, primarily in New York and California. Of the nineteen born in Europe, only one came from Bavaria, while seven had been born in Prussia, a province that in the

Table 5. Portland: Jewish Male Heads of Households and Unattached Males—Persistence by Occupation

Occupation	1860 No.	1860–1870 No.	% Persistence	Wid-ows	1880 No.	1880–1890 No.	% Persistence	Wid-ows	1880–1900 No.	% Persistence	Wid-ows
Merchant*	46	12	26.1	1	65	42	71.2	6	31	47.7	8
Agent, Broker	0	0			11	8	72.7	0	4	36.3	3
Clerk	5	1	20.0	0	26	16	61.5	0	13	50.0	0
Peddler	0				1	0	0.0	1	0	0.0	0
Professional	0				3	2	66.7	1	0	0.0	0
Skilled/service	7	1	14.3	0	22	16	76.2	1	10	45.4	3
Unskilled	0				2	1	50.0	0	1	50.0	0
Dairyman	1	0		0	0	0		0	0		0
Manufacturer	0				3	2	66.7	0	2	66.7	0
No occupation	1	0		0	1	0		0	0		0
Totals (aver.)	60	14	(23.3)	1	134	87	(64.9)	8	63	(47.0)	14

*Includes watchmakers, jewelers, opticians

1870s was supplying the majority of new Jewish immigrants. The American and European members, while presumably the products of different cultural influences, found common ground because they shared a stage in the life cycle which gave them an identical occupational niche in the Jewish mercantile network. The four men over age forty-five could join without placing an actuarial burden on the younger members because District Grand Lodge No. 4 in San Francisco (which covered the western region of the United States), had written new by-laws under which a new member over age forty-five could not participate in the mutual benefit service. The only apparent difference between the older members of Lodge 314 and those in Lodge 65 was place of birth. The former came from Prussia, whereas those in Lodge 65 came from Bavaria. The membership of men over age forty-five, as well as that of single men under age thirty, indicates that Lodge 314 offered both social and financial benefits to its members.[59]

Between 1880 and 1904, Lodge 314 attracted many white-collar employees, especially clerks and travelling agents, and craftsmen, particularly tailors. These were typical occupations for German Jewish men in their early and mid-twenties in Portland and other commercial cities.[60] Lodge members, however, did not persist in the city nearly as long as had members of Lodge 65 during its first fifteen years. The relatively high rate of transiency reflects the increasing propensity of young men who had not acquired property or become business proprietors to seek employment elsewhere. Among Jewish heads of household and unattached men in 1880, almost three-quarters of the proprietors and four-fifths of the craftsmen remained through 1890, but only 60 percent of the clerks and salesmen did. While over half of the young men coming into the labor market in the 1880s began as clerks (the others were

partners in family businesses, travelling agents, craftsmen, and two professionals), only 50 percent of their older brothers who had been clerks in 1880
remained in the city through 1890. This pattern of higher transiency among
clerks than among either proprietors or craftsmen is reflected in Lodge 314,
because most of its clerks and travelling agents left the city prior to 1890. The
same pattern of higher transiency for Jewish clerks than for other white-collar
categories held true in the late nineteenth century for other commercial
cities of similar size, like Los Angeles; Atlanta, Georgia; and Columbus,
Ohio. Fragmentary evidence suggests that, far from falling into a migratory
proletariat like American farm boys and especially Irish immigrants, the
young Jews found clerical work in San Francisco or opened general stores in
the Oregon hinterland.

Table 6. *Sons, 1880—Persistence and Entrance into Labor Force by Occupation*

Occupations, ages 17 and over*	1880	1890			1900		
		Persistent from 1880	New, 1890	Total	Persistent from 1890	New, 1900	Total
Merchant	2	2	6	8	6	2	8
Clerk	16	8	25	33	25	5	30
Skilled, service	7	5	9	14	6	2	8
Professional	2	2	2	4	3	1	4
Other	0	0	5	5	4	1	5
No occupation	2	1	0	1	0	0	0
Total	29	18	47	65	44	11	55

*Unemployed sons under age 17: ages 0–5, 33; ages 6–16, 70.

The residential pattern for members of Lodge 314 indicates further how
a new generation of merchants fit into the community. In 1880 the great
majority lived in the downtown area, where clerks and small shopkeepers
generally resided, but from which the majority of the established members of
Lodge 65 had already moved. As more clerks and tailors joined Lodge 314
during the 1880s, they too settled in the downtown areas. But by 1890, the
more successful members were moving west of the Park blocks into residential
districts which had been pioneered ten to fifteen years previously by members
of Lodge 65. By 1895, some newcomers and merchant tailors began to open
businesses and establish homes south of the major business district, while still
others moved to the Park Street area. By 1900 a large number of the most
successful, like Sig Sichel, Charles and Gerson Kahn, Henry Litt, Hyman
Salmonson, and Benjamin Cohen, now well into middle age, had moved to
the North 16th Street neighborhood. Those members who persisted in
Portland through the turn of the century had moved to established middle-
class neighborhoods at about the same stage in the life cycle as had the

members of Lodge 65. However, just as they had not become entrepreneurial leaders by founding new commercial emporiums, so they inherited older but sturdy housing rather than developing new residential districts or erecting mansions as the pioneer Wassermans, Goldsmiths, Hirches, Jacobs, and Loewenbergs had done.[61]

Table 7. *Comparative Jewish Male Persistence, 1880–1890, selected cities*

	Portland	Los Angeles	Columbus	Atlanta
heads of household	64.9%	58.4%	N.A.	N.A.
others over age 18	64.4	54.7	64.6%	56.8%

SOURCE: M. Gelfand, "Mobility in L.A.," AJH (1979), 421; M. L. Raphael, *Jews and Judaism* (1979), 55 (Table 18); S. Hertzberg, "Unsettled Jews," AJH (1977), computed from Table 1

A further indication of the aspiring clerks, tailors, and merchants attracted to Lodge 314 can be deduced by comparing them with the new members joining Lodge 65 in the 1880s. In 1885, partly in response to the action of District Grand Lodge No. 4 in raising death benefits to $2,000 (twice as high as for most other district), Lodge 65 inducted thirty new members.[62] Only two were clerks, and only two were travelling agents. Of the others, eleven owned stores and seven were independent agents in real estate, commission brokerage, and law; none were tailors. A few, like Bailey Gatzert of Seattle, had lived in the Pacific Northwest for many years and though no longer residing in Portland retained membership in Jewish communal institutions. The persistence rate in Portland for this cohort over fifteen years was 50 percent higher than for the older members of Lodge 65 and for the total membership of Lodge 314. The nine located in the 1880 manuscript census were already in their mid-thirties to mid-forties and had families. Compared to the young clerks and tailors who were then joining Lodge 314, the new members of Lodge 65 had already found a secure occupational niche and remained in the city as it grew.

The occupational profiles of Lodges 65 and 314, when compared with that of all Jewish men in Portland in the 1880s, suggest that the community was not yet formally stratified along class lines. Only two laborers who were probably Jewish appear in the manuscript census, and their omission from the lodges suggests that a sense of social distinction applied to a small minority. Men of great wealth, however, had not created distinctive institutions, although Beth Israel was becoming the preserve of an aging elite. While the division between the south Germans and the Prussians and Poles remained in the synagogues, it was blurred by the generational divisions in the lodges, and common membership in the benevolent association. Indeed, before the 1890s Portland's Jews should be divided into those who were "established" and those who were "aspiring." The social data for Portland's Jewish men through 1880 modifies somewhat the findings of scholars who have examined other small cities in the American hinterland. Most Jews who ventured west may have had skills upon which they hoped to rely to earn a living, but they depended even more on relatives and fraternal organizations to assist them in their mercantile careers.[63]

III

An examination of the third and fourth B'nai B'rith lodges, which were founded in the 1890s, indicates how a more complex and hierarchical class structure developed within the Jewish community. Although individuals in one lodge might befriend individuals in the other, the two institutions symbolized the coalescence of separate social strata. In 1891, Portland Lodge 416 was founded by primarily American-born sons of German Jews. In 1897, Sabato Morais Lodge 464, named after Philadelphia's famed orthodox rabbi (who had just died), was founded by Eastern European immigrants.[64] The appearance of Eastern Europeans, however, some of whom had been trickling into Portland since the 1870s, did not by itself create the social cleavage. Rather, a new sense of elite status among the children of the Germans—accompanied by profound changes in their family life, which will be discussed in the next chapter—disrupted the patriarchal patterns through which newcomers had previously been absorbed.

The elite of German descent and the newcomers from Eastern Europe became separated more than previous subgroups had been, in part because they resided in neighborhoods that were miles rather than blocks apart. But more important, in the greatly expanding city of the years from 1890–1914, the newcomers—unlike those of the 1870s and 1880s—could not expect at set stages in their life cycle to follow in the footsteps of their predecessors. The Portland Jewish community had never been unified, particularly after the influx of immigrants from Prussia and the Posen area of Poland. But by the time a generation of wealthy American-born and educated men and women came to share a nominal Jewish identity with more traditional Eastern Europeans, the social divisions were as acute as the cultural differences. While the officers of the old lodges 65 and 314, for example, had attended each other's meetings and shared social activities,[65] those of 416 and 464 apparently never did so. Both of the new lodges provided members with companionship and some benefit services, but rather than creating fellow feeling among men of similar interests but different stages in the life cycle, they symbolized a new cleavage. The great numbers of Eastern European immigrants *after* 1900 only added to a social division that lasted for an additional half century.

Lodge 416 was established to meet the mutual benefit and sociability needs of a very self-conscious elite. The mean age at induction of the

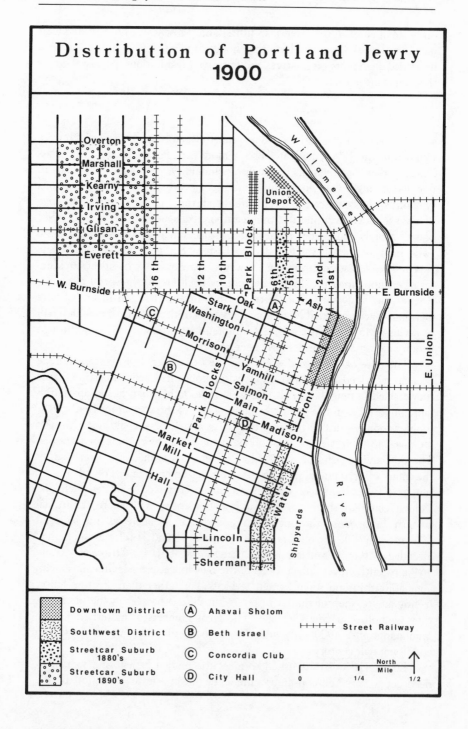

Distribution of Portland Jewry
1900

Overton
Marshall
Kearny
Irving
Glisan
Everett
W. Burnside
16 th
12 th
10 th
Park Blocks
6th
5th
2nd
1st
E. Burnside
Union Depot
Willamette
Stark
Oak
Ⓐ
Ash
Washington
Morrison
Ⓑ
Park Blocks
Yamhill
Salmon
Main
Front
Ⓓ
Madison
Ⓒ
E. Union
Market
Mill
Hall
Lincoln
Sherman
Water
Shipyards
River

▓ Downtown District	Ⓐ Ahavai Sholom	
░ Southwest District	Ⓑ Beth Israel	┼┼┼┼ Street Railway
∴ Streetcar Suburb 1880's	Ⓒ Concordia Club	North
° Streetcar Suburb 1890's	Ⓓ City Hall	Mile

0   1/4   1/2

seventy-seven men who joined between 1891 and 1896 was thirty-two years, about the same as for those who joined the older lodges. All new members who were married subscribed to the mutual benefit services and obtained the medical certificates to verify vaccination.[66] In addition to the young men, however, a large number in their forties also joined. Members in their twenties were clerks, bookkeepers, and travelling agents, as the young members of Lodge 314 had been a decade previously. But the white-collar workers in Lodge 416 were sons of the Meier, Frank, Fleischner, Blumauer, Mayer, Wolfe, and Kramer families, as well as department managers for Meier and Frank. Gus Rosenblatt, though only twenty-eight in 1891, was already an independent insurance agent and famous for his race horse, "Thousand Dollar."[67] Newcomers like Sig Sichel and Isaac Leeser Cohen were related to older families and were accumulating money and participating in civic affairs. Among the occupations represented were physician, attorney, and U.S. customs inspector—Henry Blackman. It was the first lodge to have over 10 percent of its members in the professions, and, needless to say, it did not include tailors, peddlers, or expressmen.

Lodge 416 provided the capstone to the formation of a Jewish elite similar to those coalescing in many other middle-sized American cities at the time. Many of the men who joined Lodge 416, or their close relatives, had in the 1880s helped organize the convivial Concordia Club, one of only four social clubs whose membership lists were published in the first Portland "400" Directory in 1891.[68] Concordia clubs were being formed throughout the United States by Jews of German descent in emulation of exclusive city clubs being formed by gentiles. In the "instant cities" of the West Coast Jews had a unique position in that their ambitions were acknowledged by gentiles who were themselves newcomers in search of wealth and status. The Corbetts, Failings, and Ladds had not arrived much before the Fleischners, Mayers, and Goldsmiths, and were quite aware of the contribution the Jewish merchants were making to the city's wholesale distribution and financial institutions. Gentiles in Portland and elsewhere did not admit Jews to their clubs like the Arlington.[69] But Jews never expressed displeasure at such exclusion, because they met gentile merchants as equals in Masonic lodges, partisan politics, and business partnerships. Instead, wealthy Jews retained sociability for themselves through the Concordia Club and the B'nai B'rith, and their emissaries met those of gentiles with increasing frequency in civic and philanthropic endeavors.

Concordia in Portland had been founded in 1879, but its evolution by 1887 further pinpoints the moment at which a Jewish elite emerged. According to the *Portland City Directory for 1879*, Concordia was "a new institution recently organized in this city."[70] Its officers were clerks, salesmen, and partners in small businesses. *The Portland "400" Directory, 1891,* however, gives the date of founding as 20 October 1887, when its officers were the merchants Ben Selling, Nathan Baum, and Edward Bernheim, and the lawyer Julius Silverstone. By then it had been formally incorporated. Its board of trustees now consisted of the city's most prominent Jewish merchants: Louis Fleischner, Adolph Wolfe, Emil Frank, Adolph Bissinger, Edward Ehrman, and Frederick R. Mellis. It inducted one hundred men of German descent, and new members were limited primarily to the sons and other male relatives of the founders. By 1888, Concordia had moved from rented rooms to its own hall on the northeast corner of 2nd and Morrison Streets, in the heart of the business district. It segregated the elite in a whirl of card parties, "full dress balls," and galas, which emulated the social events of the late-nineteenth-century gentile upper-middle class. In 1891, Concordia included twenty-three future members of Lodge 416, and by 1901 over one-third of its members also belonged to the lodge.[71]

Concordia in turn was largely an outgrowth of Congregation Beth Israel, which by the mid-1880s has become the preserve of the old south German families. The social network of synagogue (dominated by older men), city club (including some older and many younger men), and B'nai B'rith Lodge (composed of younger men) can be traced through the overlapping memberships of individuals and especially of families. In 1887, the year of Concordia's expansion, Beth Israel decided to construct a temple on a new site west of the business district, closer to the residences of members, and adjacent to the new structures of elite Protestant churches. They hired an architect who designed an elaborate building in a Byzantine motif which was in many respects a graceful wooden replica of San Francisco's magnificent Sutter Street Synagogue, Temple Emanu-El. Of the ninety-two members who contributed to the building fund, fifty-one were also members of Concordia, and their average pledge of $250 was six times the average pledge to the congregation's first building fund less than twenty-five years before. Of the seventy-eight men who were members of Lodge 416 through 1897, forty-five had contributed or had an older relative who had contributed to the Beth Israel building fund.[72]

A further measure of the successful business connections and high social standing of the members of Lodge 416 was their extremely high persistence in Portland. Of the seventy-seven inductees between 1891 and 1896, fifty-five were still in Portland in 1905. Jewish men at their stage in the life cycle before 1890 had far more frequently sought employment opportunities elsewhere. By 1905, however, the businesses which most members of Lodge 416 had inherited or the capital they had been able to bring to new ventures provided the economic base and in many cases the pioneer heritage to promote successful careers. The residential pattern and trajectory of the members of Lodge 416 further indicate their privileged start in life and their ability to utilize wealth to insulate their elite status. Of the seventy-two inductees between 1891 and 1896 for whom addresses could be found, 50 percent lived in the West Park Street area and 25 percent in the North 16th Street area when they joined the Lodge as young men. In addition, eight inductees lived in the still more exclusive section west of 17th Street. By 1900, following construction of the streetcar lines and the centrifugal mobility of the city's upper middle class, members of Lodge 416 left the West Park Street area for the northwest suburbs. Like the wealthy Jews of San Francisco, they also clustered on specific streets. Those settling in the northwest also tended to retain their place of residence for longer periods than had the members of prior lodges who had previously settled in older parts of the city.[73] Their wealth and the available public transportation allowed them to select homesites in residential neighborhoods far enough from the downtown to be protected from the rapid expansion of the commercial district and from continual contact with the working class. By 1905, twenty-five of the fifty-four members still residing in Portland for whom addresses could be obtained lived in the North 16th Street region. They had ceased the continual search for better lodgings that had occupied most Jews until the 1890s.

Despite the affluence of many of its members and the enthusiasm of the officers, Lodge 416 was not at first supported with great diligence. But as the leadership created innovative activities that expressed their changing social status, the lodge became more popular. At many early meetings it failed to obtain a quorum, and some of the officers were asked to resign because of their sporadic attendance. Initially, members took special interest in the traditional lodge functions of visiting the sick and accepting fraternal visits from the officers of older lodges. On 15 October 1891 all three lodges held a pleasant joint celebration of the forty-eighth birthday of the B'nai B'rith order. The officers of the three lodges even considered following the precedent set in San Francisco, where the lodges combined to erect B'nai B'rith hall.[74] Despite the general malaise that seemed to affect the B'nai B'rith lodges nationally in the 1890s, Lodge 416 grew. To attract new members the officers solicited individuals. But more important, under the leadership of Samuel Friedlander, manager of the city's exclusive Marquam Opera House, they initiated more lively entertainment. The performance in October 1893 included vocal and instrumental solos by the wives and female friends of members.[75] The operatic arias, romantic ballads, and classical piano and violin recitations may have symbolized the decorative character of bourgeoise women in the Victorian era and suggested a hierarchical division between the sexes.[76] But the performances by women *at lodge meetings*, combined with other changes in family structure and female life patterns, which will be discussed in Chapter 2, indicate closer relations between men and women and a further decline of patriarchalism among the American-born.

Although innovations within Lodge 416 reflected more egalitarian tendencies within families, they accentuated the social distance between its members and those of the other lodges. As the status of Lodge 416's membership rose and as their social patterns became more typical of an urban elite, the older lodges became inactive, while the newest lodge contained far more traditional Eastern Europeans. By 1900 members of Lodge 416 were reaching middle age, assuming leadership of the Jewish business network, and establishing residences in the suburbs. One mark of their greater individual affluence and more modern resources for meeting personal welfare needs was the virtual termination of the beneficiary membership. Over half of the members of Lodge 65 and over 70 percent of the members of Lodge 314 had dropped the benefit service during the 1890s, but eighty-eight of the eighty-nine members of Lodge 416 had discontinued the service by 1904.[77] The virtual disappearance of the service for members of Lodge 416 probably reflects their greater youth, which would predispose insurance companies to accept them as actuarial risks while rejecting the older members of Lodges 65 and 314. But the greater affluence of the members of Lodge 416 would also allow them to buy insurance from private companies—whose agents in Portland now included lodge members—in greater amounts than they could through the lodge's mutual benefit service.

The discussions at meetings of Lodge 416 and the increase in membership and in size of the treasury by 1904 further indicate the social distance developing between it and the other lodges. Its membership remained stable at about ninety between 1902 and 1907, while its treasury grew from $2,200 to $3,150.[78] The lodge, like Concordia was no longer actively recruiting newcomers, and the German families by the turn of the century were much smaller and capable of producing fewer recruits than the previous generation. Discussions at meetings had shifted from the health of missing members and local lodge business to potential charitable contributions to civic endeavors similar to those supported by the Hebrew Benevolent Association. Like the members of the association, those in Lodge 416 saw themselves as moral guides rather than as comrades of the majority of Jews arriving in Portland. The lodge cooperated briefly with Lodge 314 to form a local relief board for Jewish newcomers, and it contributed to the Neighborhood House, a settlement organized by the local Council of Jewish Women. It raised money to assist the Jews of Cracow who had suffered from fire and the Jews of Silesia who had endured a pogrom. Locally, the lodge contributed to the building fund of Congregation Ahavai Shalom and to a fund for constructing an industrial school as part of the public system.[79]

Information about the Sabato Morais Lodge 464 is harder to obtain than for Lodge 416, although surviving initiation data and references to it in the minutes of other lodges suggest an active membership consisting of Russian Jews of diverse skills and great energy but limited funds. Information gathered from the 1900 federal manuscript census and the records of other institutions, however, indicates that many members had far more complex backgrounds and would play crucial roles in the community's future. Like the founders of the other lodges, the members of Lodge 464 were also young men with family responsibilities. Of the 152 inductees between 1897 and 1904, eighty-one could be located in the census, and their median age was then thirty-four. Since the lodge had then been in existence for three years, the median age of its members at founding was approximately the same as for the other lodges. The median age, however, does not indicate the greater range of ages than in any previous lodge, with its implications of more varied social interests. Several generations were included: two members were below age twenty-one and thirteen were between twenty-two and twenty-five in 1900, while nine were then fifty years old or more. Elite German Jews might refer to those in Lodge 464 as "Russians" in need of Americanization, but their actual acculturation was already substantial. As Table 8 indicates, 62 percent of the men located in the census listed Russia or Russian Poland as their place of birth, almost 20 percent listed Germany, and 6 percent listed Austria. Furthermore, the great majority were not newcomers to the United States. Twelve percent had arrived prior to 1880, and 55 percent had arrived during the 1880s. Many had been brought to America as children and spent their formative years in public schools, and almost all had become American citizens. Isaac Swett had arrived from Odessa in 1882 with his father, who acquired a small berry farm at Buxton, west of Portland. Isaac had studied law and practiced in Portland, although he spent several weeks each year working on the farm.[80] David Nemerovsky and Israel Dautoff became inermediaries between the Hebrew Benevolent Association and the poorer Russian Jews who arrived after 1900 and sought financial assistance. Both men encouraged their children, including their daughters, to pursue professional careers, and in the next generation those children provided important services to the community. Isaac Swett, Nathan and Sam Weinstein, Ben Pallay, Leon Semler, and the Holzman brothers became pillars of Ahavai Shalom and led its move from orthodoxy to conservatism.[81] Far from being "greenhorns,"

Table 8. *Portland: Lodge 464 Membership by Place of Birth and Years of Arrival in the United States*

Place of Birth	No.	%	Year of Arrival in U.S.	No.	%
Poland, Russia	50	61.8	1858–1868	2	2.7
Rumania	1	1.2	1869–1879	7	9.6
Germany	15	18.5	1880–1889	40	54.8
Austria	5	6.2	1890–1895	21	28.8
Hungary	1	1.2	1896–1900	3	4.1
England	1	1.2		73	100.0
United States	8	9.9			
Total	81	100.0			

men like these turned to an American institution, the B'nai B'rith, rather than to *landsmenshaften* to meet their needs for secular sociability. They were not, however, "sons of the pioneers," and their social ascent would be within their own set of institutions.

The occupational profile of Lodge 464 was most similar to that of Lodge 65, founded thirty years previously. Almost 60 percent of those for whom occupations could be located in city directories were proprietors, almost 17 percent white-collar employees, and another 17 percent were skilled or semiskilled workers. By occupational distribution alone the members of Lodge 464 seem to have been of higher status than the members of Lodge 314 in the 1880s. The status of an occupation, however, is not intrinsic, but depends on the larger economic and social structure of the setting in which it is practiced. The proprietors who predominated in Lodge 65 in the 1860s and 1870s were pioneer merchants serving the needs of the city's entire population and maturing with the locale.[82] The clerks and tailors who predominated in Lodge 314 were employed by established firms in a small commercial city and were part of a social network that stretched from the wealthy proprietors to their sons and other employees, who were often nephews and cousins. By the turn of the century, in a city of almost 100,000, the status of the small general proprietor had shifted dramatically downward. Most of the merchants who predominated in Lodge 464, though going through a similar procedure to establish a small business as had the pioneer peddlers, served the city's poorer classes rather than the general public. Its twelve peddlers sold their wares in the city's alleys as well as in the countryside. Of its fifty-five retail merchants, twenty-one specialized in second-hand goods and were pawnbrokers. Their stores along Front Street, 1st Street, and North 3rd Street were adjacent to saloons, houses of prostitution, and rooming houses for unattached men and poor young couples of American and mixed foreign background. Sixteen other members of Lodge 464 were clerks working primarily for the ten clothing merchants who also belonged to the lodge. A few members, for example, Philip Gevurtz and Joseph Ricen, owned expanding furniture and drug stores, and Samuel Barde was starting a junk business on the waterfront that would become a steel manufacturing plant. But most merchants in the lodge operated marginal businesses.[83]

The low economic status of the members of Lodge 464 can be discerned in several ways. While no member of Lodge 416 lived at his place of work, many of the merchants and a few of the clerks in Lodge 464 lived in their stores in the second-hand goods district along Front Street. Others boarded in the area. The lodge also experienced a high rate of transiency, and the treasury was so low and the members so hard-pressed for funds that the lodge could not initiate a mutual benefit service. The District Grand Lodge had by the turn of the century grown indifferent to mutual benefits, and its past president, Hugo Asher, in a talk in Portland in 1906, suggested that all local lodges abolish the benefit service and focus on cultural and philanthropic work. Aaron Tilzer, a physician and former member of Lodge 464, argued instead that members of his lodge were leaving the B'nai B'rith and joining the Rose City Lodge of the new Order of B'nai Abraham precisely for the mutual benefit services. Most men he knew, Tilzer continued, joined a fraternal lodge for the mutual benefits and could "not yet afford to be altruists."[84] Furthermore, of the 132 members for whom occupations could be found when they joined the lodge, only 58 percent remained in Portland through 1910 (i.e., from 6 to 13 years). This persistence rate was more than double that of the pioneer men of the 1860s, but it was almost 10 percent lower than for the Jewish men of the 1880s. As with other lodges, clerks, peddlers, and skilled workers were more likely to leave than sedentary merchants, but only about two-thirds of the latter group remained through 1910. Overall persistence was higher than for the Russian Jews studied by Howard Chudakoff in Omaha during this period, but the propensity of the lower occupational strata to leave was about the same for both locales.[85]

The residential pattern of the members of Lodge 464 also reflects their background as small shopkeepers and craftsmen serving the urban proletariat. In addition to the intensive clustering of the second-hand goods dealers along Front Street between Oak and Salmon, sixty-nine others lived along the streetcar lines to the south in a thin strip bounded by 2nd and 3rd streets, Madison on the north and Arthur on the south. A few members resided even further south, adjacent to the new industrial district along the waterfront. Lodge 464 was also the first to have a contingent settle across the Willamette River in East Portland.

The members of Lodge 464, however, hardly belonged to the city's proletariat. They followed most of the occupations of the Jews of the Lower East Side of New York or of the Russian Pale, but in much different proportions. I. M. Rubinow, in his classic study of the employment of Russian Jews at the turn of the century, demonstrated that they clustered in the manufacturing of ready-made clothing and wood and metal products, and in commerce and domestic service. Among the immigrants, thousands were skilled workers, especially tailors, but thousands more were laborers and servants. On the Lower East Side of New York, in East Harlem, and in Brownsville in Brooklyn, tailors and skilled workers predominated, while the laborers and servants found work in semiskilled capacities.[86] But the Polish and Russian Jews in Portland, as in most middle-sized commercial cities, were already small-scale merchants. Even most peddlers and expressmen were self-employed, and their American-born children were finding white-collar work. They contributed to a mercantile rather than a proletarian environment.

For reasons that remain unclear, Portland's two oldest B'nai B'rith lodges declined sharply in membership in the late 1890s. Possibly death began to claim members of Lodge 65, while several men with political and social ambitions, like Sig Sichel and Henry Ackerman, left Lodge 314 for Lodge 416. The District Grand Lodge noted the decline with alarm and suggested that Lodges 65 and 314 merge with the small but vigorous Lodge 464. In 1904, the president of the District Grand Lodge, Wallace Wise, visited Portland and encouraged consolidation. Lodge 65 held aloof for a year, perhaps because its members took pride in their southern German origins or perhaps because their treasury was the largest of the three. Lodge 314, comprised of older men of Prussian or western Polish origins and some Russians, voted almost immediately to consolidate with the younger men of Polish and Russian origins in Lodge 464. Some were relatives, and a few shared membership in Ahavai Shalom. By mid-1905, even Lodge 65's members had reconsidered, and all three formed a new Lodge 314, named after Theodore Herzl, the recently deceased founder of modern Zionism and the key promoter of Jewish secular communal consolidation.[87]

Still, membership declined precipitously in the consolidated lodge, in part because of the class cleavages now apparent in the community. Although Lodge 416 grew wealthier and its members considered requests for charitable contributions from Jewish and even nonsectarian sources, it would not assist the other lodge financially. During the years when consolidation was being discussed, the members of Lodge 416 never considered the matter at their meetings, and their officers never suggested that they might join the movement. The spokesmen simply assumed that the task of "Americanizing" the immigrant belonged to Lodge 464, and that less financially secure lodges had to find their own means to survive. In a growing Jewish community after 1907, the B'nai B'rith revived. A new prosperity among members of Lodge 314 led to new recruits and the organization of an independent B'nai B'rith Building Association to erect a center that might meet their new social interests. Final unification of the lodges, however, did not occur until 1919, as part of an effort to consolidate all Jewish communal services because of increased welfare needs and new interest in developing Palestine as the Jewish homeland.[88]

By 1900, the successive founding of B'nai B'rith lodges provided a fairly clear picture of how social strata emerged within the Jewish community. The career trajectories of the members and the operation of institutions like the Hebrew Benevolent Association explain how Jewish men created and sustained a stable economic niche. The data also allow for comparison with other ethnic enclaves. Like Jewish communities in other middle-sized towns, such as Columbus, Ohio; Atlanta, Georgia; Syracuse, New York; and San Francisco, California, the enclave in Portland focused on mercantile pursuits from the outset. Even craftsmen saw themselves as small businessmen and were integrated into the lodge network of the community. Unlike the huge settlement in New York and communities of 100,000 Jews or more in Philadelphia and Chicago, a Jewish proletariat did not exist in the smaller cities which have so far been studied. The midwestern and western stereotypes of the Jews as clothing merchants, peddlers, and successful traders in fact corresponded to Portland's Jewish occupational profile. Jewish merchants also opened stores and rented or built houses close to one another, though not in densely settled areas as in the largest industrial cities. By 1900, Jews numbered about 2,200[89] out of a total population of 93,000, and were creating a socially varied and distinctive bourgeoise enclave. They had not come from such communities, however, and like the American farm boys and young women, and the European peasants who had settled in the new town, their life styles and ideologies had to be created anew. In their families, especially in the lives of women and children, and in the development of a civic consciousness, the major changes to a modern sense of social order were developed. To the issues of social modernization and civic order we turn in the next two chapers.

2. Jewish Women and Social Modernization 1870–1930

Observing the extraordinary changes that had transformed American Jewish families by the early 1920s, Rabbi Stephen Wise wondered, "What manner of children are to be reared by a generation of bridge experts, of women half-crazed with the pleasure of card tables to whom no prize of life is as precious as the temptations of bridge whist."[1] Wise may have been overcome momentarily by his passion for rhetoric, but he hardly exaggerated the changes in life options for women and in the structure of Jewish family life that had occurred since the 1880s. Tamara Hareven has noted that family organization and habits seem particularly resistant to change even in industrial societies. In Buffalo, New York, for example, Italian families remained intact despite separation during the year and promoted smooth resettlement. Multi-generational Czech families in south Texas provided the mutual assistance that enabled many to rise from renters to farm owners.[2] For German and Eastern European Jews family networks also eased resettlement in America. But for them, over two generations the family became the scene of more rapid and fundamental changes than even the world of work. Men may have risen from itinerant to sedentary merchants, from retailers to suppliers, but their form of work and even lines of trade remained substantially unchanged over two or three generations.

For women and children of both German and Eastern European families, the demands and opportunities of American cities disrupted the patterns of dependence that presumably had existed for many generations. Changes in their life cycles were far more dramatic than for men. While the family traditions of German Jews differed substantially from those of East Europeans, the American-born daughters of both groups began to exercise options for employment outside the home, for decisions about marriage and family structure and even for civic participation that differed radically from those of their mothers. Indeed, they very quickly came to resemble one another despite continuing differences in wealth. In addition, women's voluntary associations, which had slowly evolved in Europe, were quckly founded in America. They responded to major changes in Jewish community structure as quickly as did men's groups like the B'nai B'rith. While multifamily assistance eased resettlement, drastic changes in family structure and roles gave women new authority and encouraged their ability to provide leadership and to influence community values.

I

The term most often used to characterize traditional Jewish families is "patriarchy," which implies not only that property and name are passed from father to son, but that within the families the sexes socialized separately and that men made the major decisions linking the family to the outside world.[3] The term, however, has been very broadly applied to describe most families in agricultural societies, from West Africa to the mid-nineteenth-century American Middle West.[4] By implication, the families of rural pioneers who crossed the plains had much in common with the German Jews whose discontented sons sought commercial opportunities along the water routes. Nevertheless, recent studies of family life in Bavarian villages, in the American Middle West, on the Oregon Trail, and in the early settlements of the Willamette Valley suggest substantial variation in the organization of "patriarchal" families. Many differences in the timing of family formation, in the social characteristics of the spouses, and in family structure suggest that "patriarchy" arose for different reasons, took different forms, and in cities like Portland was highly susceptible to erosion. While the term does help us understand particularly the organization of German Jewish families, women and their daughters in Portland seem to have shown far more independence than their counterparts in Germany. Their ability to organize for mutual assistance and to create an independent cultural life which paralleled and at some points merged with that of their husbands also seems far greater than for Oregon's rural women.[5]

With husbands and most wives reared in Germany, we might assume that their new families retained many social traditions despite the frontier setting in which they were formed. Unfortunately, no modern studies exist of Jewish families in nineteenth-century German towns, so we know little about their size, their composition, and their propensity to change over several generations. Bernard Goldsmith, for example, noted that his family had lived in Weddenberg, a small town midway between Nuremberg and Munich, for generations and that his mother had had ten children, suggesting both

7. The German patriarchal family: The Ehrman brothers and their wives, 1892
(Oregon Historical Society)

continuity in residence and the traditional large rural family. But he also
noted that his father had substantially expanded the family's fortunes, thus
suggesting the prospect of economic mobility even in an old town, and that
the business had been moved to Munich, thus contributing to substantial
change in regional trade patterns.[6] Furthermore, all of his brothers and sisters
survived childhood, which was remarkable in an area that reported infant
mortality rates of about 45 percent as late as the 1880s.[7] "Patriarchy"
prevailed among South German families, at least through the early
nineteenth century, because the laws required that all men—Jews as well as
gentiles—be established as craftsmen or merchants before they could obtain
marriage licenses in the towns. Women had neither civil rights nor the means
to become economically independent. The process of migration to America
to some extent reinforced the patriarchal tradition by emphasizing the man's

8. The first women professionals: Ida & Zerlinda Lowenberg, front row; Rose Loewenberg Goodman and daughter Laddie Goodman Trachtenberg, 1946

role as explorer and provider. But it also helped erode that tradition by requiring that the wife initiate organizations for women's welfare and by exposing her to new educational and economic opportunities.

The reinforcement of a patriarchal tradition in an American city like Portland can be seen most easily in family structure and emerging sex roles. In Portland, as in Bavaria, men tended to marry at a substantially later age than they do in mid- and late- twentieth-century America. An intensive study of parish records for Anhausen, a village 13 kilometers southwest of Augsburg, indicated that in the nineteenth century Bavarian men did not contract an initial marriage until about age thirty.[8] This was about the same as for native-born middle-class men in a suburb of Chicago at the same time.[9]

Table 9. *Portland Jewish Women, 1900: Age at Marriage by Place of Birth and Age*

Place of birth and age group (1900)	19 or under		20–25 years		26–29 years		30 years or over		Total
	No.	%	No.	%	No.	%	No.	%	No.
German-born									
40 yrs or over	34	37.4	44	48.4	6	6.6	7	7.7	91
Under age 40	15	34.9	23	53.5	5	11.6	0	0	43
American-born of German father									
40 yrs or over	13	40.6	16	50.0	1	3.1	2	6.2	32
Under age 40	23	24.2	60	63.2	10	10.5	2	2.1	95
East European-born									
40 yrs or over	37	52.1	25	35.2	5	7.0	4	5.6	71
Under age 40	52	63.4	27	32.9	2	2.4	1	1.2	82
American-born of East European father									
40 yrs or over	1	100.0	0		0		0		1
Under age 40	6	28.5	13	61.9	1	4.8	1	4.8	21
American-born of American father									
40 yrs or over	1	20.0	2	40.0	0	0	2	40.0	5
Under age 40	7	30.4	15	65.2	1	4.3	0	0	23

SOURCE: *United States Manuscript Census, 1900*

However, while men in Bavarian villages generally selected women two to four years younger than themselves, almost two-thirds of Portland's German Jewish men in 1880 had married wives seven to ten years younger. The choice of substantially younger women suggests that men already accustomed to becoming financially secure prior to marriage found that migration had separated them from the cohort of women to which they would have ordinarily turned for wives. As Table 9 indicates, younger women, in turn, would not have had to wait so long to establish families, and they could now find men who would promise them a reasonable prospect of financial security. Stephen Wise, writing in the 1920s, reminds us that for Jewish merchant families, at least, marriage provided the only legitimate opportunity for a young woman to leave her father's house.[10] The reappearance in the home village or even in larger cities like Munich of successful young merchants from America enhanced this opportunity.

The difference in age and experience, however, reinforced the authority of the husband in the marriage and indicated that the wife would neither be expected nor required to exercise independent judgment in financial or most other matters. The welfare demands of life on the urban frontier would in fact require young women to assume major communal responsibility, which the demographic profile of households fails to indicate. Nevertheless, the pattern of youthful marriage to men substantially older than themselves continued after the pioneering era. The abolition of marriage restrictions even in conservative Bavaria in 1870, as well as the achievement of a far more even sex ratio among Jews of German descent in America, had only a limited effect on marriage patterns. In 1900 most women in Germany did not marry until their mid-twenties and then they married men about three years older than themselves.[11] Again as Table 9 indicates, among American-born women of German descent *under* age forty, only 24 percent had married in their teens, a percentage substantially below that of American-born women *over* age forty. But as Table 10 demonstrates the majority of the younger women still married men at least seven to ten years older. They saw, as had their older sisters, the importance of selecting a spouse who could provide an established home, and they faced a social setting in which men who sought wives would still be in their late twenties and early thirties.

Despite a patriarchal structure, Portland's German Jewish families were

Table 10. *Portland Jewry, 1880–1900: Age of Wife Relative to Age of Husband*

Place of Birth and Age	Wife Older than Husband		Wife 0–3 Years Younger		Wife 4–6 Years Younger		Wife 7–10 Years Younger		Wife 11 or more Years Younger		Total
1880	N	%	N	%	N	%	N	%	N	%	N
German-born	2	03.0	9	14.0	14	21.0	18	27.0	23	35.0	66
American-born	0	00.0	2	08.0	8	33.0	7	29.0	7	29.0	24
1900 German-born											
40 yrs or over	5	07.0	19	25.0	8	11.0	16	21.0	27	36.0	75
Under age 40	1	02.0	11	25.0	11	25.0	11	25.0	10	23.0	44
American-born of German father											
40 yrs or over	1	04.0	6	23.0	4	15.0	6	23.0	9	35.0	26
Under age 40	1	01.0	17	18.0	24	26.0	29	32.0	21	23.0	92
East European-born											
40 yrs or over	5	9.0	30	56.0	9	17.0	5	9.0	5	9.0	54
Under age 40	3	4.0	42	51.0	19	23.0	14	17.0	5	6.0	83
American-born of East European father											
40 yrs or over	0		0		0		0		0		0
Under age 40	0	0.0	6	35.0	4	24.0	5	29.0	2	12.0	17
American-born of American father											
40 yrs or over	2	29.0	2	29.0	1	14.0	2	29.0	0		7
Under age 40	1	05.0	7	32.0	5	22.5	4	18.0	5	22.5	22
											420

SOURCE: *United States Manuscript Census, 1880; 1900*

hardly traditional in the sense meant by contemporary students of family history. Men did remain responsible for family income, while married women, as in Bavaria, rarely were listed as employed. But in Portland, as opposed to European villages or even Willamette Valley farms, women were neither confined to the home nor emmeshed in their own economic and social sphere.[12] Instead, they created institutions parallel to that of the men, so that they might in a frontier setting carry out traditional household responsibilities. In the process, however, they gained administrative skills, which they passed on to their daughters—who, in the next generation, organized a far more politically conscious and socially innovative institution, the Council of Jewish Women.

The activities of the major voluntary association among the pioneer women, the First Hebrew Ladies Benevolent Society, founded in May 1874, demonstrated how women created a flexible institution for their needs as wives and mothers. In the mid-1860s men had established health and death benefit insurance for themselves through the new B'nai B'rith lodge, and in the early 1870s they reinforced the economic side of the male sphere through their benevolent society. In a community of increased and growing families in the early 1870s, the young wives found that their husbands might be long distances from home on buying or selling trips, and they pooled their resources to aid one another. They assumed tasks which in Germany had accrued gradually, over many centuries. The Hebrew Ladies Benevolent Society was organized "to administer relief to the poor, the needy, the sick, and to prepare the dead for interment" among "ladies of the Jewish faith."[13] The Society regularized the female responsibility of visiting the sick and caring for children by empowering the vice-president to recruit members for the tasks. When members found it impossible to remain with the sick overnight, the society raised funds to pay for nurses, as well as to pay doctors for visits at home and hospitals for treating the very will. They supported several destitute women whose husbands had died or deserted them, and provided travel funds for wives and children desiring to rejoin husbands in distant cities.[14]

Initially the women were under the direction of men, perhaps because so many members were so young. The president and secretary, who could jointly dispense small charitable donations without the consent of the all-female board of directors, were under the constitution allowed to be men. For the first five years they were men, until Mrs. Cecelie Friedlander became secretary in 1879. As the society grew, the women gradually asserted their independence from male control. In 1884 the president, Edward Kahn, a fifty-year-old hide merchant and the patriarch of a large family, resigned; he was succeeded by Mrs. Bernard Goldsmith. Goldsmith himself was one of the most forceful and politically prominent of Portland's Jews, having served as mayor from 1869 to 1871. In 1891 he was named on a committee of three, along with Julius Loewenberg and Ben Selling, to advise the Hebrew Ladies Benevolent Society on the proper investments for its endowment. But Mrs. Goldsmith clearly had strong managerial skills as well. As Judge Matthew Deady volunteered in an interview about Goldsmith in 1889, "His wife is an excellent woman, an admirable woman. She is a woman of a great deal more than ordinary ability."[15] With her next-door neighbor and close friend Mrs. Philip Wasserman as treasurer during the 1880s, Mrs. Goldsmith gave the society strong leadership, and it never again turned to men for officers.[16] With the officers continuously stressing the need for recruitment, the society grew from 43 in 1875 to 177 by 1893.[17]

The women's role as source of nurture in the family was reinforced by the sharing of responsibility, because only women served on the Benevolent Society's various committees and provided the nursing services. So exclusively maternal was nurture considered that when Fannie Barman died in 1885, her children were referred to as "orphans" even though her husband, a successful dry-goods merchant, survived her.[18] Through the society women faced the single most serious form of continual grief: the death of children. Requests for burial in Beth Israel cemetary in the 1870s and 1880s indicate that far more children than adults were then interred. From August of 1872 through Decmeber of 1873, for example, nine of the eleven special requests for burial were for children.[19] Records of death kept by the rabbis of Beth Israel for the northwest region from 1877 through 1900 showed a more balanced incidence of mortality through the life cycle. As Table 11 indicates, however, through the mid-1880s children under ten years of age were still almost 43 percent of the total, and children under one year old were almost 25 percent. By the early 1890s, the proportion of children under ten years of age among the dead fell below 18 percent, and in the years from 1895 to 1900 they were less than 8 percent of the total, reflecting both better health care and smaller families. The aging of the pioneer generation had also by then pushed the proportion of deaths in the sixty-year-old-and-above age group to almost 50 percent of the total, and for the first time this age group provided the largest proportion of the deaths.[20]

The best documented case of bereavement and of collective care is that of Henrietta Goodman, who had been born in Louisiana in 1849 and in her late

Table 11. *Deaths Recorded by Rabbis of Beth Israel, 1877–1900, by Age Group*

Time Span	(yrs.)	0–9 Years	(%)	10–17 Years	(%)	18–59 Years	(%)	60 + Years	(%)	Total Deaths
1877–1885	(9)	33	(42.8)	6	(7.9)	30	(38.9)	8	(10.4)	77
1886–1894	(9)	10	(17.5)	1	(1.8)	33	(57.9)	13	(22.8)	57
1895–1900	(6)	5	(07.5)	1	(1.4)	30	(44.8)	31	(46.3)	67

SOURCE: Compiled from *Record of Deaths*, Beth Israel, Portland, Oregon, Papers, AJA

teens had married an L. Goodman, sixteen years her senior and an immigrant merchant from Bavaria. The couple had arrived in Oregon in 1867, where their two daughters were born. By 1873, however, Mrs. Goodman, then still only twenty-four years old, had lost her husband and one of her daughters. Beth Israel provided the burial plot and the carriage for the child's funeral. Two years later, Mrs. Goodman left Portland for a "distant part of the country," perhaps to return to her native state. So moved by her losses and impressed by her personality were her colleagues of the Benevolent Society that they passed in her honor the only resolution to a living member in the nineteenth century. It read in part, "She was very zealous in the holy cause of charity, and who having undergone many trials and tribulations herself, knew well how to sympathize with the suffering and distress of others."[21]

By American standards in the late nineteenth century, the percent of children who died in Portland's Jewish families was actually rather low. This might be attributed partially to the mild climate, which pioneers had recommended since the 1840s. Although a few cases of smallpox and the suspicion of other diseases led to the quarantine of Chinese laborers in 1869, Mayor Philip Wasserman by 1872 reported that the city had never experienced diseases which had become epidemic elsewhere. By 1910, Mayor Joseph Simon commended the health department for its diligence and in his annual message, cited both the absence of epidemics and the low death rate. The death rate rose from seven to eleven per thousand between 1909 and 1910, but it remained among the lowest in the nation.[22]

A comparison of the proportion of children who died among the various segments of Portland Jewry in 1900, indicates first that all segments had a lower childhood mortality rate than the general American population. Only the Eastern European immigrants approached the American average, and many of their children were reared, at least for a part of their lives, in European *shtetls* and ghettoes. Nevertheless, their relatively low mortality rates—as compared with the American average and with that of Italian and Polish immigrants—may be partially attributed to the relatively high number of Jewish midwives and nurses in Russian cities and to their appearance in Portland as well. Although Stephen S. Wise was quite critical in 1902 of one Jewish doctor used frequently by the Hebrew Ladies Benevolent Society to care for the poor,[23] the women did act quickly when cases were brought to their attention. It is perhaps surprising that, according to Table 12, the children of second-generation German Jews should have had a higher mortality rate than the children of second-generation Russian and Polish Jews. The number of women in the latter group, however, was small, and their families were very young. Half of the women had had only one child, and for all segments of the community women having three or fewer children rarely experienced any childhood deaths. A few large families suffered severe childhood mortality. Among the Germans, Caroline and Julius Walter had had nine children, only two of whom were alive in 1900, whereas among the Russians, Lizzy and Morris Applestone had lost four of seven children, and Bertha Spiro, only forty years old in 1900, had had with her husband Abraham ten children, only three of whom survived. Nevertheless, only a dozen families in the community in 1900 had had seven or more children over half of whom had died.[24]

Table 12. *Portland, 1900: Childhood Mortality for Mothers 50 Years Old and Younger*

Mother's Place of Birth	No. Women	No. Births	Individual Birth Rate	No. Children Died	% Children Died
Germany–West Europe*	60	241	(4.02)	21	8.7
U.S.†—German father	95	214	(2.25)	18	8.4
East Europe‡	124	584	(4.71)	77	13.2
U.S.—East European father	14	29	(2.07)	2	6.9
U.S.—U.S. father	23	54	(2.35)	3	5.5
U.S.A.		1186		186	15.7

SOURCE: *Historical Statistics of the United States, Colonial Times to 1957* (Washington, 1960), 28, Series B, columns 144–147
*Includes France, Austria
†Includes England, Canada, Australia
‡Includes Russia, Poland, Hungary, Rumania, Bulgaria

Assistance for the bereaved typified the individual acts of charity to which the Benevolent Society continued to devote itself. It also responded to the growth of the Jewish community by welcoming a few women of Eastern European descent, like Mary Dautoff, who continuously made requests for aid for families that needed food, clothing, or wood. As older women died in larger numbers in the 1890s, the society appointed a committee of five with rotating membership to assist in the burials, and also placed limits on expenditures for members' funerals. Similarly, "visiting" with sick members was better organized when a permanent committee of six, also with rotating membership, replaced the informal recruitment of volunteers by the vice-president.[25]

By 1900, the society was run by older women, who seemed reluctant to alter either their conception of welfare or the relationship between Jewish women and their gentile counterparts. The scope of their charity was expanded slightly when they donated $100 in 1903 to the victims of the Kishineff pogrom and $500 in 1906 to the Jews who had suffered in the San Francisco earthquake. But several of the latter must have been personal friends or relatives, and their donations in both emergencies were part of a city-wide fund-raising effort led by the men of the B'nai B'rith, the First

Hebrew Benevolent Association, and the synagogues.[26] Although in 1903, under prodding probably from Rabbi Wise, the society joined the National Conference of Jewish Charities, it discretely tabled a motion by Mrs. Wise that it amend its constitution to allow donations to non-Jewish causes. When Mrs. Bertha Loewenberg, perhaps at the suggestion of her daughter Ida, who was active in social work, reintroduced Mrs. Wise's resolution in 1909, it was defeated.[27] Perhaps a sign of the society's growing isolation from the mainstream of Jewish communal life can be seen in the dwindling attendance at meetings. In the 1890s it usually reached twenty-five, while by 1907 the annual meeting attracted only eleven members.[28] For the ladies of the Benevolent Society philanthropy continued to mean the village notion of piecemeal charity.

Table 13. *Incidence of Spinsterhood and Bachelorhood, Portland Jewry, 1900*

Social Origins	Unmarried Women 25 yrs and over	All Married Women	Ratio	Unmarried Men Over 35 yrs†	Over 30 yrs‡	Ratio
German & descendants	56	268	1: 4.8	40	xx	1: 6.7
Eastern European & descendants	6	154	1:25.6	xx	6	1:25.6

*Age 25 selected because 87.4% of married women of German descent and 92.0% of married women of Eastern European descent had married prior to age 25
†Age 35 selected for men of German descent because over half (54.8%) were married to women at least 7 years younger than themselves and would be married by age 35
‡Age 30 selected for men of Eastern European descent because over 70% were married to women 0 to 6 years younger than themselves and would be married by age 30
SOURCE: *United States Manuscript Census, 1900*

Another remnant of the patriarchal tradition was the high incidence of spinsterhood and bachelorhood. Several scholars have recently noted the unique conditions in eighteenth- and nineteenth-century Western Europe, in which far more adults than in Eastern Europe never married. In societies where a small number of guild masters and landholders demanded intensive social control, particularly over population, marriage licenses were difficult to acquire.[29] Despite new social freedoms in America, many Jewish men and women of German descent found bachelorhood and spinsterhood satisfying, and they were not stigmatized as were the far smaller number of unmarried adults in the Eastern European families. When questioned about his decision not to marry, one Jewish resident of Baker, Oregon, simply replied that he had been preoccupied with establishing a business. Several Jewish women in the same town remained spinsters, perhaps because they found no suitable men for mates.[30] Most of the daughters of very successful merchants like Soloman Hirsch, Julius Loewenberg, and Max Friendly also chose not to marry, or married quite late, perhaps as their nieces have suggested because they could not find men who matched their fathers' forceful character.[31] Some women, like Ida and Zerlinda Loewenberg, developed professional ambitions when the death of their father left the family with a much diminished income. But their experiences were hardly unusual. The ratio of unmarried women of German descent over age twenty-five (when the great majority wishing to marry had already done so) to all married women of German descent in 1900 was 1 to 4.8. For women of Eastern European descent the same ratio was 1 to 25.6. Indeed, the decision not to marry by women of German descent in Portland was made in a city with a sex ratio in which men substantially outnumbered women at least through 1910.[32] Not the lack of men, least of all the desire to marry gentiles, but rather a social tradition that accepted the single life as a very common alternative, led many women and men to remain unattached.

The family, however, remained the context in which unmarried people carried out their lives. Unmarried men as well as women, regardless of age, invariably lived with their parents. Anselm and Fred Boskowitz, whose parents lived at the turn of the century in Eastern Oregon, came to Portland as young men for white-collar employment and lived with their grandmother, Adeline Bloch. Most of Anselm's aunts and uncles never married and resided together in the family home and later in an apartment. Anselm also remained a bachelor and resided for decades with single brothers and sisters a short distance from the Blochs.[33] In other cases, as the parents died, the unmarried adult children moved to the home of a married sister or brother. If several unmarried adults existed in the same family, like the Blochs and the Boskowitz brothers, they eventually moved to a residential hotel.

The patriarchal family faced dramatic erosion, however, not only because so many who were reared in it never married to recreate the form, but because American-born women had substantially lower fertility rates than did their mothers. The United States manuscript census returns for 1900 provide data not only on the composition of households, but on the number of children ever born to each woman. A comparison of German- and American-born women in the same age groups suggests some of the effects of the new setting on family composition. Because women under age thirty, despite in many cases having been married over ten years, are presumed to be still at the beginning of their child-bearing years, we include for comparative purposes here only those women in the age categories 30 to 39 years, and 40 years old and older. Among women in their thirties, who would have begun to have children in the late 1880s and early 1890s, 33 percent of the German-born had at least four to six. Among the American-born in the same age group, only 5 percent had at least four children, and none had over five. Among women forty years old and over who bore at least one child, half of the German-born had had at least six children, but only 5.5 percent of the American-born had borne that many. The great majority of Americans had had no more than three, thus emulating the general American fertility rate of 3.56 children per married white woman in 1900.[34] From this data and other sources it seems clear that birth control was not widely practiced in rural Germany, regardless of the occupation and social status of the head of the household. The move to an American city, even on the frontier, did not induce the German-born to limit family size. The American-born, however, not only married several years later than the German-born women and were thus less susceptible to pregnancy during the child-bearing years, but clearly also had a strong desire to substitute human agency for submission to nature's dictates in the determination of pregnancy and family size.

Table 14. *Portland Jewish Women, 1900: Fertility of Married Women by Age and Place of Birth*

Place of Birth and Age Cohort	Number of Live Births				
	0	1–3	4–5	6 and over	Total
German-born					
Under age 30	3	9	1	0	13
30 to 39 yrs old	3	17	6	4	30
40 yrs and over	9	21	21	43	94
American-born of German father					
Under age 30	16	21	1	0	38
30 to 39 yrs old	7	44	3	0	54
40 yrs and over	3	24	10	2	39
East European-born					
Under age 30	5	27	9	1	42
30 to 39 yrs old	2	15	12	13	42
40 yrs and over	1	12	14	39	66
American-born of East European father					
Under age 30	6	8	0	0	14
30 to 39 yrs old	1	4	2	0	7
40 yrs and over	0	0	1	0	1
American-born of American father					
Under age 30	5	5	0	0	10
30 to 39 yrs old	1	4	2	0	7
40 yrs and over	1	6	0	1	8

The dramatic decrease in fertility has no precise explanation, although it occurred in late-nineteenth-century German cities like Berlin, Hamburg, and Munich, as well as in the cities of the United States.[35] For Portland's middle-class Jewish women, to marry later and to practice birth control probably stemmed from a general pattern of social emulation rather than from any economic necessity. Far less economic pressure to limit offspring

9. Presidents of the Council of Jewish Women, ca. 1910, left to right: Mrs. L. Altman, Mrs. Ben Selling, Mrs. Alex Bernsteinn, Mrs. Julius Lippitt, Rose Selling, S. M. Blumauer, Mrs. Max Hirsch, Mrs. Isaac Swett

existed in the city than had faced Jews in German "home towns." Many men in the 1880s were creating large businesses, which could have absorbed sons and daughters, and many Jewish clerks came to Portland to seek work. Fertility decline in the 1890s, however, accompanied not only a higher average age at marriage for women and a more even sex ratio among German Jews, but the emergence of the sons of the pioneer generation as a self-conscious elite. The second-generation merchants were creating the exclusive Concordia Club and were being included in the Social Register. They had founded a new B'nai B'rith Lodge where their wives and fiancés were encouraged to develop personalities in interaction with men.[36]

Elite women, both married and unmarried, formalized their new status by organizing a local chapter of the Council of Jewish Women in 1896. The national organization had been initiated specifically by women who were dissatisfied with their subordinate place in Jewish activities at the Columbian Exposition in Chicago in 1893.[37] Local councils were founded to demonstrate that women had an equal stake with men in Jewish education. While formal instruction even in basic Hebrew never proceeded very far in Portland, the council's social activities do demonstrate new efforts both to share experiences fully and to exercise public responsibility more equitably with men. The scope and evolution of the council will be discussed later, but here it will suffice to note that its meetings featured readings, musical solos, and frequent talks by men as well as women, and by gentiles as well as Jews. By 1899 it was recognized by Portland's gentile women's clubs as the Jewish voice on civic issues.[38] Leisure for these activities was available because over 40 percent of married German Jewish women over age thirty, and 25 percent under age thirty, hired live-in servants. For this service they turned to the same pool of young Scandinavian and German girls and their American-born kin who served the middle-class gentile families.

Table 15. *Council of Jewish Women, Marital Status, 1900*

Marital Status	No.	%*
Married	55	67.7
Widowed	6	7.3
Single	21	25.6
Data not available	42	
Total	124	100.0

*Of those for whom data are available

Table 16. *Council of Jewish Women, Age Profile, 1900*

Age Cohort	No.	%
29 yrs & under	28	34.2
30–39 yrs	29	35.3
40–49 yrs	16	19.5
50 yrs & over	9	11.0

The expanding welfare functions and increased political sophistication of the council's leadership indicates how women came to share with men responsibility for defining community interests to the city as a whole. Indeed, within the work of the council it is easier to trace a more modern sense of communal responsibility than in men's groups like the B'nai B'rith. Richard Sennett, in his influential study of middle-class families in a residential Chicago neighborhood, argued that by the 1890s women came to assume responsibility for charity and welfare. Middle-class men, lacking social status, turned in on themselves and their families and abandoned civic responsibility.[39] For Portland's elite and middle-class Jewish men some sense of responsibility at least for the ethnic group remained. Though intent on earning a living, they did not retreat to their homes, despite their movement to residential districts. Through their Benevolent Association the Germans continued to raise money for charity, while through the B'nai B'rith lodges the German, Polish, and Russian men contributed to national and even international Jewish causes and to public projects like the vocational school in the immigrant district. The women simply eclipsed the men in their understanding and organization of welfare, and they thereby gained a far larger civic role. Women not only established a new agency to consolidate social services, but trained themselves in the rudiments of professional expertise. In expanding from piecemeal charity to the operation of a settlement house, they became enmeshed in the full panoply of progressive issues affecting women, children, and the "scientific" organization of the home.[40]

The council was initiated ostensibly to revive religious consciousness among Jewish women, as Rabbi Bloch explained to the thirty-six women attending the founding meeting in Portland. Initially, five neighborhood Bible-study circles were organized to make it more convenient for women to attend weekly sessions. They were reduced to two, which met irregularly, and by 1900 Mrs. Dora Altman reported little interest among the members in study-circle work or in forming a Sabbath school. In December 1897, Dr. Bloch spoke for over an hour on "Torah," but he seems to have spoken only rarely after that. Men like David Solis Cohen and Benjamin Cohen were looked to for leadership in discussing matters like the essentials of Judaism, modern approaches to interpreting Talmud, and topics in Jewish history. But council activities prior to 1900 generally reflected the romantic affectations and sympathy for the afflicted so common in late-nineteenth-century American and British upper-middle-class households. Entertainment, for example, was usually provided by the members, who demonstrated their ornamental skills in piano, violin, and vocal renderings of popular ballads. Miss Loewenberg spoke on the "Romantic School of Music," and others read papers on the Biblical patriarchs and their wives. An effort initiated by the national headquarters to develop support for Captain Dreyfus culminated in a talk by Miss Loewenberg comparing him to the Prisoner of Chillon. Indeed, through the Dreyfus Affair the women seemed most concerned about the proper form for a telegram of sympathy to be sent to Mme. Dreyfus.[41]

Many of the early officers of the council, like Mrs. Ben Selling, Mrs. Aaron Meier, and Mrs. Sol Hirsch, were also leaders of the Hebrew Ladies Benevolent Society. But they were not representative of the council, which became very popular and grew rapidly. Despite a turnover as familes arrived and left the city, membership reached 84 in 1897, 233 in 1902, and 298 in 1907.[42] A list of 124 members compiled through 1900 shows that of the 82 who could be located in the federal manuscript census, 25 percent were unmarried and 70 percent were under forty years of age. They had very little religious training, but did come from families with a strong heritage of communal self-help. The single members included five teachers, three of whom taught in the public schools, and others, like Ida and Zerlinda

Loewenberg, Mrs. Isaac Leeser Cohen, and Mrs. Marcus Friede, who became involved in public service institutions that radically altered the council's focus. The great majority of the women were of German descent, but by 1903, Mary Dautoff and Sarah Savaransky, both of Russian birth, had joined the council and brought their intimate knowledge of the immigrant district to the attention of the members.[43]

The arrival of Stephen S. Wise in Portland in 1900 provided the focus and plan for women with the leisure time, the family background, and a growing knowledge of community social needs. Prior to Wise's arrival, the council sponsored classes in sewing, preparation of a kitchen garden, and some vocational training for both Jewish and non-Jewish young people living in South Portland. They expressed a desire to initiate a "mission" and heard talks on "friendly visiting" by gentile social workers conversant with the settlement work undertaken in eastern cities. Their desire for professional supervision of the work is reflected in their intention to have several of the members take classes at the local "normal school" in the preparation of the kitchen garden; their sewing school was graded, to move girls from the less to the more complex techniques through a "graduation" ceremony. When Wise agreed to become rabbi at Beth Israel and religious mentor to the women in the winter of 1899, he imparted to them a far broader vision of ethical rehabilitation. He prescribed that they read Israel Zangwill's *Children of the Ghetto* rather than Torah, and though he held a small Bible class for several years, he understood that the interests of the women lay elsewhere.[44] On arriving, he initially suggested that the women establish a religious school with volunteer teachers, as they had for their other ventures. But by April 1901, he presented a plan for coordinating the "homemaking" classes with comprehensive settlement work, and by May 1902, plans for a "neighborhood guild" similar to those in New York and Chicago were announced. The classes, which had met in rented rooms, were to be consolidated, and a separate building was to be erected, with baths and a gymnasium to be added as funds allowed.[45] Women like the Loewenberg sisters and Mrs. Blanche Blumauer, all in their late twenties and early thirties, were enthusiastic supporters of the project. By January 1905, after extensive fund-raising of over $5,000 for construction, a neighborhood house was erected and dedicated in South Portland. Its board of directors was controlled by six members from the council, though it also included one male representative from Beth Israel and one member of B'nai B'rith Lodge 416. Pledges of annual support from the synagogues, lodges, and benevolent societies, and from wealthy individuals were solicited, and a sinking fund was established. With the acquisition of property and responsibility for the maintenance of an institution like the settlement house, the council was formally incorporated under state law in April 1905.[46]

10. Neighborhood House, ca. 1910

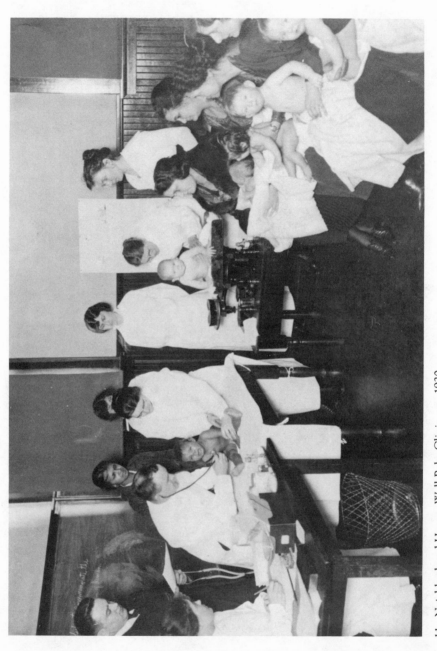

11. Neighborhood House, Well Baby Clinic, ca. 1920

From the beginning, Neighborhood House, like the individual classes that had preceded it, was open to all children living in the South Portland area. Mrs. Ben Selling, who presided over the sewing classes, complained that more gentile than Jewish girls were enrolled, and the same was true of the manual training classes for boys and the classes for both sexes in gymnastics.[47] The extension of Jewish philanthropy beyond the ethnic group, however, symbolized the new civic consciousness of the generation of young women who had matured with the city in the 1890s. They retained a sense of ethnic distinctiveness which the council solidified in various social events and which the individual women experienced by attending dances and banquets with their husbands at Concordia and elsewhere. But they also shared civic interests with gentiles of similar social background. Whereas the Hebrew Ladies Benevolent Society—dominated by older women—continued to confine itself to Jewish communal charity, the council broadened its scope by inviting speakers from the Portland Women's Club, the public schools, and the YMCA, and eventually by sponsoring local speeches by national figures like Mary Antin.[48]

The council, in addition, was continuously appraised of activities promoted by the national headquarters. The dynamic executive secretary, Sadie American, spoke in Portland on 29 August, 1900, and communications from her on immigration bills before the Congress, on entertaining Jewish troops during the Spanish-American War, and on various cultural matters, reinforced the powerful impact that she had made.[49] By 1901 the Portland Council began to send a representative to the triennial national convention, and lengthy reports on the proceedings were made at subsequent meetings. But the local council also affiliated with the State Federation of Women's Clubs as early as December 1899, and from then on it was perceived as the Jewish voice on matters affecting community welfare. Usually with prodding from the Portland Women's Club (referred to in the minutes as "our sister club"), the council was enlisted in crusades for expansion of the public schools and the placement of women in administrative positions, higher salaries for teachers, the creation of a public employment bureau to place and protect young women, and in the battle against prostitution and venereal disease.[50] The Jewish man most active in local civic reform, the lawyer Joseph N. Teal, Jr., despite being married to a gentile woman, donated funds to the council on several occasions and organized a program of speakers on various aspects of conservation.[51] By supporting women's and children's issues through their separate organization, the council brought Portland's elite Jewish women into closer contact with national Jewish affairs and into local civic crusades.

One might argue that members of the council merely brought the social sciences to the female role of nurture, and in fact in feminist issues they did generally follow the lead of the gentile Portland Women's Club. After serious debate in 1912, the council reluctantly refused to endorse women's suffrage in the state election, as the Portland Women's Federation had urged. But in 1913, with the adoption of women's suffrage in Oregon, the council appointed its own committee to monitor the legislature. In 1916 it endorsed its own candidate, Mrs. Blanche Blumauer, with her wealth of experience at Neighborhood House, for the Portland school board.[52] In fact, council members did develop a more sophisticated understanding of how government—a sphere of life from which they, like all women, had been excluded—might be utilized to protect and rehabilitate children, to improve the status of women, and to defend the reputation of Jews. Mrs. Isaac Leeser Cohen, for example, was appointed to a committee of the new juvenile court in 1906, and brought from her experience a wide range of issues to the attention of the council. Mrs. Cohen at first encouraged other women to work for the court, but then became very critical of judges who denigrated the physical appearance of Jewish children. She also criticized references by newspapers to defendants as "Jews." The council quickly acted to combat both practices. It passed a resolution condemning the court for overstepping its jurisdiction when criticizing personal habits, and another upbraiding the newspaper for discriminatory reporting. It also sent a delegation, which gained concessions from the editor, and a team of "friendly visitors" to the schools attended by the immigrant children. The principal of the Failing School in particular was grateful for the council members' assistance in improving the hygienic habits of the children, and the council in turn became a strong advocate for improving the funding and quality of the schools.[53]

As part of her investigation into the lives of poor children, Mrs. Cohen also encountered the newsboys, who were so conspicuous through their hawking at major intersections during rush hours. The boys fought among themselves for prime locations, and were also exploited by circulators who distributed the papers on commission and refused to redeem unsold copies. As Manly Labby, a former newsboy, recalled, "I was ten years old when I started selling papers. It wasn't very safe to go downtown and sell papers before you could handle yourself on the street. The boys were very jealous of the corners on which they sold and interlopers were made unwelcome. . . . Competition was very heavy; it sometimes resulted in fights, black eyes and bloody noses. Each one had to bring money back to his family."[54] Mrs. Cohen tried to lobby protective legislation for the newsboys through the state legislature and then visited the clubhouse, which had been donated to the boys by a local philanthropist. When the clubhouse seemed poorly supervised, she suggested that it be merged with Neighborhood House, which was close by. The newsboys, however, were a particularly independent group, who enjoyed the old building and the privacy it afforded them. Mrs. Cohen's

12. The newsboys at their clubhouse, 1912

criticism of their decorum represented an irresolvable conflict between working-class and middle-class standards. Indeed, the successes of the news-boys in dealing with the circulators and the city's newspapers came from a strike and their organization into a union rather than from the lobbying of Mrs. Cohen. Nevertheless, she did express a legitimate concern for their rights as minors in an era that initiated child labor laws, and she also educated her colleagues on the council to the practices of the legislature.[55]

Only a few of the unmarried members of the council were formally employed, but the organization emerged at a time when women were increasingly moving into the labor market. In conjunction with the decision to limit family size, the employment of women in white-collar jobs prior to marriage (which accompanied an increase in age at marriage) constituted the primary sociological points at which the patriarchal family tradition was being eroded. In 1880, for example, only six of 116 Jewish women over age sixteen were listed as employed, while nineteen who were unmarried were listed as "at home." The rest were married and apparently not in the formal labor force. By 1900, among the American-born women of German descent over age fifteen, forty-one out of 251 (or 17 percent) were employed, almost all as white-collar workers. This was an even higher percentage than women finding work in trade and manufacturing in Germany at the time. Neverthe-less, as Patricia Branca has noted, women through new white-collar work were expressing a traditional proclivity for "warm, human relationships at work."[56] Jewish women in Portland, in addition, were largely confined to the familiar ethnic business network. A few were proprietors of small shops and private teachers of music and dance, while more were teachers in the public schools. But the majority were clerks, sales girls, and stenographers in the expanding Jewish department stores of Meier and Frank, and Lipman, Wolfe and Company. As Flora Steinberg Rubenstein recalled her work career at Meier and Frank and elsewhere, "Of all the jobs I've had, they really weren't that awful . . . they were all clean and I always dealt with people. . . . I could have gone to work in factories, but I never did."[57]

Just as Italian women chose to work with their families in the canneries near Buffalo, New York, so they might maintain familial social control within the work sphere,[58] so Jewish women sought employment with friends and relatives in a comfortable setting. The Jewish women, of course, were not impoverished, nor were they as tightly controlled by male relatives, as were the Italians. Although work did not yet hold out the promise of a career for many women, it nevertheless eroded rather than reinforced patterns of male dominance within the family. While retaining an ethnic social ambiance, employment also exposed women to a wider public than their mothers had known, and prepared them to expect some financial independence. By 1905, fourteen more young women who had been under age fifteen in 1900 had

Table 17. *Portland Jewry, 1900: Female Employment, Type of Job, by Place of Birth*

Place of Birth	Type of Employment						No. Employment	Under 15 yrs	Total
	Proprietor, Professional	Clerk	Craft, small merchandise	Semi-skilled	Labor	School			
Germany	5	4	1	1	0	0	160	4	175
America, German father	17	17	3	4	0	10	201	83	335
Eastern Europe	0	7	4	9	0	4	177	37	238
America, East European father	2	5	0	4	0	7	26	144	188
America, American father	1	5	0	0	0	2	30	60	98
Totals	26	38	8	18	0	23	594	328	1034

Table 18. *Entry of Persons 18 and Under, 1900, into Labor Force*

	Years of Entry											
	1901–1905				1906–1910				1911–1915			
Place of Birth	Level of Entry				Level of Entry				Level of Entry			
	I	II	III	IV	I	II	III	IV	I	II	III	IV
American-born of German father												
Male	1	16	13	1	5	19	17	0	6	32	16	3
Female	2	8	2	2	6	9	1	2	4	3	0	0
East European-born												
Male	0	5	8	7	0	4	3	3	0	5	6	3
Female	0	5	3	4	0	1	0	0	0	0	0	0
American-born of East European father												
Male	0	19	6	6	1	19	15	4	4	14	26	7
Female	0	10	3	0	0	9	3	1	1	14	2	0

I = Professional; II = Clerical; III = Family business; IV = Craft skills and laborer

entered the labor force, almost all as clerks or as public school teachers. By 1910, although some had left the labor force, several of their younger sisters had taken their places. In one generation's life cycle options for women of German descent had shifted dramatically. They married at an older age, were somewhat closer in age to their husbands, had far fewer children, and were encouraged to seek genteel employment. In addition, organizational outlets continuously encouraged women to participate in civic endeavors and to share social experiences with men. While the patterns approximated that of the gentile middle class, it was conducted almost entirely within a Jewish occupational and social network.

II

The arrival of Eastern European Jews in America between 1881 and 1914 is traditionally treated as a separate epoch in American Jewish history. It is assumed that the Jews of Eastern Poland, Lithuania, Rumania, and the Ukraine emigrated for different reasons and in a different manner than did the Jews of Western Europe. Many of these assumptions seem correct, even when applied to the Eastern Europeans who were willing to cross still another continent to arrive in Portland. A fuller discussion of Eastern European emigration, settlement, and social mobility will be considered elsewhere. Nevertheless, to understand how Jews of very different backgrounds might coexist and eventually coalesce in a medium-sized city, it seems appropriate at this point to compare the family structure and the role of women in the Eastern European families with those of the Germans. A statistical comparison of the two groups based primarily on data from the 1900 manuscript census suggests that Eastern Europeans came from a different family system, but one peculiarly adaptive to the opportunities of an expanding commercial city.

Though subordinate to their husbands in law and lore, Eastern European Jewish women were part of a patriarchal system in substantial decay. Patterns of age at marriage, very small age differentials between husbands and wives, and extensive female employment all suggest a more assertive role for women and a sharing of responsibility among husband, wife, and children which one might call "mutuality." As the authors of The Jewish Woman in America remind us of Eastern Europeans, "Women, in addition to their domestic duties, were accustomed to functioning as part of a family economic unit, a pattern typical in preindustrial societies where husbands rarely earned enough to support entire families."[59] Although in Portland Jewish women did not engage in sweatshop and factory labor, they found employment in large numbers partially in handicraft work but increasingly in occupations that had been "pioneered" by daughters in the German families. Combined with changes in family size and composition which were as dramatic as those undermining the German patriarchal system, the work experience of women of Eastern European descent provided them with the personal background to create modern, middle-class families.

As many scholars have noted, Eastern European Jews arrived in America in full or partial family groups, rather than as single males. The exodus from Eastern Europe seems to have been less connected with persecution after 1881 than with the relentless displacement of Jewish craftsmen and peddlers as railroads brought factory goods deep into Eastern Europe. As handicraftsmen, the Jews were as much displaced by increased industrial production as the small farmers of Sicily and Central Europe were hemmed in by the expansion of commercial agriculture.[60] Exacerbating the high rates of unemployment for Jewish craftsmen, Russia's May Laws of 1892 severely limited urban self-government, particularly the power to tax for improvements, because urban reformers did not want Jews and other minorities to participate in city government. As Michael F. Hamm has recently noted, "Provinicial cities with large non-Russian populations often fared the worst, for their residents endured the twin burdens of urban stagnation and minority discrimination."[61] Many Jewish businessmen then left cities like Odessa, Kiev, and Bialystock for Lodz or Warsaw, which were becoming heavily industrialized. Others willing to take even greater risks trekked to Berlin, Paris, London, or even New York.

Impoverishment and political restrictions induced people to emigrate, but Eastern European Jews came in family groups because of their specific family traditions, some of which they shared with the majority of the Christian population. Few civil restrictions on marriage existed in the Russian Pale, Galicia, or Rumania, and women there were even more likely to marry at a very young age than were their German counterparts of the mid-nineteenth century. In the Portland group of Eastern European origins in 1900, 25 percent of women *over* age forty had married in their teens, but for women *under* age forty this figure *rose* to 63 percent. Over half in each cohort were married to men no more than three years older than themselves. A recent study of nuptuality patterns among Russian Jews in the late nineteenth century indicates that the average age at marriage for women in the 1870s and 1880s was about 22 years, with husbands about four years older. The emigrants, at least those in Portland, seem to have married slightly younger and to have been slightly closer in age. Furthermore, age at marriage for Jewish women in Russia rose slightly by 1900 to about 24.5 years, and for men to about 28 years, reflecting to some extent increasing Jewish urbanization. Comparison with the Portland group suggests, however, that those choosing to emigrate had intensified traditional nuptuality patterns and had suffered severe economic consequences. Rather than choosing to delay marriage to seek employment in Russian cities, they had married young and eventually had been forced to emigrate. A sample of non-Jewish families of peasant origins in the Moscow region in the early twentieth century showed the same trend of increase in age-at-marriage as did the Jews who remained in Russia. The non-Jews also had a corresponding decrease in family size from that of their rural parents. [62] Since American-born Jews of Eastern European descent in Portland also delayed marriages and had far fewer children than their parents had had, it appears that urban migration in general rather than the move to America created new options for young people, which eventually eased economic pressures.

Those who emigrated all the way to America, however, faced special problems. The young husbands were not attached to commercial networks dominated by patriarchal relatives, as had been true of the German youths of the 1840 to 1870 period. Instead, the bulk of East European male immigrants were craftsmen or at least semiskilled workers, whereas others hoped to start as peddlers and perhaps become small merchants. This was as true in Portland as in New York, except that in a middle-sized commercial city relatively few became industrial workers. Several Russian Jews did find work initially as upholsterers, tailors, and varnishers. Abraham Labby manufactured hats on concession from Alex E. Miller's clothing company, and later had his own small "factory." [63] But the Russian immigrants of the early 1890s, like Henry and Sam Hochfeld, Isaac Savaransky, Harry Nusbaum, and David Nemerovsky had opened second-hand stores or pawn shops in the waterfront district, and they encouraged newcomers to peddle wares. Joseph Shemanski, probably the most successful Polish immigrant, managed a large cut-rate clothing store and hired many newcomers as peddlers. The growth of a small Jewish clothing industry in Portland by 1920 induced several Jewish men and women to become cutters and machine operators, [64] but the great majority of newcomers found work in second-hand stores or as peddlers.

The poor Eastern European men and women felt more adrift in the migration streams of the early twentieth century than had the wandering German brothers of the mid-nineteenth century because so many more family ties had to be reknit. Though most families who settled in Portland came on their own initiative, several hundred came with the assistance of the Industrial Removal Office (IRO), whose records provide valuable data for reconstructing the structure of Eastern European families and the process of migration. The IRO was founded by the Baron deHirsch Fund in 1901 to disperse unemployed Jewish workers from New York City, where so many had clustered, to jobs in the interior. [65] In large industrial centers like Detroit many Jewish employers requested workers, but in commercial cities like Atlanta, Georgia; Columbus, Ohio; and Portland only a few small manufacturers requested occasional shirt-makers, upholsterers, or butchers.[66] Indeed, the Portland file shows far more requests by women in particular to send children, parents, and brothers and sisters, for whom they believed they would be able to find jobs. The agent for the IRO in Portland for most of the period 1905–1917 was Ben Selling, who served simultaneously as dispenser of charity for the Hebrew Benevolent Association. His job was to combine the meager funds of the immigrant families with the stipends from the IRO central office and loans or grants from the Benevolent Association, to finance the transportation of the relatives sent out from New York. In every case he assessed employment prospects in Portland, the reputation of the local family for hard work and thrift, and the skills of the immigrant to determine if he or she should be sent. Selling believed that Portland was a poor place to send men trained for modern industries like electrical work or machine tooling because better jobs existed in the eastern industrial centers. But he always encouraged sending children to reunite families, and he saw good prospects for skilled hand craftsmen. Through the Benevolent Association he was also willing to provide loans to start men as peddlers, and he expended about $2,000 annually on immigrants either for transportation or for business loans.[67]

Though the IRO-assisted families hardly constitute a systematic sample of immigrants, their experiences suggest the burden that women bore, much of which can be further substantiated by data on persons who could be traced through the manuscript census. While Eastern European Jews did emigrate as families, the units were often separated for many years and women were expected to bear much of the financial burden. Rose Cohen, for example, arrived in New York from Kishineff in 1908 at the age of eighteen and was apparently already a widow. She had no trade and hoped to join her grandmother, Zlata Nudelman, who kept a small rooming house in South Portland. Freda Weiss, apparently separated from her husband and supporting herself and two children by practicing as a midwife, wanted to bring a third child, her sixteen-year-old daughter Annie, from Philadelphia. In both cases Ben Selling strongly recommended that the IRO assist in reuniting these young women with their families, and Rose Cohen on arrival found employment as a seamstress.[68]

Unlike the German immigrants, for the Eastern Europeans connections through female relatives were as important for resettlement as were connections through men. Nathan Tonitsky and his wife Leah, as well as her two children by a previous marriage, moved between Portland and New York several times between 1907 and 1917, each time eliciting the aid of the IRO. They seem to have travelled together only rarely and to have accepted separation as part of the search for employment and security.[69] Beirach Olschansky, in his mid-thirties and with no trade, left his wife to look after their five children in Hungary when he came to New York to seek work. Abraham Shapkin, a forty-four-year-old Hebrew teacher, left his wife and six children in Russia when he did the same. Hershel Shamas and Morris Kessler, both tailors in their early thirties, had also left their wives and children in Russia. All of them had trouble finding work in New York and each turned to his sister and brother-in-law in Portland for help. Max Brill, who came to Portland in 1907 to work as a varnisher for $12 a week, soon brought his family out from New York. It consisted not only of his wife and two children, but also of his wife's two brothers. In every case women were not only expected to scrape together subsistence while husbands were thousands of miles away, but were expected to assist their brothers, sisters-in-law, nieces, and nephews to find employment and resettle. David Bressler, executive secretary of the IRO, stated women's responsibilities very explicitly in discussing the case of Wolf Goldberg, who at age eighteen was destitute in New York. "He came here as a seventeen year old boy who should be taken care of by his [married] sister," Bressler stated. "He came to the United States intending to join his sister in Portland. Instead, he tried to make a living in New York and spent his money. We do not feel that we should pay the price of his experience."[70] While in a formal sense Russian Jews lived in nuclear families, mutual assistance was continuously extended from settled sisters to unsettled younger brothers rather than through unmarried travelling brothers, as had been generally true for the Germans. As Gaulda Jermuloske Hahn recalls, her father left Poland alone at age eleven to seek work in London. Within two year he had joined his two older married sisters in Council, Idaho, and on reaching marriageable age he joined other relatives in the larger Jewish settlement in Portland.[71] Despite its limited appearance in the census, the extended family, with women playing major connective roles, provided the backbone of Eastern European Jewish resettlement.

Not all families were easily reunited, however, and the population pressures of Eastern European villages heightened the desperate plight of many families. The census records of families already in Portland in 1900 reveal the large size of Eastern European families, while the places of birth of the children document their wanderings. But as early as 1900 American-born daughters of Eastern Europeans began to decrease their family size in much the same way as had the American-born daughters of the Germans. The tradition of the "mutual" family continued, as will be noted especially in the discussion of female employment. But the pattern of teenage marriage and persistent childbearing was quickly broken in America, and by World War I pressure on poor households was diminishing.

Comparison of Eastern European-born women with their American-born younger sisters and daughters shows a dramatic decline in fertility. Because in 1900 the Eastern European migration had not yet peaked and only one American-born woman of an Eastern European-born father over age forty could be identified, the age cohorts chosen for comparison here will differ slightly from those used to compare German-born women with their American-born relatives. Although the conclusions for Eastern Europeans must therefore be more tentative, the trend seems clear. Of the Eastern European women over age forty, 60 percent had borne six or more children, a percentage similar to the findings of the United States Congress's Dillingham Commission, which studied a sample of immigrant families from the 1900 manuscript census returns. Their survey found that of Russian-born Jewish women between ages 20 and 49, 50.5 percent had borne five or more children. This percentage was exceeded only by Polish-born women, presumably of the Catholic religion.[72] In Portland, among the forty-two Eastern European-born women in their thirties, twenty-five had borne at least four children, and thirteen of them had six or more; among American-born women in the same age category, only two had four children, and none had more than five. Among the forty-two married Eastern European women under age thirty, ten already had borne four children; among their fourteen American-born cohorts, none had borne more than three. The American-born women could react quickly to reduce fertility, in part because of the tradition of mutual responsibility for family security. Husbands and wives were close in age and mutually dependent for support, and their daughters as well as their sons could be directed to employment rather than teenage marriage. In addition, Dr. Lena Kenin, the Oregon-born daughter of David and Netti Nemerovsky and probably the first gynecologist and psychiatrist of Russian descent to practice in Portland, affirmed in the 1930s that her Jewish patients were fully aware of birth control methods. A cultural commentary on the break with family custom was noted by Dorothy Fain Fisher, daughter of Portland's orthodox rabbi, whose mother in the 1920s and 1930s helped supervise the *mikveh*, or women's ritual bath. American-born women, Mrs. Fisher noted, used the bath usually only once, just prior to marriage to satisfy their mothers, and not after each menstrual period, as ritual prescribed.[73]

Through employment, Jewish women continued to contribute substantially to family finances. A few, like the widows Tobe Bernstein and Zlata Nudelman, ran small grocery stores and boarding houses by 1907. Many women, however, were employed in the family business without being listed as employed either in the census or the city directories. Hanna Robison, for example, worked with her husband Lazarus in their second-hand clothing business at 575 Front Street. By 1910 their store had become the major general store in South Portland. For over twenty years the family resided only four blocks west of the store, which was the center of family life. Unlike Aaron Meier, the German entrepreneur of the late nineteenth century,

Lazarus Robison relied on his wife and daughters, Celia and Bessie, rather than recruiting male relatives and other young men as clerks. When Robison's son Charles became a lawyer and his daughters married, what had become a neighborhood institution faced extinction.[74] Gaulda Hahn also recalls that her mother and most of her aunts worked with their husbands in small South Portland businesses, but would never have considered seeking formal employment.[75]

Nevertheless, the pattern of female employment from 1900 through 1930 suggests that Eastern European families used the tradition of mutual responsibility to gain economic security. In doing so, however, they prepared young women for fuller participation in the modernized ethnic community by exposing them to work experiences and family patterns very similar to those of daughters of the more affluent German Jews and of middle-class gentiles. European-born women usually held jobs of lower status than that of their American-born daughters, sisters, and cousins. The shift from semiskilled and handicraft labor to white-collar employment may not have resulted in substantially higher wages, but marked a decided improvement in status and contact with a more sophisticated clientele. In 1900, only thirty-one Eastern European-born women and their American-born younger sisters were formally employed, a proportion only slightly higher than had been the case for German women in 1880. By 1905, however, twelve Eastern European-born and thirteen American-born girls between ages fifteen and twenty had entered the labor force. Over half the Eastern Europeans worked as seamstresses or in the family business, while almost all the American-born daughters followed the daughters of the German families to the department stores. Like Italian women, very few Eastern European Jews ever sought domestic service, by far the most popular form of female employment in Portland as late as 1910. By then the Eastern European-born women from the 1900-to-1905 group had disappeared from the formal labor force, while many of the American-born women persisted and were joined by younger sisters, again almost entirely as clerks for large firms. These women, unlike those in the German Jewish group, were not simply exercising an option of respectable employment in place of remaining "at home." Instead, they provided important financial support for the immigrant family. As among the women of German descent, however, as yet few of the women from Eastern European families pursued careers. The number of those listed as employed between 1905 and 1915 scarcely changed, while the number of their brothers listed as employed increased by two-thirds during those years. As a recent study of contemporary family patterns explains, these women "participated" in the labor force, and very few became "attached" to self-fulfilling employment.[76]

To demonstrate the importance of female employment for supporting immigrant families, a later sample of women has been selected. Employment data has been gathered for the 216 families of the Jewish children enrolled in two different public schools in 1920.[77] The Failing School was located in the immigrant district along the southwest waterfront, while the Shattuck School was located to the north and west in a district where families of slightly greater affluence were likely to reside. The families of the two schools were similar in social origins and many were related to one another. Almost all had arrived in Portland after 1900, and were part of a business network of second-hand dealers, grocers, junk gatherers, tailors, and small-scale manufacturers of hats, mattresses, umbrellas, and bottles. The families, however, were very stable, as shown by the high persistence in Portland during the 1920s of the heads of households, including widows. For the Shattuck School, 78 percent of heads of households, and for the Failing School, 82 percent remained in Portland through the 1930s, percentages matched only by the affluent German Jews of the 1890s. Several of the families became financially successful, but only one professional, an orthodox rabbi, could be identified among the heads of households. By 1930 none of the families had produced a doctor, lawyer, or dentist who still resided in Portland, though oral histories suggest that several younger sons and daughters did eventually launch professional careers. The heads of household from the Shattuck group were probably somewhat more successful than those from the Failing group, because many more headed incorporated businesses rather than small craft-related shops or groceries. Shattuck School families also seem to have had fewer children, based on the lower number of pupils per family enrolled in the Shattuck than the Failing School, and the smaller number of young men and women from the Shattuck group who resided at home.

Nevertheless, the employment of daughters in both sets of families was very similar and reinforced the pattern initiated by the American-born daughters of both German and East European families. Of the thirty-two older sisters of Failing School pupils living at home in 1920, twenty-seven were employed, with twenty-one working for large firms, especially Meier and Frank and Lipman-Wolfe and Company. Of the twenty-two older sisters of Shattuck School pupils, fifteen were employed, again primarily in the department stores. The very high employment rates for young women and the identity of their employers takes on added meaning when compared with the employment patterns of their brothers. The employment rate of 84 percent for daughters from Failing School families was almost 13 percent higher than for their brothers and almost as high as for their fathers. The small family businesses in South Portland could not provide enough jobs for young Jewish men, and while many sought work in larger firms they were far less successful than were their sisters. This is hardly surprising because

Table 19. *Employment in Failing and Shattuck School Families, 1920*

Head of Household	Prof. & semi-prof.	Incor. bus.	Mfg., contrac-tor	Small store, peddling	Employee, small store	Employee, large firm	Craft, semi-skld	No empl.	Total	% emplyd.
Failing	3	2	4	49	5	4	20	13	100	87.0
Shattuck	0	10	9	33	5	4	19	14	94	84.9
Other Male										
Failing	0	0	0	3	7	12	11	13	46	71.7
Shattuck	1	0	0	1	11	1	5	10	29	65.5
Other Female										
Failing	1	0	0	1	3	21	1	5	32	84.4
Shattuck	0	0	0	0	2	12	1	7	22	68.2
Widows										
Failing	0	0	0	1	0	0	0	4	5	X
Shattuck	0	0	0	0	0	1	0	2	3	X

Portland's male employment between 1910 and 1930 increased by only 15 percent, while female employment more than doubled.[78] Although employment in trade and clerical work for men did increase, similar jobs for women grew much faster. For the Shattuck School group the employment for both men and women was lower, but again the female employment rate was higher than the male rate. Of the sons employed, almost all were working in local stores, primarily for their fathers.

During the 1920s when family income was rising, employment exposed young women from immigrant families to wider influences, even more complex work situations than those of their brothers who continued to work in retail stores in the immigrant district. As Shattuck School male pupils entered the labor force in the late 1920s, a few who did not work for their fathers found jobs with the fathers of school mates. But female pupils from both schools followed their older sisters to the department stores and other large firms. Indeed, of the 112 unmarried daughters residing with Shattuck and Failing school families in 1930, seventy-two (64 percent) worked in clerical or sales capacities for large firms. Only two could be considered professionals, two worked in family businesses, and two were doing semi-skilled work. The others were either at school or not employed. By the 1920s, also, a few women were being promoted to positions as private secretaries and buyers for department stores rather than remaining as stenographers or stock girls. Female labor continued to meet basic family financial needs and in addition subsidized the higher education of their brothers. In 1930 thirty-seven males as opposed to only eleven females from these families were listed in the city directory as students.

The experiences of American-born daughters of Eastern European Jewish women were substantially different from those of second-generation German Jews in Portland because the latter were raised in families which were formed when the husband was well-established and affluent and which matured in less self-consciously ethnic enclave. The latter point will become clearer after a discussion of the civic consciousness of German and East European men in the next chapter. But the patterns of social adjustment for second-generation German and East European women were surprisingly similar. In part they were simply a small contingent in the vast migration of village people who moved to large cities from Odessa to Berlin, to London or to New York. Mercantile elements for other ethnic groups underwent similar internal transformations, though very little demographic research has been done to demonstrate these patterns. For Jews, certainly, several different forms of patriarchal families rapidly gave way to forms in which women and men shared in most basic decisions. Despite the continuing view that the education of daughters was less important than that of sons, even Orthodox Rabbi Isaac Faivusovitch took it for granted that his daughters as well as his son would continue their education in subjects of their own choosing at Reed College.[79] Women were now far freer to choose their spouse, limit family size, and participate in the work and civic arenas of the city. While the Council of Jewish Women remained in the 1920s largely a preserve for women of German descent, it included over twenty members from Ahavai Shalom, as well as a larger contingent from Beth Israel. Although it sponsored card parties and entertainments which Stephen Wise in his more righteous moments might decry, its members both in their family lives and in their organizations acted on serious social and political matters. In addition, as American-born daughters of East Europeans married and moved from South Portland to residential and middle-class neighborhoods, they came to approximate in family patterns those of the wealthier German women. Along with Jewish men, Jewish women developed a common American consciousness, based on ethnic ties through work and voluntary associations and on a strong faith in the new freedoms of the American city. While the men alone until 1913 could exercise the franchise, from the beginning a sense of dual participation in ethnic and civic welfare affected women as well as men. To the development of this ideology of community service we now turn.

3. Civic Activism: The Public and Private Sources of Ethnic Identity

Jews migrating to America found not only opportunity to utilize their entrepreneurial and craft skills, but a culture fostering innovation and free of the legal constraints that had tied them to a subordinate status in Central and Eastern Europe. As the Israeli historian Ben Zion Dinur has noted, with the migration to America "the masses entered the stage of history" and individuals had to make their own decisions about the value of tradition.[1] The full implications of the removal of corporate constraints from men and women accustomed to hierarchical authority and collective responsibility have not been recognized by American Jews or studied by scholars. But from the beginning of large-scale migration to America in the 1840s, men and women had to reconstruct their identities as Jews and as Americans with neither the aid nor the coercion of the state. Unlike France with its state-supported Jewish *consistoire*, or England with its centralized board of deputies and chief rabbinate, America provided its Jewish immigrants with no traditional guidance for maintaining their values and for organizing communities. In France the *consistoire* and chief rabbi might promote religious reform and support local ritual observance. In England Sephardic and Ashkenazic central synagogues might offer alternative models of ritual and the board of deputies might bring local problems to the attention of British Jewry.[2] But in America the lack of a central authority, exacerbated by great distances, meant that Jews had to adjust simultaneously to their new status as citizens of the Republic and as sons and daughters of a voluntary covenant of Israel.

Their new dual identity, however, did not necessarily lead to inner tension. The conflict between generations which Oscar Handlin has documented for Eastern European Jews primarily in New York is not visible among the German Jews in Portland.[3] Nor does it seem significant for the Russian and Polish Jews. In the West Jews were not in a stigmatized class position which might lead them to question the value of their traditions or of their

very humanity. Freedom came to the Jews in America not through emancipa-
tion in a land conditioned to perceive them as pariahs, as in Germany;[4] nor
had they been recruited for their labor like the Irish in the East and the
Chinese on the Pacific Coast.[5] Despite the wide-spread questioning of their
business ethics, Jews were perceived to be fully human and to possess badly
needed mercantile skills. As merchants, Jews beyond the industrial centers
subscribed to an ideology of "boosterism," which allied them with the local
elite struggling to create a civic order.[6] In Oregon, in particular, Jewish civic
participation received greater public recognition than elsewhere because
without a mining boom as in California, more farm families in proportion
needed long-term mercantile services,[7] and no corporate giants like the
railroads appeared, creating a managerial elite that eclipsed the status of local
distributors.

To suggest, as Daniel Elazar has done,[8] that in the West Jews succeeded
as individuals and felt no need to create an ethnic community is to
oversimplify both the Jewish sense of identity and the structure of politics in
the urban West. German Jews were just as eager to meet their ritual and
welfare needs as they were to participate in the creation of political order.
Because young men rather than families predominated in the frontier towns,
their ritual and social needs at first were simpler than the needs of families in
the larger eastern cities. As men with limited religious training, the young
German pioneers did not generate the debates over theology and ritual that
marked Jewish life in New York, Philadelphia, and Cincinnati. By the 1880s,
however, institutions proliferated as social needs expanded. Men like Jacob
Fleischner, Bernard Goldsmith, and Joseph Simon served in local militia and
fire companies, and later Jacob Mayer, Adolphe Wolfe, and David Solis
Cohen became master masons.[9] In addition, all helped create Jewish burial
societies, synagogues, and lodges, because secular and religious institutions
helped define social boundaries and establish an orderly city.

In an era like our own when the functions of the state have expanded so
dramatically, we may exaggerate the importance in nineteenth-century
America of politics as the mechanism for resolving social problems. In a
frontier locale like Portland where most public offices carried a per diem
stipend rather than a salary, elections at least through the 1880s integrated
civic leaders from a variety of familial factions more than it provided
opportunities to distribute patronage.[10] It allowed for variations on the theme
of "boosterism" rather than for channeling class tensions. Despite the lack of
ethnic bloc voting, Jews, like Protestant and Catholic merchants, did not
participate in politics solely as individuals. As members of the same lodges,
partners in business ventures, and relatives by marriage, they helped one
another find security in their private lives and recognition in the public
arena. As Don Doyle has noted, "voluntary associations performed very

special covert roles by integrating community leaders, enhancing individual opportunity, safe-guarding the middle class family, and serving as schools that taught organizational skills and group discipline."[11] For Portland's Jews, participation in fraternal orders like the Masons and in ethnic organizations like the Hebrew Benevolent Association and the B'nai B'rith were as vital to their private security and public status as was participation in politics.

I

, The effort to create order, like the ability to generate capital in frontier settings, was dominated by the merchant class, and Jews participated in both ventures. In Portland, as elsewhere, men were most frequently able to participate in the initial venture in governance if they had had prior experience. Bernard Goldsmith, for example, had first participated in civic activities as a member of St. Francis Hook and Ladder Company No. 1 in San Francisco in 1853. He had subsequently been elected a fire warden in Crescent City, California, in 1856 and a member of the city council one year later.[12] Louis Fleischner, the leading local member of the wholesale house Fleischner–Mayer and Company, gained his title of colonel in the local militia.[13] The store keeper as guardian of civic order became a tradition among Jewish merchants, and many of those who settled in Eastern Oregon towns in the 1880s and 1890s served as members of town councils and as mayors. In the Willamette Valley towns like Salem, Albany, and Eugene, and even farther south in Roseburg, the stability of the Jewish merchants was symbolized in the brick and stone structures they erected to protect their merchandise. Leo Samuels, a young Prussian immigrant and editor of the most important "booster" journal in the Northwest, *The West Shore*, wrote admiringly of a store erected by Samuel Marks and Company of Roseburg in 1878 for $18,000. The structure, he said, "was the most substantial brick building in southern Oregon," and marked the success of a firm that had been in business for over twenty years.[14] In Portland in the late 1860s and 1870s, the city council held its bimonthly meetings in the store of Rosenblatt and Blumauer. As large iron and masonry buildings were erected in Portland's central business district, Jewish merchants rented space side by side. In 1870, when Portland's population exceeded 10,000, Mayor Bernard Goldsmith suggested that several merchants be invited to build a public market whose second floor might be used by the city as a permanent hall and record-keeping repository.[15]

Young Jews who were not yet successful merchants usually clerked for established relatives, but they identified sufficiently with authority to seek work occasionally as deputy sheriffs or county clerks. It was an employment option, of course, that would not have been open to them in the towns and cities of their birth in Germany and Poland. D. Jacobi, listed as a bookkeeper in the 1870 census, was also sexton of Beth Israel and in 1869 and 1870 warden of the city jail and apparently janitor for the council chamber.[16] Jewish firms like Emil, Lowenstein and Company and L. Goldsmith also received small contracts to supply the city with commodities for the police, the jailor and other city employees. Jewish property owners, in addition, felt as free as other citizens to petition for building permits, to complain against faulty grading of streets, and to request better street lighting that would improve their safety and promote their business prospects.[17]

Participation in elective politics for most Jews in Portland in the 1860s and 1870s was not an effort to create permanent access to patronage, as was the case, for example, with many saloon keepers in towns like Kansas City, Cincinnati, or even Boston.[18] Although Jews dominated the wholesale liquor trade and several owned saloons, most Jewish merchants saw their political activity as an extension of their effort to oversee economic growth amidst social stability. By 1869 two men who were probably Jewish sat on Portland's city council, which consisted of three representatives from each of the city's three wards. Though identified only by their last names, one was probably Charles Fechenheimer, a general merchant and member of Beth Israel.[19] In the subsequent election neither was returned to the council, but the new mayor, who took office in July 1869, was Bernard Goldsmith. He succeeded Henry Failing and other gentile merchants, and after serving a two-year term was succeeded by his close friend and fellow Bavarian immigrant, Philip Wasserman. Though Goldsmith had been a Democrat before the Civil War, he had voted for Lincoln in 1864 and eventually supported the liberal Republican insurgency in 1872. From then on he remained on the fringe of the Democratic Party, while Wasserman remained more active in the Republican Party caucus.[20]

As mayors, both Goldsmith and Wasserman faced problems of rapid urban expansion, as the village of clustered frame buildings and indiscriminate land use grew into a regional port. Just as they turned to their families in Germany for advice in organizing their synagogue, so they relied on their predecessors like Henry Failing and their fellow merchants on the city council for meeting civic needs. They had to deal particularly with the demand for fire protection. Although Goldsmith in his annual message in 1870 argued that wooden buildings should no longer be allowed in the central business district, on 22 December 1872, Portland experienced its worst fire to that date. Mayor Wasserman, acting in the emergency, had to call fire companies from as far away as Salem and Albany to assist. The Oregon and California Railway sent a special train to bring the fire companies from the outlying towns, but many blocks were devastated. In his report to the council, Wasserman noted not only that the myth about the fire resistance of fir timber had been exploded, but that the city lacked the facilities to deal with such a conflagration. It needed larger water mains and more hydrants, hoses, and fire wagons. In addition, ordinances against wooden construction in the central business district and in streets leading to the river wharves had to be enforced. [21]

The question of laying water mains pointed to a series of problems in planning that symbolized both a new era in city government and portended new methods of political organization. Because of the logging of hills for the initial construction of suburban residential districts, the city now required storm drains to control the increased run-offs and to dispose of sewage. Decisions on financing the storm drains would delay the construction of more permanent street paving, which was now required because of the heavier commercial traffic and the new demand for street railways with permanent tracks leading to the suburbs. [22] Financing these improvements would require both higher taxes and the creation of new city departments, which would create new jobs upon which a political system based on patronage could be erected. Wasserman in 1872 recommended that a special election of taxpayers be held to determine how a municipal waterworks should be financed and that the state legislature amend the city's charter to create a department of streets, which could oversee future city growth. [23]

Goldsmith and Wasserman held paternal views of the city as a social and fiscal entity. As in the synagogue over which they presided, they tried with the city to keep costs low while providing the necessary services and planning for gradual expansion and beautification. Certainly neither man had the control over the council which Joseph Simon, then state Republican Party leader, was able to exercise during his mayoral term forty years later. Despite his prior town council work, Goldsmith entered office apologizing for his limited experience in city government, and the city council under both men rejected the committee assignments which the mayor under the charter was authorized to make. [24] Both men, though, showed much initiative in meeting emergencies. Goldsmith, for example, was forced to veto a measure increasing the auditor's salary because he felt the city revenue did not warrant what was otherwise a deserved raise. To obtain reasonable police protection, he and the city marshal hired special policemen at salaries above those authorized by the city council. As the responsible authorities, they spread the allotted funds over fewer positions. [25] Both Wasserman and Goldsmith supported the raising of funds to acquire land for municipal parks, so that in a city where most people resided within walking distance of work and of one another, areas for relaxation might be available to all. In addition, they argued that permanent open space would insure higher land values around the parks, which would benefit both the city and the property owners. Goldsmith presided over the acquisition of the park blocks which remain the major open space in downtown Portland, and Wasserman recommended the establishment of a permanent tax to acquire land for small parks throughout the city as it grew.[26]

Both men supported municipal ownership of water works, and as early as 1870 Goldsmith argued that the city in prior years had been too liberal in granting franchises to private developers. But most of all, in an era of mass immigration and transcontinental railroad construction, they hoped to lure a trunk line and settlers to their city. In 1871 Wasserman suggested that the city appropriate the funds to support a bureau of immigration and statistics after the state had ceased funding such an agency. He argued also that the city, like so many at the time, should deal liberally with any major railroad that would link Portland to eastern markets.[27] Goldsmith, however suggested a tax on the gross premiums of commerical and life insurance companies. He and his fellow merchants paid heavy premiums as well as property taxes, while the insurance companies escaped taxation because they owned no real property in the state. By taxing their premiums, Goldsmith argued, the city would simply be spreading the tax burden to those who were best able to pay.[28]

Presiding over a town dominated by transient young men, neither Goldsmith nor Wasserman was interested in controlling the clandestine service establishments of gambling and prostitution. Though not connected with illicit activities themselves, both had been among the transient population less than ten years before, and neither was alarmed by a lack of police protection. Of the 404 arrests in 1872, almost half were for assault and battery, and most of the balance were for petty theft. With only four murders, the town seemed relatively free of serious crime, and the merchant class seemed to flourish on the free flow of men and the commodities to keep them amused.[29] Liquor and peddler licenses provided much of the city's revenue, as was true in most commercial towns in the South and West in the nineteenth century,[30] and neither Wasserman nor Goldsmith jeopardized this source of income or increased taxes on property.

On one social issue, however, Wasserman and Goldsmith showed a more liberal view than most of their colleagues, a view which seemed to reflect their own background as the offspring of a stigmatized people. Both showed a regard for the living conditions and the civil rights of the Chinese laborers. In July 1869, Goldsmith had to oversee the treatment of Chinese passengers who had arrived on a ship suspected of carrying smallpox. Without state quarantine laws or agents, the mayor had to deal with contagious diseases as a police matter. Goldsmith selected a doctor to determine if the men were ill and supervised their landing and quarantine in a make-shift tent area just beyond the city limits. They seemed to be in good health, and local Chinese firms agreed to feed them for three days, after which the extension of quarantine was to be in the hands of the city council.[31] In a more pointed defense of the civil status of the Chinese, Wasserman in 1873 vetoed a council ordinance which would have prohibited contractors with the city from hiring Chinese laborers on municipal construction. Citing the Fourteenth Amendment, which forbade local governments to discriminate on the basis of race, and a treaty with the Chinese government which gave their nationals reciprocal "most favored nation" status with the United States and equal protection of federal law, Wasserman concluded that "the power to act in the matter in my judgment lies solely with the congress of the United States."[32]

Presumably any mayor would have had to face the constitutional issue in dealing with such an ordinance, and Wasserman did refer his veto message to the city attorney for further action.[33] Nevertheless, he could have agreed with the majority of the city council and sustained their discriminatory ordinance. That he did not demonstrates some willingness to protect the civil rights of an unpopular people in a spirit of social stewardship. His view also reflected that of the merchant class, which in Portland as in San Francisco defended the employment of low-wage Chinese labor. They saw their defense of the Chinese as an assertion of their right to uphold civic order rather than as the expression of any special regard for an ethnic minority. In the 1870s in San Francisco and the 1880s in Oregon City and Portland, merchants led the special deputies enrolled to protect the Chinese from attack by unemployed working men.[34] Ben Selling, among those recruited as a special deputy in Portland in 1886 to defend the Chinese quarter, emphasized his duty to maintain order, though he also expressed concern for the vulnerability of the Chinese. Writing to a friend he noted, "We have been threatened with serious trouble on account of the Chinese agitation. At Oregon City the Anti-Coolie Club drove the Chinamen out of town. The better classes of citizens deprecate this and here in Portland have enrolled about two hundred deputy sheriffs."[35]

People like Goldsmith, Wasserman, and Selling may also have felt some sympathy for the Chinese as a stereotyped and ghettoized minority. A younger colleague, the lawyer and merchant David Solis Cohen, in a lengthy manuscript on "The Chinese Question," presented a sympathetic analysis of the Chinese as "unwelcome sojourners," which expanded upon rather than contradicted the opinions of Wasserman and Selling. Cohen was not an immigrant, but the product of a prominent Sephardic family, which traced its roots on both maternal and paternal sides to the pre-Revolutionary era. Cohen himself had been born in Philadelphia in 1865. His sister had married Alexander Bernstein of New York, and both families had migrated to Portland, where Cohen and Bernstein established a joint law practice and real estate business.[36] Cohen's sister, Salome Bernstein, became a very active member of the Council of Jewish Women.[37] Cohen became not only a venerated lay leader of Ahavai Shalom and a frequent guest speaker at Beth Israel, but as a Mason, Elk, and reform Republican, a prominent public speaker. As a well-educated easterner and regional officer of many lodges, his views may have been somewhat broader than those of the German immigrants; but on the Chinese question it is not possible to detect a significant difference.

Cohen appreciated that China's culture was sophisticated and its social structure complex, though his image of most of the immigrants to America was generally not complimentary. The educated classes, he noted, remained at home, while only those forced from China by overpopulation and economic depression came to America to seek work. Though he did not ignore the hostility expressed against them by white Americans, like so many detractors of the Chinese immigrants Cohen also emphasized their meager living standards, particularly in housing and food, their ancestor worship, which seemed superstitious, and the prostitution among the women.[38] Nevertheless, he found both individual initiative among some of the Chinese and a respect for a traditional culture with which he could strongly sympathize. A few men among the original Chinese immigrants, he noted, like most of the German Jews had begun as peddlers and opened small stores in interior towns. The more successful had moved to the larger cities where they also frequently served as labor bosses for newcomers. Still others had acquired craft skills. When they offered their services at lower rates than established white craftsmen, the latter had responded violently in defense of their livelihoods.[39]

Although Cohen respected the initiative shown by Chinese merchants and craftsmen, he deplored their apparent unwillingness to accept American economic and moral standards. Even worse, for Cohen, Chinese ancestor worship violated the fundamental creed of nineteenth-century liberalism by isolating the individual from the opportunities for intellectual growth that America offered. His own emphasis in talks to Masonic, Elk, and B'nai B'rith lodges on brotherhood and fellowship as the basis of social order in an ethnically diverse nation also explains why he should have been so offended by the Chinese rejection of social intermingling.[40] Nevertheless, Cohen showed a special regard for the intense cultural life of Chinatown. Despite its horrible overcrowding, gambling, opium dens, and prostitution, it also housed flourishing legitimate businesses, which sustained an ancient culture, and a theater, which dramatized its current problems. Indeed, the major theme in Chinese plays, which were written especially for the sojourning males, was the struggle to maintain filial piety over great distances.[41] As Cohen noted in many talks to Jewish youth in Portland, maintaining respect for the language and faith of one's ancestors was the central spiritual problem of their own community.[42] The presence of an identical problem among the Chinese enabled Cohen to present an ethnic group so different from his own as sympathetic human beings. Indeed, Cohen's depiction of the intense isolation of Chinese culture and the discrimination faced by Chinese in America provided a stark—if perhaps only subconscious—contrast with the conditions from which the Jews of Eastern Europe were fleeing and the new freedoms they were finding in America's West-Coast cities.

The Jews in America, unlike the Chinese, not only could hold elective office, but could form a permanent clique of political spokesmen whose high civic status enhanced the respectability of the community and helped create a mutually sustaining public and private identity. Goldsmith and Wasserman represented the initial stage of civic participation. As pioneer merchants they moved from one short-term partnership to another in search of wealth, while in public life they temporarily fulfilled their duty as mayor. Within their ethnic group they were active in the synagogue, but they remained aloof from the lodges and very close to one another's families by residing in adjoining houses. As Judge Deady noted of Goldsmith in the 1880s, "He sometimes joins with his brother [Leo], although very seldom in doing something for their church."[43] Starting in the 1870s, however, men like Solomon Hirsch and Simon Blumauer emerged as a different kind of civic activist and ethnic spokesman. As wholesale merchants supplying the general stores throughout the interior, they had permanent ties to the regional economy and were major employers within the ethnic community and officers in multiple ethnic organizations. They also developed a permanent interest in the political arm of the merchant class, the Republican Party. Hirsch and Blumauer ran for city and state office in election after election, with Hirsch elected several times to the state senate and barely losing an election within that body in 1885 for the United States Senate.[44]

By the mid-1870s young Joseph Simon became the leading Republican politician in the state, based on training and subsequent partnership in the law firm of Dolph, Mallory and Simon. As a partisan politician he was joined in the 1880s by Ben Selling and in the 1890s by Sig Sichel, both young relatives of very successful merchants. As a partner in a firm that did much work for railroad interests, Simon kept a close watch on political developments throughout the state.[45] Selling and Sichel, through equally widespread commercial contacts, were able to do the same. Because he was a lawyer and speculator in real estate rather than a merchant, Simon began to look on partisan politics as a major part of his career. At age twenty-six in 1875, he was appointed secretary of the Multnomah County Republican convention through the intercession of his senior partner, C. A. Dolph, who served for many terms as mayor of Portland and United States Senator. A year later Simon was one of three men elected to the party's county committee. In 1877 he was elected to the city council, and by 1881 he ran for mayor of Portland. Although he received exactly the same number of votes as the incumbent, the banker D. P. Thompson, the city council awarded the election to the latter. The state supreme court upheld the decision the following December. Simon, though, remained Republican county chairman through most of the 1880s, and on several occasions the Party's state central committee met in his office.[46] He served several terms in the state senate and was finally elected to the United States Senate in 1898, where he served for one term.

Simon was never comfortable in Washington, because he had to assume a junior status after holding so much power locally for several decades. Writing to Jonathan Bourne, Jr., in 1898, he observed, "I find the conditions in the Senate much different from what I expected. It is very difficult for a new Senator to get very deep inside of the little ring that controls legislation . . . I am not particularly impressed with life at Washington. I would infinitely prefer to be at home." Simon returned to Portland in 1904, and despite continual political opposition was elected mayor in 1909. His influence continued to rest on his support by business interests rather than on "ethnic" patronage, and very few if any young Jews were appointed to city jobs during his administration. Instead, he called on his friends among the Jewish businessmen to help finance civic projects like the Broadway bridge. Their ingenious reasons for declining his invitations to purchase bonds to finance the proposed structure make amusing reading.[47]

Over the years Simon provided legal services without charge to Beth Israel, the First Hebrew Ladies Benevolent Society, and the Council of Jewish Women.[48] But he was so embroiled in political, financial, and real estate matters that he did not play a major role in the ethnic community's life.[49] Perhaps the fact that he remained a bachelor predisposed him to prefer participation in a volunteer fire company to the B'nai B'rith,[50] while his law practice led him into far more ventures with gentile developers and speculators than was typical of Jewish merchants. In this regard Ben Selling and Sig Sichel represented more acurately the balance between ethnic and civic affairs that characterized the second generation. Selling married in 1880 and Sichel in 1889, and both became leaders of the ethnic community's welfare institutions while remaining within the general merchandising, tobacco, and clothing businesses typical of the German Jews. While Simon displayed a certain flamboyance and willingness to mix sound real estate investments with speculation in mining stocks, Selling stuck close to his trade. Writing to a relative in 1883, he argued, "When it comes to buying patent rights or in fact *anything* outside your legitimate business, my advice is to let it alone." His account books indicate he followed this advice, at least through 1910.[51]

Simon and Selling were equally known in national Jewish circles for having influence in Portland's civic life, though Simon more for his political prominence and Selling for his philanthropic zeal.[52] They were also able to work together to deal with threats to the community, especially in the form of anti-Semitism. The subject of anti-Semitism seems especially elusive in the history of the Pacific Northwest, which lacks celebrated cases like that of Leo Frank in Atlanta, occasional riots such as occurred in New York city, and notorious social discrimination like that against the Seligmans at Saratoga.[53] Nevertheless, the local credit reporters for Dun and Bradstreet used the same negative stereotypes to describe the business reputation of local Jewish merchants as were used in other cities, and suspicion of Jewish usury or over-charging was widespread.[54] In a marketing era before set retail prices, when store owners used verbal cues to alert their salesmen on prices appropriate to each customer, shoppers might well have been suspicious.[55] But men like Ben Selling were particularly careful to monitor the sales techniques of new merchants to warn them from antagonizing customers. When his own store in Prineville burned down in November 1883, after failing to make a profit, he was scrupulous in his search for inventory records to satisfy the insurance adjuster.[56]

Jeff Hayes, in his popular pamphlet on business men and social life in Portland in the 1880s published in 1911, presented a combination of crude stereotypes, rough toleration, and personal affection for Jewish merchants which probably prevailed among the gentile middle class. Although referring to an anonymous money lender with a heavy German accent as a "Shylock," he also noted the "high standards" established by Fleischner–Mayer and Company ("the foremost and most enterprising business house in Portland"), Koshland Brothers, Albert Feldenheimer, and Meier and Frank. His effort at ethnic humor was a reference to Henry Ackerman, who, in describing his crockery store, would say, "upstairs we have the electric lights and downstairs we have the Israelites."[57] What the joke lacked in sophistication Hayes' retelling lacked in malice. Few overt instances of discrimination against Jews were recorded, and when newspaper reporters or vaudeville comedians resorted to stereotypes, complaints from Jewish organizations received prompt apologies.

Nevertheless, Ben Selling felt that, especially in rural areas, "there are many Jew haters in Oregon." In 1886 he called on his cohorts in towns like Prineville, The Dalles, and Pendleton to thwart the candidacy for the state supreme court of a Judge Waldo, whom he described as a "bitter Jew hater and he said he never knew a Jew to come into court with a straight case."[58] Waldo's prejudice, Selling felt, made him unfit to render impartial justice, and the Jewish merchants of Portland influenced as many people as possible to vote for his opponents. Wide-spread suspicion of Jews, however, required that the campaign against Waldo be based on his general unfitness rather than his specific anti-Semitism. "To make a public race fight would insure his election," Selling believed.[59] Significantly, though, his contacts were all respected Jewish merchants, and their influence within the Republican Party in small towns led to Waldo's defeat. Selling then feared that Waldo's friends would seek revenge by trying to unseat Joseph Simon as state Republican Party chairman. Again contacting his friends, Selling was able to avoid that as well.[60]

Anti-Semitism, then, existed in the popular imagination in Oregon, as it did in much popular American literature of the time.[61] David Solis Cohen felt that it was the product of Christian religious prejudice, American xenophobia, and resentment against the success of so many Jewish immigrants, especially of those in eastern cities. But anti-Semitic sentiments did not prevent ambitious men like Sol Hirsch, Joseph Simon, and Ben Selling from pursuing successful public careers based on their mercantile prominence. Although they constituted an ethnic clique, they did not perceive themselves to be creating a voting constituency, and they often disagreed. As Cohen noted, "Political organization founded upon racial or religious cohesiveness is sternly discountenanced by Jews generally, and the effort by politicans to such an end is as far as possible prevented."[62] Cohen's remarks could hardly be applied to his native Philadelphia or to the immigrant district of New York, but they applied to his adopted Oregon very well.

If Jews seemed more successful politically in Oregon than even in California, the explanation probably lies in the persistent power of the merchant class, of which they were a prominent part. With no major corporate interests like the railroads to eclipse their economic and financial preeminence, and with no organized industrial workers such as those led by Dennis Kearney in San Francisco to challenge their power, the Jewish merchants—like the Failings, Corbetts, Thompsons, and DeLashmutts in whose shadow they operated—continued into the second generation the prestige of the pioneers. Compared to Seattle and even Spokane, let alone San Francisco, Portland had very weak labor unions as late as 1912. As Ben Selling informed a New Yorker, "The open shop predominates. In the clashes that have been had, the employers have been successful in the main."[63] Although the Southern Pacific became increasingly important in Portland city development and eastern interests acquired control of local utilities by the turn of the century, their agents blended with rather than trying to supercede the local social and civic elite.[64] Not so much a lack of popular stereotypes about Jews, but rather a lack of social classes which might see in Jews specifically an obstacle to influence, precluded the rise of anti-Semitic politics. Indeed, in 1885 the defeat of Sol Hirsch for the United States Senate was attributed by local newspapers to his identification with the Portland merchant class, as the state senators from the Williamette Valley

13. Bernard Goldsmith,
    Mayor of Portland, 1869–1871

14. Philip Wasserman,
    Mayor of Portland, 1871–1873

15. Joseph Simon,
    Mayor of Portland, 1909, 1911

16. D. Solis Cohen,
    ideologist of civic reform

17. Isaac Swett,
    rural pioneer and romantic Zionist

and Eastern Oregon, most representing farming constituencies, opposed him. By the same token, in the 1890s several Jewish lawyers like David Solis Cohen and Joseph Teal, Jr., who identified with national reform interests rather than the local merchant class, both became outspoken opponents of the "Simon machine." And even Sol Hirsch on occasion supported reform Republicans against Simon.[65]

II

The political activities of men like Wasserman, Goldsmith, Hirsch, Simon, and Selling led Portland's Jewish spokesmen to a deep appreciation of the distinctive citizenship that America afforded. During the pioneer era Jews relied primarily on familial interdependence and benevolent institutions which allowed them to create a community in a town where transients predominated, and gentile merchants clustered in much the same way. The maturity of the second generation in the 1890s allowed the Jewish community to assist more systematically in sustaining moral authority in a rapidly growing and ethnically diverse city. Materially, the creation of Neighborhood House and the contribution of the B'nai B'rith to public education and other projects suggest how the Jews as a community took greater responsibility for civic betterment. Symbolically, the election of Joseph Simon as mayor in 1909 allowed for the appointment of men like Selling and Sichel to prestigious city boards. It allowed Sichel to tell his eastern friends on a trip in 1910, that "I have the honor to serve on the executive board under the best mayor Portland ever had."[66] Selling continued the political adventure by being elected president of the Oregon state senate in 1911, and defeating the incumbent Republican United States senator, Jonathan Bourne, Jr., in the primary election in 1912.[67] He was defeated in the general election by the former mayor of Portland, Harry Lane, who ran as a populist insurgent.[68]

The clearest expression of the social ideology of the second-generation Jews can be seen in the speeches of David Solis Cohen. Speaking at the dedication of veteran's cemeteries, the installation of lodge officers, July 4th rallies, and on religious holidays and temple dedications in the Jewish community, he applied consistent criteria for citizenship to disparate groups. His views on the professional monitoring of government through civil-service reform and on the organization of new constituencies in the market place through labor unions and in the polity through women's suffrage differed from those of Joseph Simon and others.[69] But his interpretation of the social and civic values of Portland's Jews of German descent and of many of the Eastern Europeans arriving before 1900 was reflected in their behavior. He combined their regard for individual freedom and their role as merchants in maintaining public order with their consciousness as heirs of an ethnic heritage.

For Cohen, citizenship was defined largely to meet the needs and encourage the achievements of minority peoples. Like many Afro-American writers at the time, he saw in the traditions of his own people a unique message of brotherhood and toleration for the American republic. He here adopted a common theme of nineteenth-century liberalism, which retained from prior religious thought a belief in the teleological character of society. Because the laws of nature were presumed to be guided by divine purpose, Cohen felt that the accumulated happiness of individuals would yield a prosperous and humane society. Happiness, in turn, arose from an appreciation of the ethical laws embodied in the Jewish tradition, which had provided the Biblical basis for the individual freedoms enumerated in the Declaration of Independence and codified in the Constitution.[70] If Black writers like W. E. B. DuBois saw in the abolition of slavery and the eradication of racial stigma the fulfillment of the American promise of freedom,[71] Jewish writers like Cohen felt that respect for their people would arise from the appreciation of freedom's origins in the Jewish tradition.

Neither brotherhood nor freedom as ideals were unique to the Jewish people, however, and Cohen as a member of a variety of secular institutions sought in their creeds similar values. Indeed, he believed that civic duty could be fulfilled not primarily through government action but through participation in voluntary associations, which provided moral guidance. In talks to Masonic and Elk lodges on "Citizenship" and "Prejudice" he argued that the basis for an ethical society lay in the guarantee of civil rights to individuals, the separation of church from state to guarantee toleration for all races and religions, and the commitment by voluntary associations to moral surveillance of their members. Masonic ritual, he noted, emphasized symbols which enlightened men of all backgrounds to the physical and moral laws governing God's universe. As an international order the Masons had ritualized "flashes of inspiration, treasured through all the centuries, which Masonry has gathered for its own, but merely as conservator, to make them the property of mankind"[72] in the struggle against prejudice. Although the Elks were limited to American citizens, Cohen saw them also as an institution promoting social solidarity by emphasizing good fellowship and brotherhood. Less formal and ritualistic than the Masons, the Elks had a greater responsibility to reconcile local practices with the ideals of the Constitution.[73]

In talks to synagogues and the B'nai B'rith Cohen emphasized especially how their religious and fraternal ritual promoted a humane and progressive world order. For the benefit of non-Jews he often refuted the charge that Jewish ritual was anachronistic by noting that the various innovations and denominations that had recently appeared testified to the vitality of Judaism.[74] For the benefit of Jews he emphasized how the ritual and purpose of Jewish life contributed to the ethical traditions of the American republic. Speaking at the dedication of Ahavai Shalom in 1904, he noted, "It is the inherent consciousness of a mission uncompleted which has preserved Israel, and in that consciousness, with the wrecks of passing ages around him, he stands like a rock in the ocean of time with the light of Sinai shining from its topmost peak." And when dedicating a synagogue in Tacoma he argued, "The place of the Jew is upon the broad highway . . . . that is the only path worthy of Israel's faith."[75] Although he rejected many ritualistic innovations, Cohen adopted the ethical messianism of liberal Judaism to justify the social separation yet full civic participation of Portland Jewry. He conducted an exercise in secular and religious boosterism to solidify the social order and the place of Jews within it. Torah and Talmud, for example, he believed provided the sources for the tradition of human rights and fellowship among peoples; these values were then given their clearest political expression in the American Constitution. Jews, therefore, had to study the Torah, observe their ritual, and revitalize the Hebrew language if they were to interpret to their fellow citizens the ethical sources of America's enlightened civic order. In a lengthy talk on the Talmud to the Council of Jewish Women he emphasized how in the nineteenth century many gentile as well as Jewish scholars had begun to understand it as an historical document of high ethical standards rather than as a catalogue of obscurantist superstitions. Through the dark ages the rabbis had not succumbed to dogma, but on the contrary had sustained the highest ethical standards from which the modern world might still learn.[76]

Cohen did not interpret American society as a culturally plural order, as would writers like Horace M. Kallen a generation later, because he saw Judaism as a religion rather than a culture.[77] For Cohen, pluralism existed within the individual, whose esthetic and rational powers would lead him or her to recognize God's purpose in a variety of sources. God's moral law was expressed in the symbols of Masonry, the humanitarian fellowship of Elks, and the philanthropic projects carried out by the B'nai B'rith and the Council of Jewish Women. It was most articulately expressed by the Hebrew prophets and embodied in the ritual of the Jewish religion. Jews and others who participated in the range of secular and religious voluntary associations would avoid the dangers of egoistic individualism and fulfill their duty to the civic order. The multitude of rituals and esthetic symbolism would inculcate habits of liberal fellowship, which would in turn maintain a stable social order.

The most serious theoretical challenge to the identity of Jews as American citizens upholding the social order through voluntary associations came from the rise of Zionism. Indeed, it is hardly surprising that the leading organ of Jewish civic self-expression in America, the B'nai B'rith, should have forbidden discussion of the subject for over a decade. Its leading spokesmen in Portland after 1900, like Stephen Wise, Isaac Swett, Moses Mosessohn, and David Solis Cohen, were predominantly European born. But they were also very secure in their status as American civic leaders. They had all been educated in America to professional careers and were widely respected in a city where Jews for two generations had been thoroughly integrated into mercantile and political leadership. They achieved intellectual consistency by equating Zionism with American democracy as dual agents for a more enlightened world order. Wise, who had substantial sympathy for Zionism's cultural as well as political aspirations, found local support for Zionism from Protestant clergymen, who saw in the return of the Jews to the Promised Land a fulfillment of biblical prophecy.[78] Cohen in many speeches tried primarily to equate support for practical projects and for political asylum in Palestine with the ideals and purpose of America. He told the Masons, for example, that they should see in Zionism a means for verifying the ethical intent of their own symbols. Masonry held Solomon's Temple as its most sacred symbol because it demonstrated how man's constructive skills could be dedicated to God's design for the universe. Zionism, by revitalizing the humanitarian Jewish spirit on the site of Solomon's Temple, would literally fulfill Masonry's creed.[79] In addition, he told the B'nai B'rith, support for Zionism would enable American Jews to share their heritage of civic equality with their brethren then suffering under despotism.[80]

Several American-born descendants of established German Jewish families, like Otto Kraemer and Ben Selling, accepted the more pragmatic rationale for Zionism emphasized by Solis Cohen. They supported it not as a cultural expression of European Jewry, but as a projection of Western Jewry's philanthropic impulse. Kraemer knew victims of Russian pogroms, like the Swett family, and under the direction of Rabbi Wise he had toured Palestine. While seeing himself and other American Jews as comfortably settled, he thought it quite logical that the dispossessed Jews of Europe should find refuge in the land of their forefathers, which he perceived as "empty." Selling even more pointedly saw ethnic cohesiveness in America as a means for rescuing world Jewry. Responding favorably in 1904 to a request for funds from Rabbi Joseph Krauskopf, founder of the National Farm School in Doylestown, Pennsylvania, and an outspoken Zionist, Selling praised the school's work because it trained only Jewish youth. If it were nonsectarian, he said, he would not contribute. "Not that I object to helping our Christian neighbors," Selling wrote, "but because I believe the efforts of the American Jew should be *concentrated* on allevaiting the distress and improving the condition physically first and morally afterwards of our sorely tried Russian brethren."[81]

Like most American Zionists, Cohen vacillated on the idea of a Jewish state in Palestine. As a leader of nonsectarian political and fraternal organizations, he could no more support a state based on religious law than he could a politics based on ethnic cleavage. The closer the prospect of a Jewish state in Palestine appeared, the more vague Cohen became as to its proper form. He defended the idea of a *secular* state controlled by the Jews not only because of their need for a refuge from Europe's oppression, but because the Arabs seemed to lack both democratic ideals and the desire for economic development. Rather than explaining how a secular Jewish state might come into existence, he reverted to a teleological image of God's will. He hoped that the various technological and educational projects in Palestine might bring prosperity and thus toleration to all of the land's inhabitants.[82] Such a society would not only be recognized as fit for statehood, but would also justify Cohen's vision of the American Jew as philanthropic citizen and voluntary religious loyalist.

Cohen's view of American Jewry as a fraternally active citizenry with special responsibility for embattled world Jewry was shared by most native-born lay leaders.[83] In addition, however, a special frontier ethos of free-booting capitalism and latitude in the imposition of moralistic restraint sustained the self-esteem of Portland's Jewish male elite. While their social status, residential dispersal, and religious beliefs were very similar to those of Jews of German descent in southern, and midwestern cities,[84] the Jewish elite in Portland also expressed a provincial pride based on their pioneering legacy. Occasionally this pioneer ethos led to social contradictions. On the basis of wealth accumulated selling pots and pans to miners and farmers, men like Philip Selling, Adolph Wolfe, Ignatz Lowengart, and William Ehrman vacationed at Baden-Baden and attended High Holiday services in Munich and Vienna. Julius Loewenberg, after a career as master of mule teams, promoter of railroads, speculator in mining stock and real estate, and banker, tried in the 1890s to import refined European culture. He acquired a marble bath and classical furniture for his new mansion and a music teacher for his wife and daughters. While erecting the home he kept his family in Germany, with his wife taking the baths, his son attending the gymnasium, and his daughters taking voice lessons. Loewenberg's extravagance led to serious financial overextension, and the depression of the 1890s, which adversely affected most Portland supply businesses, exacerbated his problems.[85] After his death in the late 1890s, the family fortunes declined precipitously. The census taker in 1900 found the widow Loewenberg and her grown children residing in a hotel, with several of the daughters giving voice lessons.

In a more serious cultural clash, David Solis Cohen and Stephen Wise, both educated in eastern cities and promoters of personal moderation and social control of morality, were appalled at the indifference of many Jewish merchants to the gambling and prostitution that flourished. Joseph Simon owned property on which houses of prostitution were operated, yet much to the disappointment of the more moralistic citizenry he never expressed the notion that sin should be eradicated. As mayor, Simon apparently intended to localize the bordellos in an area north of Burnside Street. One irate citizen responded that "if this great city deliberately admits that it must have its leperous spot where the very children, boys, the hope of the race, may be legitimately tainted with the poisons that are rapidly damning the civilized peoples of the world, then indeed may hope for the perpetuity and betterment of our race and civilization be well abandoned."[86] Despite a national crusade which led to passage of the Mann Act in 1910, Simon did not change his mind. Nor did Sig Sichel object to the use of his cigar store for modest gambling during a crusade led by Rabbi Wise to prevent gambling's legalization. Wise had worked closely with Sichel planning B'nai B'rith programs which featured speakers on civic reform, and at the height of the anti-gambling crusade, during which his life had been threatened, he stopped at Sichel's store. He was appalled to see members of his own congregation playing the slot machines. In frustration he wrote his wife, "Disgustedly I blurted out, 'What's the use of preaching to stone walls?' The rotten, Golden West!" Wise ultimately left Portland, not only because it was remote from the Zionist and Jewish reform activities available in New York, but because members of his congregation tried to discourage his reforming zeal.[87]

Cohen saw himself in the image of Theodore Roosevelt of New York bringing efficiency and honesty to vital civic services through impartial public scrutiny. In the mid-1890s he participated actively in successful campaigns to introduce the Australian ballot in place of the party caucus for nominating candidates, and for altering the composition of the police commission to eliminate patronage from the department. Denying the charge of self-righteous elitism, he reasserted the desire of genteel reformers throughout the nation "to carry out the will of the people, which I believe to be the elimination of politics from the police department."[88] During the campaign to introduce the Australian ballot he denied that he was trying to undermine the party system, especially the Republican Party, of which he was a member. Instead, he charged that a few men, obviously referring to the Simon faction, had assumed control of county politics for their own financial interests. After 1900, with Stephen Wise and Joseph Teal, Jr., he supported women's suffrage and the drive led by the largely female Consumer's League to outlaw child labor. In his attack on child labor Cohen most clearly explained how "moral fellowship" must combat the impersonal tendencies that promoted centralized exploitation. In a daring analysis for a Jewish lawyer and businessman, he linked the department stores, which he felt had created mass markets, to the demand for cheap child labor to produce mass quantities of cotton and wool for cheap garments. After quoting from pathetic interviews with children in Birmingham, Alabama, cotton mills, and citing his own observations of sweat shops in New York, he called on the women of the Consumer League "in a spirit of kinship" to form neighborhood associations. These would sponsor the relocation of poor families from the East to Portland so that they might escape the sweat shops; they would also organize against the local exploitation of child labor.[89] Against the centralizing tendencies of modern industry and politics, Cohen desired a *"gemeinshaft"* of the best educated to control the exploitative aspects of the pioneer spirit.

Joseph Simon, of course, opposed interference by the righteous in the control of society, which he hoped to regulate through the imposition of party discipline and the trade-offs of the market place. He struggled in the 1890s to retain control of the Republican Party in Portland and he complained that President William McKinley had given all of the patronage to his opponents.[90] He was accustomed to the use of special deputies to control anti-Chinese mobs and was attuned to the gambling, prostitution, and hard drinking of frontier towns where men outnumbered women. He and his friends resented the efforts by eastern "intellectuals" like Rabbi Wise and David Solis Cohen to bring new standards of authority to a city which had been founded by the fathers of Simon and his friends and built by Simon's generation. To maintain order during strikes in 1910, for example, Simon authorized the recruitment of special deputies to protect factories and generally to assist the owners and managers. When his friend William Corbett of Williamette Iron and Steel Works requested the arming of a special deputy to patrol his plant, Simon and the city council readily agreed. Corbett appreciated the special police protection, though he added, with no intent at irony, "the only feature of it that does not look right to us is the apparent inactivity of these officers to keep a lot of loafers from congregating around and indulging in what they call peaceful picketing." Simon replied that the police would protect "every man who desires to work . . . . I have no sympathy with people who will not work themselves and at the same time insist that others shall not take the place they vacate."[91]

A self-image as successful urban frontiersmen gave the German Jewish elite in Portland the confidence to preside over a paternal integration of Eastern European immigrants. Unlike the elite in New York and other eastern cities, men like Sichel, Selling, and Sol Hirsch—as well as younger newcomers like David Solis Cohen and Isaac Swett, and leaders of the Council of Jewish Women like Hanna Baruch, Blanche Blumauer, and Ida Loewenberg—felt neither pressure from gentile anti-Semites nor fear of inundation from the immigrants. Certain nagging self-doubts about their isolation from cultural centers did remain, though. In the mid-1880s Ben Selling boasted to his brother that a local restaurant was "just as good as New York." He also noted plays like *My Geraldine* and *Michael Strogonoff*, which had appeared in Portland and which suggested that the town had more cultural sophistication than outsiders might suspect.[92]

The recruitment and effort to maintain the rabbinical services of young Stephen Wise between 1899 and 1906 typified the social aspirations of the German Jewish elite. Wise was recruited to Beth Israel directly from New York, where he was rabbi of B'nai Jeshurun and a graduate student at Columbia University. In 1899, he had spoken in Portland as part of a tour of the Pacific Coast to raise funds for the nascent Zionist movement. His extraordinary gifts as an orator obviously impressed the local audience, which was composed of wealthy gentiles as well as Jews. Sol Hirsch, Simon Blumauer, and Charles Kohn of the Beth Israel recruitment committee raised a special fund of $3,000 to guarantee Wise's salary, which at $5,000 a year was double that of Rabbi Bloch and much higher than what Wise was then receiving at B'nai Jeshurun. Although Beth Israel's board had had complete control over Rabbi Bloch, they were willing to accede to Wise's request that he work without a formal contract. Expressing their own sense of accomplishment, the Beth Israel board tried to attract Wise with the boast that their temple was over forty years old; but Wise was ultimately attracted by the unformed character of the community rather than the age of the congregation.[93] He was also the first rabbi who was neither recommended by a European relative of a Portland merchant nor recruited from a closer western pulpit. Indeed, he was chosen over several such men.

Wise became an immediate favorite with his congregants because he gave people with economic and political influence the social and cultural veneer which they as yet lacked. The best educated among them could boast at best of having attended a provincial law school.[94] Wise described his meals with the various Portland clans—the Meier–Franks, the Wassermans (who were related to his wife, Louise), the White–Blumauers, and the Kraemers— with affection for their hospitality and relish for their frontier delicacies like wild duck. They in turn were delighted with his ability to double membership in two years, to free the synagogue from debt and from antiquated fund-raising methods which now seemed undignified, and to promote modern views of philanthropy at Neighborhood House.[95] Equally important, they were impressed with his political influence and his reputation in the community at large. When Theodore Roosevelt, for example, visited Portland in 1903, Wise spoke with him privately at length on the plight of Jews in Rumania and on the need for the development of Palestine as a Jewish homeland. The B'nai B'rith in Portland, at Wise's instigation, had previously passed a resolution praising the president for denouncing the Rumanian government, and they now saw the President of the United States responding to their own rabbi.[96] The governor of Oregon appointed Wise to the state board of charities, and he spoke at numerous public institutions, including universities around the state, and in Idaho. He also addressed the Masonic and Elks lodges, and became a close friend of most of the liberal clergymen, including the venerated Unitarian minister, Thomas Lamb Eliot.[97] Although he supported reforms like women's suffrage and the eradication of gambling which Simon and Sichel might not publicly endorse, he provided the Jewish community for the first time with broad public recognition in the most genteel social and political circles.

Wise, along with Selling and Sichel, also provided the institutional mechanisms, through the Industrial Removal Office and Neighborhood House, to help integrate many of the Eastern European immigrants into the Jewish community. The migration, of course, constituted the major demographic and cultural shift in the community, and Selling estimated in 1912 that both Russian and Rumanian contingents outnumbered the original German settlers and their descendants.[98] However, most of the newcomers turned to second-hand shops, peddling, and the junk business for a livelihood and never faced the Germans in class antagonism as industrial workers against factory owners. As the city's proletariat grew, it saw Jews neither as employers nor competitors, but as pawnbrokers and shopkeepers, while the Jewish newcomers could count on the patriarchal assistance of the German elite in any anti-Semitic encounters that might transpire.

The treatment of the IRO migrants from 1905 through World War I demonstrates more specifically how the Jewish elite oversaw the integration of newcomers as an extension of their own sense of civic responsibility. Shortly after his arrival in Portland, Rabbi Wise was informed by Philip Cowen, publisher of the *American Hebrew*, of the influx of immigrants from Rumania and the role the B'nai B'rith would play in distributing the newcomers. "The main thing is to scatter them everywhere," Cowen wrote, "and the farther West they are to go the more careful will be the selection of people, for the reason that where so much money is being spent for transportation, they will not want to make a failure of any that are sent out."[99] He agreed with Wise's suggestion that they be sent in family groups so they might assist one another, as the prior German immigrants had done. Only indirectly, however, did the B'nai B'rith in Portland become the IRO agent. When Wise volunteered for the role in 1903, he was informed by David Bressler that Sig Sichel, one of the lodge's leading members, had already helped several families. As the influx increased Ben Selling, largely because of his position as treasurer of the Hebrew Benevolent Association, assumed responsibility for the new families.[100]

In part, men like Selling and Sichel saw the newcomers like the migrants of the 1890s, as families in need of temporary financial assistance. And the migration in fact proceeded much as Cowen and Wise had agreed, with cousins and in-laws as well as brothers and sisters helping one another.

Selling had also been lending small sums to needy families since at least the early 1890s. By 1908 he had made loans of under $200 each to twenty-six different people. Some were men like Israel Dautoff, Meyer Wax, and Louis J. Sax, who had been in town for over a decade, whereas others were newcomers like Hirsch Kulchinsky, Sam Jankowitz, and the Rogoway family.[101] All of these men were trying to establish small businesses rather than seeking employment with others, and Selling encouraged the growth of entrepreneurial business among them. Correspondence between Selling and David Bressler established a system for matching the funds of individual families with donations from the Hebrew Benevolent Association and stipends from the IRO. Selling's judgment in balancing the three sources constituted not a "professionalization" of the service, but the application of traditional paternal responsibility over greater distances and to larger numbers of people. Sig Sichel, who apparently lent none of his own money to newcomers, assumed responsibility for cases when Selling was out of town. His correspondence with Bressler also indicates the informal character of IRO operations in Portland, despite formal guidelines for selecting cases and the official forms on which records were kept. Indeed, his letters with Bressler, like those of Selling, are filled with references to family activities as well as personal comments on the persons seeking IRO assistance. Bressler pursued many cases despite their failure to meet IRO criteria because he felt a personal attachment to Selling, Sichel, and their social circle, many of whom had visited him in his office in New York.[102]

The Russian and Rumanian families, in addition to being individuals in distress, were also a distinct cultural element. Most clung to an orthodoxy which Selling and his friends had never experienced, and they established their own synagogues. Jacob Tonitsky, the center of a cluster of IRO immigrants, was listed in their records as unemployed and a relative of a J. Schneiderman, an old man who spoke no English and worked in a junk store. Tonitsky was also, however, an unordained rabbi and became spiritual leader of Congregation Linath Hatzedek, where for over thirty years he conducted religious services.[103] Selling and Sichel could not help referring to the immigrants with some condescension and were in turn the object of suspicion because of the cultural gap between themselves and the newcomers. Sichel, for example, described one series of transactions covering the transportation payments for Freda Greenblatt in the following manner: "I have been getting this in two and three dollar payments, and each time these parties paid the amount I had to sit down and write them a receipt, as they would not take the endorsement I made on the note in their presence sufficient guarantee that they would not have to pay it again. You can see how much confidence some people have in me."[104]

Many of the newcomers, in turn, seemed to Sichel or Selling either untruthful or ungrateful. Many were unprepared for the jobs as bakers, upholsterers, or tailors for which they had claimed to be qualified. Often without telling Selling, they would leave the skilled jobs that they could not perform and try to subsist as laborers, dish washers, varnishers, or seam-stresses. A few who had been part of the IRO's "Galveston Project" were unable to find work.[105] Others, from a contingent that had been sent originally to Spokane, had come later to Portland, where they solicited Selling for charity and complained about the failure of the IRO to find them work.[106] Still others refused to pay their debts either to the Hebrew Benevo-lent Association or to Selling, while others refused to take money from their businesses to assist in transportation costs for their relatives. Writing about the Landau family from Suwalki, Russia (a town from which many Portland families came), Selling told Bressler, "these people have relatives here . . . who can help pay transportation, but who at first said they would help only *after* they arrived. When I threatened to write to you advising you not to send them, they changed their attitude. They will probably come back next week with $50."[107]

Families assisted by the IRO who could be located in the city directories settled among the Eastern European immigrants, the Italians and other poor families in South Portland, with several families clustering on a few blocks, much as Rabbi Wise had envisioned. Their persistence rate in the city for a decade was somewhat lower than for members of Lodge 464 in the previous decade, for example, but it was not extraordinarily low. In cities like Atlanta the persistence rate seems to have been much lower, while in industrial cities like Detroit large numbers of workers may have passed through.[108] In Portland, though, the newcomers were usually sent for by relatives, provided with lodging, and assisted in their efforts to find work. Selling's complaints were largely those of a patriarchal philanthropist whose "charges" did not fulfill his personal code or who perhaps failed to heed his advice, as his cousin Alex Sinsheimer had done twenty years before. Even he, though, admitted that most of the Eastern European immigrants were finding steady employ-ment and contributing to the good name of the Jewish community.[109]

III

A very different image of frontier enterprise was expressed by men of Eastern European background who were enthralled by the notion that Jews should return to the soil. Some were influenced by the *Am Olam* movement, which was centered in Odessa in the Ukraine, and which saw in communal agricultural life a revitalization of the Jewish spirit. Others apparently were simply attracted to farming, which some Jews in the Ukraine were able to practice despite the formal injunction against Jewish-ownership of land in

Russia.[110] Jews with agrarian ideals in either case reflected a collective rather than a familial sense of social cohesiveness and portended a much stronger ethnic consciuosness than had existed among the German Jews of the nineteenth century. Socialism as a philosophy seems to have had very little currency among Portland's Jewish men; however, a broader sense of communalism grew with the increased social status of the newcomers who had had some farming experience.

The most prominent of the young men with rural ideals was Isaac Swett. His father Leon had sympathized with intellectuals from Odessa who had established an agricultural colony near Roseburg in southern Oregon in the early 1880s, but because of his young family he felt unable to participate in the idealistic community. Settling instead in Portland in 1882, he accumulated enough capital to purchase a farm near Buxton, about twenty miles northwest of the city. Though always a small vegetable and fruit farm with additional acreage devoted to wheat, dairy cattle, and sheep, and supplying a local market, it provided young Swett and his older brother Zachary with a special enthusiasm for Jewish pioneering. Although he graduated from a local law school in 1896, Isaac Swett assured Rabbi Joseph Krauskopf, founder of the National Farm School for Jewish youth near Doylestown, Pennsylvania, that "I am no less a farmer for being a lawyer. . . . The money to go to university I made on the farm, my vacations are spent working on [the] farm, and [I] now practice in winter months in Portland and farm the rest of the year. Indeed, my love for the soil is so strong that even when practicing I board out of town about three miles, where there is a little land I can work at, morning and evening."[111] By 1900, Leon Swett had sold the Buxton farm and purchased a smaller one just east of Portland's city limits at Mt. Tabor. Isaac continued to assist his father, and his sister Nadia seems to have married a gentile farmer in the area.[112]

Many other Jewish families in Portland had tried farming in North Dakota in the 1880s before coming to the city. Approximately a dozen families still in Portland in 1900 had farmed in a communal arrangement from the early 1880s through at least 1889. The age of the last child born in North Dakota in each family suggests that the families left in small groups or perhaps together in that year. Two families went to Minnesota, where the next child in each was born. The others took the Great Northern Railroad in the opposite direction, ending in Portland. The heads of these families settled into careers as proprietors of second-hand stores and of clothing and furniture stores on Front and 1st streets, but they had experienced a sympathy for the rural as well as the urban frontier. Like the Swetts, families like the Brumbergs, Lautersteins, and Calofs had seen in the rural frontier the setting for a revitalized Jewish life.[113] They would provide not only support for the pioneering image of Zionism, which promised to revitalize traditional agriculture, but for the Portland Hebrew School, which would bring a modernized instruction in the ancient language to the burgeoning frontier town. Even greater numbers of families of Russian and Polish origins in Portland had younger children born in Minnesota, Missouri, and Kansas before making the final move to the Pacific Coast. They too had some familiarity with rural America and a decade or more of experience as "Westerners."

A moral reformer like Stephen Wise, who had never lived on a farm, had supported Rabbi Krauskopf's farm school even before coming to Portland. Wise believed that a "return to the soil" would be physically healthful and morally beneficial to Jewish youth. On visiting Portland in 1899 to promote Zionism, he was immediately attracted to the isolated setting. He wrote to his wife, "I wish to begin work all over again, in a new, untilled and unexplored land." Over the years Ben Selling, Isaac Swett, and Sig Sichel, as well as others, also cooperated with Rabbi Krauskopf, who felt that through these men he maintained contact with America's remaining true frontier. To Easterners like Jacob Riis, Portland seemed so remote as to be mythic. As he wrote to Stephen Wise after receiving a few letters in early 1901, "I must at last believe that there is a Portland."[114] But Jews actually living there saw themselves shaping a sophisticated society on a much unformed frontier. The land of opportunity provided the option not for rejecting but for revitalizing their ancient culture.

Like the immigrants of the 1890s, those after 1900 were left to organize their religious and fraternal life on their own, though Neighborhood House was now provided as a center for social rehabilitation. Recognizing that the newcomers were arriving as families in a well-established city rather than as individuals on a frontier, the founders of Neighborhood House had provided a range of services. Cooking and sewing classes were provided for the girls, and the boys were instructed in handicrafts until they transferred to new classes for manual arts in the public high schools. While South Portland was not densely settled like the immigrant areas of eastern cities and had many undeveloped hillsides where children might play,[115] Neighborhood House nevertheless provided a very popular range of organized athletic programs to integrate immigrant children into the social world of American youth. The classes in gymnastics attracted many boys and girls, but far more popular were the basketball facilities and the teams, which played teams from other community centers. Funds to build a swimming pool were not raised until 1926, when Ida Loewenberg finally gained sufficient funding and the assistance of a local Jewish architect. The pool supplemented the numerous clinics that were held at the house, because in an era when public school officials complained constantly about the lack of cleanliness among South Portland's children, public bathing and swimming were important as hygienic and recreational outlets.[116] When a nearby Methodist mission introduced a story-telling hour that attracted many young Jewish children, Neighborhood House quickly countered with its own version to recapture their wayward clientele.[117] Of lesser ultimate importance for social integration but of greater ideological concern, Neighborhood House also offered many classes in the English language and American citizenship. Underlining the acculturative intent of the settlement, David Solis Cohen spoke on Flag Day to emphasize both the liberty from oppression symbolized by the Stars and Stripes and the responsibility of new citizens to respect America's traditions and laws.[118]

Neighborhood House under the close supervision of Ida Loewenberg tried to impress immigrant Jews with a sense of civic responsibility and ethnic self-reliance, which the elite of German descent, too, considered as the hallmark of their own success. But Neighborhood House was never intended to create social bonds between the elite and the newcomers. Although the Council of Jewish Women held an annual open meeting at Neighborhood House, which was generally well attended, Blanche Blumauer, for many years head of the Council's Neighborhood House Committee, had great difficulty persuading the members to visit the house on a regular basis to observe the classes and other activities.[119] Young people growing up in the South Portland area never expected to mingle with the children of the Germans, while children of the German families attended social activities elsewhere.

The major recognition of the cultural aspirations of the Eastern Europeans came with the organization of the Portland Hebrew School. Classes had apparently been meeting since 1910 at a Talmud Torah, which as early as 1900 had been headed by Max Levin. Listed in the manuscript census as the "minister" of the Talmud Torah, Levin was identified in city directories as the proprietor of a second-hand store which over two decades came to specialize in hardware and furniture. Exuding the pioneer spirit, Levin and his wife had emigrated from Russia with their first child in 1888 and settled in Kansas, where five more children were born. Their youngest son was born in Oregon in 1898, and Levin and his children remained in the city through the 1920s.[120] By 1916, however, control of the Hebrew school passed to a board of directors organized by Neighborhood House to bring more stable support and broader community appeal to the work. Indeed, the Hebrew school should not be seen as an effort to retain antiquarian inculcation nor to promote orthodoxy in religion. In conjunction with the movement in New York, Baltimore, and elsewhere to modernize instruction in Hebrew as a language for cultural revitalization,[121] the Hebrew school in Portland was designed to combine instruction in religious ritual with a modern Hebrew that would lend support to the Zionist movement. The leading promoters of the Hebrew school were also the leading local sponsors of the United Palestine Appeal with its message of "Back to the Soil of the Homeland."[122]

The creation of a Hebrew school on the Pacific frontier was hardly as remarkable as it might appear, given the rapid social mobility yet traditional cultural background of many Eastern European families, and the comprehen-sive interest in social rehabilitation shown by the founders of Neighborhood House. The Hebrew school was supported in part by tuition fees (which were often waived), in part by dues contributed by the synagogues Beth Israel, Ahavai Shalom, and Neveh Tzedek, and by large loans from the successful Polish clothing merchant, Joseph Shemanski.[123] By April 1917, despite the prominence of the recent immigrant Rabbi Joseph Faivusovitch of Shaarei Torah on the board of directors, the board was dominated by a very sophisticated and Americanized group of immigrants like Shemanski, Dr. Aaron Tilzer, Moses Mosessohn, and David Nemerovsky, as well as Ida Loewenberg, Blanche Blumauer, and Mrs. Carlos Unna of the Council of Jewish Women, and David Solis Cohen. Its officers included men like Israel Brumberg, who had farmed in North Dakota in the 1880s, Jacob Asher, and Abe Rosenstein. Almost all had been in Portland for several decades and most belonged to Ahavai Shalom. They saw in the Hebrew school not so much a setting for religious instruction but a vehicle for instilling in their children and grandchildren an appreciation for a culture, which could contribute to their moral stability in a very mobile secular society. Indeed, the leadership of the Hebrew school was as confidant of its place in Portland's civic life as they were of the ultimate success of their educational venture. Despite the continual shortage of funds, the board contemplated the erection of a special building for the school, and on several occasions at the request of parents initiated a small school on the East Side. As Joseph Shemanski told the seventh graduating class in 1931, for pupils at the Hebrew school, "anti-semitism is not uppermost in their minds. Jewish ideals concern them much more."[124]

The pedagogical goals of a modern educational institution were not always realized. Complaints against a few elderly teachers for failing to capture the attention of American pupils led to their dismissal. Others, like Moses Maccoby, were considered insufficiently trained, and the young Niamark sisters were not always able to meet the demanding teaching schedule.[125] The salaries for teachers varied from $100 to almost $200 a month during the 1920s and early 1930s, but they were well below the average industrial wage for the decade. Nevertheless, dedicated teachers continued to appear, many recruited from the East. In February 1921, the public school authorities, seeing that many parents wished to have their children instructed in a religious atmosphere for part of the day, authorized a committee of three clergymen, including Rabbi Jonah Wise of Beth Israel representing the Jewish community, to select a larger committee to propose a system under which release time for attendance at religious schools might be granted. By the fall of 1922 pupils from Failing and Shattuck schools could be released for one hour on Thursday afternoon to attend the Hebrew school.[126] As early as 1918 Rabbi Faivusovitch had held a meeting at his synagogue to determine why so few of Portland's Jewish youngsters were attending the school, but his orthodox apprehensions were ill-founded. Under Bert Treiger in the 1920s and H. I. Chernichowsky in the 1930s, enrollment fluctuated between 140 and 185, with perhaps 40 others occasionally attending a branch at Ahavai Shalom. A survey taken by the Council of Jewish Women in 1925 showed a Jewish public school enrollment of about 950.[127] Consequently, during a decade of major Jewish migration away from South Portland, an attendance of about 16 percent of the potential Jewish youth was certainly respectable. Enrollment remained at about 170 throughout the Depression, a figure made possible, of course, because tuition could be remitted for families that could not pay.[128]

The officers of the school hoped that its graduates, who averaged about a dozen annually from the mid-1920s through the early 1950s, would lead the community to a fuller appreciation of its cultural heritage. Rabbi Faivusovich, who changed his name to Fain when he was naturalized in the early 1920s, urged his orthodox congregants to send their children to what he considered a secular, communal school. He wished his congregants, like himself, to adjust to America in name while maintaining the substance of a religious and cultural tradition. Indeed, members of the school's board did try to achieve a balance between instruction in liturgy and the study of Bible, language, and Jewish history, and graduates have felt that the school served its cultural function admirably. Young Rabbi Edward Sandrow of Ahavai Shalom in the 1930s saw the school as the basis for a revived *kehilla* movement. The graduates, many from poor families, did not emerge as a new leadership elite, though a few like Jacob Weinstein and Alvin Fine became rabbis with national reputations in the struggle for social justice and civil rights after World War II.[129] The school itself did help redefine the sensibilities of the community by becoming an agent for a culturally plural vision of American society that went beyond the views of liberal Judaists like David Solis Cohen. Particularly during the 1930s, when Portland Jewry coalesced to fight anti-Semitism abroad and at home, the social vision promoted by the school symbolized the community's intellectual and moral power.[130]

The flourishing of the Hebrew school perhaps symbolized best the moment when Jews of Eastern European descent emerged to exercise some communal leadership. Their new visibility was only one of several shifts in the Jewish community that emerged in the 1920s, an era when cities were undergoing dynamic growth and spatial dispersion. But cultural revitalization promised by the Hebrew school was a further example of the continuing balance in which voluntary associations were deemed vital for the creation of a stable civic order. The 1920s saw the beginnings of an era during which professionals like Harry Kenin, Roscoe Nelson, Sam B. Weinstein, and David Robinson, many of them from Eastern European families, appeared as leaders within the Jewish community and as spokesmen for Portland Jewry in wider civic matters. But their success in the city at large lay in their nurturing firm support initially within the institutions of the ethnic community. The vital balance between private and public activism remained as the basis for civic leadership.

4. The Immigrant District and the New Middle Class: 1900–1930

The years from 1910 to 1930, which saw so many innovations in American social reform, urban expansion, and international commitments, saw parallel changes in the structure and ideology of American ethnic communities. The Poles of Chicago became a community of homeowners around the stockyards and promoted a strong Polish nationalism. The Slovaks of Cleveland and the Poles of Philadelphia became entrenched in foundry work and established intensive ethnic enclaves.[1] The Croats and Italians in a mill town like Steelton, Pennsylvania, produced a second generation to solidify their hold on skilled work and to establish churches and fraternal societies.[2] Blacks created major settlements in Chicago, New York, and other northern cities, while their intellectuals promoted a cultural renaissance and Pan-African politics.[3] Other ethnic enclaves like the Italians in Chicago and the Rumanians in Cleveland, which were minor elements in the local labor force, scattered from their areas of first settlement, experienced substantial occupational mobility to white-collar employment, and participated in city politics.[4]

The Jews of Portland, like those of Harlem in New York city, of Cleveland, and of Los Angeles, underwent similar social transformation through residential mobility and economic improvement, as well as through the changes in family life discussed in Chapter 2. Their changes in residence were not as dramatic in magnitude as the exodus from Harlem or as impressive as the creation of Cleveland's 105th Street area or the Grand Concourse in the Bronx.[5] But even in Portland, older neighborhoods saw substantial decline or turnover, and new residential suburbs rapidly expanded. In addition, both the sources of leadership and the internal organization of the community underwent enormous change. For most ethnic groups, scholars have emphasized the creation by immigrants of new institutions and the relationship between them and the larger social world in which they searched for employment and territory.[6] Unlike the other Eastern and Southern European immigrants, however, the Russian and Rumanian Jews in Portland and elsewhere encountered a well-established enclave with which they shared religious identification. For the Jews, therefore, with their concentration in small businesses or garment trade employment, much of the story of adjustment requires an explanation of contacts between the immigrants and the established enclave of German ancestry. Jewish scholars have recognized the importance of these contacts, but the institutional and social mechanisms by which tensions were absorbed and cooperation promoted have not been fully studied.[7] Attitudes of condescension and resentment have too often been emphasized, and the actual contacts between different segments of both groups have been ignored.

For Portland Jewry, the most important social event of the years just before and after World War I was the emergence of a new middle class, which gave direction to the community. The process through which new leadership developed and a new communal ideology emerged involved a shifting relationship between three generations. The first constituted the American-born children of the German pioneers, men like Ben Selling, Isaac N. Fleischner, Anson Boskowitz, and Julius Meier, and Rabbi Jonah Wise. Some of these men, in addition to creating an institution like the Tualitin Country Club to cater to their own social set,[8] were willing to respond to issues of Jewish welfare promoted by other men and women in the community. Their wives and daughters in the Council of Jewish Women, though less willing to recruit women of East European background, did promote even broader political issues. The second generation constituted the Eastern European-born merchants and a few lawyers like Zachary and Isaac Swett, Joseph Shemansky, David Nemerovsky, Israel Bromberg, Rabbi Fain of Shaarei Torah, and Isaac Friedman (the kosher butcher). These men had high social aspirations and in their patterns of residential mobility and institutional affiliations hoped to cooperate with the more receptive individuals among the Beth Israel elite. The third generation consisted of men brought from Eastern Europe as children or born in the United States, like Joseph and Leo Ricen, David Robinson, Harry Kenin, and Harry Herzog. Most were professionals, particularly lawyers, and as part of the Jewish business network they brought a broad knowledge of civic reform and international Jewish issues to the community. During the 1910s, the first generation, those of German ancestry, provided leadership, while the Eastern European entrepreneurs recruited the rank and file for a reorganization of communal affairs. During the 1920s, the generation of Ben Selling reached old age and had few children to assume their leadership role. The successful Eastern European immigrants were not only absorbed in their businesses, but, except for their vision of a Hebrew school, they were provincial in outlook. The third generation, being far better educated than both the old German elite and their own fathers, joined the organizations their fathers had helped to create and used their expertise to emerge as community spokesmen.

During the period the Jewish community was expanding, from perhaps 5,000 in 1910 to over 10,000 in 1930.[9] With the establishment of an immigrant district in South Portland by 1906, and then the rapid dispersal of Jews to new residential districts in the 1920s, no set of spokesmen, particularly those who were not major employers, could direct the entire community. Indeed, the one institution that did attempt to integrate the community's males, a reorganized B'nai B'rith lodge, rapidly lost membership after 1925 as different strata went their separate ways. Nevertheless, as men and women chose new housing, found more remunerative occupations, and shifted institutional affiliation, the new leadership strata helped define for the community a much wider range of interests. By 1930 Portland Jewry was more scattered than it had been in 1900, but it was also approaching more uniform social standards. A patriarchal elite no longer presided over the community; instead it helped administer specific institutions like the Jewish Shelter Home or Neighborhood House, while withdrawing into its own social enclave bounded by the Tualitin Country Club and to a large extent Beth Israel. A new middle class centered in synagogues like Ahavai Shalom and in the B'nai B'rith had established patterns of occupational and residential mobility, which were being followed in turn by a few of the more recent immigrants clustering in an orthodox synagogue like Shaarei Torah. Cooperation between German and Polish merchants to support new institutions existed in Portland, as in Harlem or the Bronx. But intellectual innovations like neo-orthodoxy or Mordecai Kaplan's Reconstructionism were confined to the metropolis.[10] In Portland the process of "middle classification" and the development of an ideology of secular pluralism, which marked the community through the 1950s, was well under way by the 1920s.

I

Not all Jews who settled in Portland saw their relocation as a means to social and residential mobility. Some lacked the skills or capital to build large businesses or were too committed to the religious or cultural institutions in the South Portland area to desire to leave. By conventional measures they were socially or economically stagnant, particularly during the 1920s when the city was rapidly expanding. But their immobility in or near the immigrant district was more than a desire to remain within walking distance of a synagogue. Many men and women, particularly widows, felt most comfortable in the old district, which provided necessary services, remained peopled by familiar faces, and was pressured only moderately by commercial sprawl. Flora Rubenstein, for example, was brought to Portland from Lublin with her mother, two brothers, and a sister in 1921. She became a salesgirl and dropped out of a business school course because she preferred to attend local dances and was quite content with her work. She and her husband were married by the unordained Jacob Tonitsky, and they attended a small orthodox shul, Kesser Israel, at 2nd and Meade streets. As in most orthodox shuls, the women sat separately from the men and could gossip while the men conducted the ritual. Mrs. Rubenstein's father bought two small houses at 1st and Arthur streets, and in the 1960s and early 1970s she lived as a widow in one while her brother and sister lived next door.[11]

Others preferred the ritual and companionship of the larger orthodox shul, Shaarei Torah, on 1st Street just north of the immigrant district. Under the direction of Rabbi Joseph Faivusovitch from 1916 to the 1950s, Shaarei Torah provided the most stable base for local orthodoxy. It seems to have been supported not by annual dues, but by the traditional auctioning of seats for the High Holidays and the sale of the honors (*aliyot*) of reciting prayers in the Sabbath ritual. When a more progressive-minded woman like Anna Director refused to be seated apart from the men, she forced her husband Noah to join Neveh Tzedek, which had instituted family pews on its road to Conservatism. Mr. Director and his sons, however, continued to attend Shaarei Torah during the holidays.[12]

Many skilled craftsmen with *arbeiter ring* political connections also settled in South Portland. Although most eventually moved to Los Angeles, where their talents and cultural interests were more easily satisfied, others remained as carpenters, glaziers, or cutters in garment trades all of their lives. Jacob Cohen, for example, emigrated from Glasgow, Scotland, in 1906, and arrived in Portland in 1911, where he practiced his trade as a watchmaker. He travelled through the countryside repairing watches of farmers in exchange for produce, and he also did piecework at home for downtown stores. When his son Moses asked him why he did not charge more for his work, on which stores made substantial profits, Jacob replied, "No, that is all I am worth."[13] His intrinsic rather than market concepts of value were matched by his orthodox religion and social stolidity. For decades he lived at 3rd and Sherman streets, three blocks from Shaarei Torah, which he attended for over fifty years. The brothers Ben and Israel Simon fled from conscription in Warsaw in 1904, and settled in Brooklyn's Williamsburg district, where they were carpenters. They came to San Francisco in 1906 after the earthquake because they heard that their skills were in demand, and in 1908 they settled in Portland. Israel Simon eventually moved to Chicago, but Ben practiced his trade in South Portland for many years.[14] Abraham Labby emigrated in 1905 from the village of Golta near the Ural Mountains,

18. Front Street, looking south from Washington Street, 1902; Mark Levy & Co. on corner (Courtesy Oregon Historical Society)

19. Maurice & Anna Ostrow in the second hand store, South Portland

20. Reiser's Grocery Store, South Portland

21. Stein's Grocery Store, 1st & Carruthers, South Portland

22. Mr. Mosler, baker, South Portland

23. Nathan Sigell, second hand goods, 3rd Street (Courtesy Oregon Historical Society)

24. Mr. Stein, peddler, ca. 1910

25. Samuel & Nathan Weinstein Co., 11 N.W. 5th Street; commercial base for members of the "new middle class"

and after an unhappy year at the Baron de Hirsch Fund agricultural community in Woodbine, New Jersey, he came to Portland. Here he manufactured hats for Alex E. Miller's clothing store. Tiring of his trade, in 1918 he became *shamas* at Shaarei Torah and held the position for over forty years.[15] Men like Louis Swerdlich, Sam Tarshis, Sam Banasky, and Joseph Bachman resided in South Portland and worked for decades as furniture makers, laborers, or peddlers.

Many other men and women started small businesses, which were only modestly successful. Hyman Kirshner's father, Oscar, travelled a wagon route between Salem and Portland buying hides. Hyman took the initiative in the 1920s to resign as a cutter in a ladies cloak and suit factory to begin his own business. His father eventually came to work for him.[16] Israel Tarshis, Jacob Sugarman, and many others had a series of small grocery stores over the years. More permanent businesses along Front Street near Caruthers—like Robison's dry good store, Harry Schnitzer's butcher shop, Dora Levin's small fish market, and Benjamin Skulnick's chicken market—provided a focal point for sociability and kosher shopping.[17] Older men and women fondly remember the stores for keeping alive the culture of *kashrut* that helped to distinguish them from the gentiles in an area where Jews, Italians, and others intermingled freely.

Small tailor shops led eventually to a Jewish clothing industry and a rudimentary union movement by the late 1920s. Owners and skilled workers resided in the same neighborhood, belonged to the same nearby synagogues, and had matured in the same craft culture of Eastern Europe. In outline, the Portland garment industry went through similar initial stages as those found in larger cities, with an employee in one firm deciding to open a "factory" of his own. The small size of the local market and competition from larger eastern firms, however, retarded the growth of this industry. The only firm to reach national stature, White Stag Sports Wear, was in the 1920s still concentrating on crude water-proof clothing for loggers. It began initially as the Hirsch–Weis Manufacturing Company, when Max S. and Leopold B. Hirsch left the Meier and Frank store presided over by their aunt Jeanette to gain a modicum of personal and financial independence. They bought the Williamette Tent and Awning Company from Henry Wemme, and took on Wemme's secretary, Harry Weis, to help run the business. After World War II Max's son Harold saw the new demand for athletic clothing and leisure wear, and created the White Stag line, which soon became the mainstay of the business. During the 1920s, however, about a dozen small clothing companies existed in Portland, though only a small portion of the work force of about fourteen hundred were Jewish. As in New York, Jewish men were primarily the cutters and pattern makers, while women of Jewish, Italian, and other nationalities were pressers, machine operators, and finishers.

The Modish Suit and Coat Company, which along with Louis Olds's Beaver Coat and Suit Company were the two largest firm, was founded in 1924 by Hyman Kirshner, who had been a cutter in a small local factory, and Ben Vogel, who had been a designer. Initially they rented a loft near 13th and Burnside streets. To fight eastern competition they used only Oregon fabrics, which had a unique appearance, and employed skilled workers, each of whom assembled the complete garment from the pieces. By contrast, at Beaver Coat and Suit, less skilled workers were organized on an assembly system, with each sewing only a part of the garment. While untrained young workers like Manly Labby could more easily find employment at Beaver, especially through the intercession of neighbors employed at skilled jobs, wages were much higher for the employees of Modish. Workers would try to move from one firm to another, seeking higher pay.

Efforts to organize a union began in 1928, when Sam Schatz, Manly Labby, Cliff Mayer, and Ernest Leonette sought assistance from the International Ladies Garment Workers Union in New York. Though working conditions in Portland were probably not as severe as in New York's tenements, Labby recalled having worked "from early in the morning until late at night at a steam press where you could not even see who I was because the steam shot into my face and covered my body from my waist up." Then adding a note that characterized the primary motivations behind the local union effort—low wages and powerlessness—Labby continued, "I have worked at the mercy of employers who didn't give a damn whether I existed or not."[18] Indeed, the dark side of the extension of craftsmanship to proprietorship lay in the control taken by the owner as his prerogative over his "operatives" and "hands." Modish was selected as the initial target for unionization because the skill of the hands gave them initial leverage in the work place; they could not easily be replaced, as could the semiskilled women at Beaver Coat and Suit. Ironically, the shop that remained closest to the craft tradition provided the best leverage for a modernization of the political economy of the work place. Kirshner defeated initial efforts at unionization by moving his plant across the Columbia River to Vancouver, Washington. But the National Industrial Recovery Act of 1933 required employers to bargain collectively with employees or be denied the sanction of a "Blue Eagle" label for the finished garment. By 1934 Modish signed a union contract and returned to Portland; all of the other firms gradually agreed to union contracts as well.

The Jewish ladies garment industry in Portland, apart from Hirsh–Weiss which at the time produced only specialized men's clothing, was for both management and workers a product of the immigrant generation. Once higher wages were introduced, local factories could not compete with larger eastern manufacturers. But employment even in the skilled work appealed to very few Jewish men and women, anyway. Two of Manly Labby's brothers were a dentist and a clerk at Meier and Frank, and a third moved to Los Angeles. Hyman Kirshner does not refer to any siblings or children in his business, which is not only the sole remaining local clothing factory, but to Kirshner himself now merely a "hobby." The intense working-class culture of the lower East Side, Brownsville and East Harlem in New York had at best sympathetic echoes in Portland. Mrs. Miriam Sandrow, for example, recalls social gatherings at Annette's Tea Shop as a mecca in South Portland during the 1930s for radicals and union organizers. Rallies supporting the striking Seattle dock workers drew Rabbi Sandrow, Harry Kenin, and others. But relatively few children of immigrants became even skilled cutters and designers, while their siblings and children sought white-collar and professional work.[19]

Because there were not enough individuals from a single town or province to form *landsmenshaften,* or mutual benefit societies for men from the same home town, the welfare organizations created by the Eastern European immigrants (like those created by the Germans two generations previously) were open to virtually all Jews who wished to join. Three societies are best remembered and are still active. The Rose City Lodge, the local affiliate of the International Order of B'nai Abraham, was organized in 1905 to provide sick benefits and burial costs for the immigrants, and by 1920 it had over four hundred members. By contributing twenty cents a month, members were guaranteed nine dollars a week should they become too ill to work. The society buried not only its own members, but indigent Jews whose deaths were called to its attention.[20] With the B'nai B'rith lodges having dropped such welfare services at the turn of the century, the new immigrants utilized the traditional means of persistent and minute fund raising among themselves to meet their own needs. In 1912, Isaac Nemerovsky and Noah Director helped organize a Hebrew Benevolent Society to provide loans for small businesses and charity to those in need.[21] It was apparently quite separate from the old organization of the same name initiated by the German immigrants in the 1870s. Both the Rose City Lodge and the benevolent society held picnics, banquets, and dances to create a sense of social solidarity and to raise money for charitable endeavors. Louis Albert, an immigrant from Kiev, became president of the Rose City Lodge in the 1920s; like Louis Fleischner and Ben Selling in an earlier era, he had discretion to provide small charitable donations to people in need. Noah Director's store on 1st Street near Main became the headquarters of the benevolent society. He too was empowered to provide small loans or donations to the indigent and to distribute second-hand clothing provided by the Council of Jewish Women.[22]

The South Parkway Brotherhood and Sisterhood were separate social clubs that were organized out of Neighborhood House in 1916 and 1923, respectively. Providing separate fellowship for men and for their wives, the clubs held weekly meetings for members where dues were collected for charitable endeavors. They, too, sponsored family picnics and dances, and the ladies auxiliary held an annual social affair for their own mothers.[23] Between the meetings and the social activities of the societies, men and women as well as young people in the South Portland area had a network of entertainment, charitable support, and conviviality, which created an atmosphere to which social workers referred when they used the term "neighborhood."[23] The memories of old South Portland residents may romanticize the sociability of the area, though the network of social institutions created by their parents was even more intense than that created by the German immigrants and their descendants from the 1860s through the 1890s. Neighborhood House, of course, provided an initial meeting place for various clubs and classes for adults and children. But the immigrants themselves created the permanent organizations that provided continuity and support for lives which were otherwise very much in flux.

Above all, people reared in South Portland remembered the family as the center of social life. Fathers were occasionally away from home peddling, kept late hours at family stores, and attended lodge meetings. But family members usually shared in the business, and social occasions in the home seem to have been quite large. Leon Feldstein recalled that his household became a center for Jews of Rumanian origin. His parents came from Bucharest to join Mrs. Feldstein's brother, Israel Korn, who in turn had been assisted by the IRO. Adolph Feldstein worked briefly in Korn's junk shop and then opened a furniture store on the east side of the Willamette River. While not residing in the immigrant district, they were within a short streetcar ride, and Mrs. Feldstein held large gatherings on Saturday nights. Leon remembers the "*mamaliga* parties," where large vats of the Rumanian corn meal were cooked with garlic and served in gravy, while his mother played the piano and guests sang and danced the *horah*.[25] Estelle Director, whose parents were active in the Hebrew Benevolent Society, also recalls large gatherings of Russian Jews in her parents' household.[26] Several Director brothers settled in South Portland and some entered business partnerships with other men, so that the family and business network was extensive.

Although the neighborhood was neither exclusively Jewish nor densely packed, as in New York, Philadelphia, or even Cleveland, an examination of families whose children attended Failing and Shattuck grade schools in 1920 indicates why such large gatherings would have been easy to assemble. Freda Gass, for example, lived in 1920 on Park Street near Jackson, across from the Shattuck School, and attended the Portland Hebrew School at Neighborhood House, from which she graduated in 1934. While being serenaded by *chazzan* Abraham Rosencrantz, who rehearsed liturgy through the open

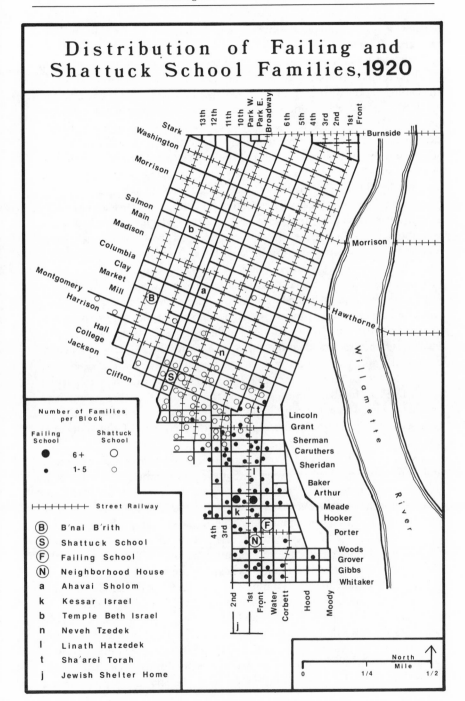

Distribution of Failing and Shattuck School Families, 1920

Number of Families per Block

Failing School	Shattuck School
● 6+	○
• 1-5	○

╫╫╫╫╫╫ Street Railway

(B) B'nai B'rith
(S) Shattuck School
(F) Failing School
(N) Neighborhood House
a Ahavai Sholom
k Kessar Israel
b Temple Beth Israel
n Neveh Tzedek
l Linath Hatzedek
t Sha'arei Torah
j Jewish Shelter Home

North
Mile
0   1/4   1/2

window next door, she felt continuously surrounded by friends.[27] In the four, five, and six hundred blocks of the streets between Park and 1st were almost seventy Jewish families whose children attended the school, not to mention childless couples, couples with older children, and unattached individuals. In the Failing School district from 3rd Street east to Moody, and from Caruthers south to Porter, were ninety-nine more Jewish families whose children attended the school. While only 38 percent of pupils attending Failing School were Jewish,[28] the five and six hundred blocks of 1st, 2nd, and 3rd streets and the two hundred blocks of the cross streets Caruthers, Sheridan, Arthur, and Meade had many Jewish families living next door to one another. In addition, in the upper grades, about half the pupils were Jewish. Young people would have from twelve to nineteen Jewish classmates in public school during the day, and many would attend Hebrew school, physical education classes, or social events at Neighborhood House perhaps as often as four or five afternoons and evenings a week.

The interlocking familial relations of the Failing school area were perhaps most clearly outlined by Gaulda Jermuloske, who was born there in 1916, and who later graduated from Reed College. She recalled that the area contained people of many races and religions, but that the "extended family" provided the focus for her social life. The block bounded by Hooker, Meade, 1st, and Front streets contained her grandparents (Pessie and Michael Rosenfeld), and "Next door to them was my aunt, my mother's sister Mrs. Calof, with three children . . . We lived next door to them. Around the corner lived my mother's brother . . . and then around the other corner lived another uncle and their family."[29] No wonder so many young people felt part of a secure social network despite the relative poverty of the individual households.

Within South Portland people were anxious to improve their residences and many acquired pieces of property, but even during the prosperous 1920s, the majority migrated only short distances. As Mrs. Miriam Sandrow observed for the mid-1930s, "Some residents of South Portland did not move away even after they were financially able to do so. They felt comfortable near their *shul*, the Kosher butcher, the *Mikvah* and their neighbors."[30] Statistical evidence from the 107 families whose children attended the Failing School and the 102 families whose children attended the Shattuck School in 1920 indicates that families changed residence in definite patterns, and rarely left their friends very far behind. As Table 20 indicates, of the eighty-four heads of household, including widows, from Failing School families still in Portland in 1930, forty-three still lived in South Portland (twenty-five were in the same houses) and twenty others had moved only a few blocks north and west into the Shattuck School district. Of the seventy-five heads of household, including widows, from the Shattuck School families still in Portland in 1930, forty-one still lived in the area of the school, and only six had moved farther south. If we add to these the 172 grown children from these families listed in the city directory for 1930 as residing in the two districts, we can see how many familiar faces remained.

Within the general pattern of communal stability, however, there were two major migration routes. About one-third of those residing in South Portland had moved to the somewhat more desirable area closer to the Shattuck School. The children recalled that this often required a shifting of allegiance from attendance at social events at Neighborhood House to attendance at the new B'nai B'rith building, whose significance will be discussed later. Another 20 percent in both groups moved to the East Side, finding homes from East 14th to East 28th streets and in the newly developed Ladd Addition. A few opened grocery stores, furniture shops, and clothing stores on the East Side, which served a predominantly gentile clientele. No kosher meat market seems to have been opened on the East Side, and only one small orthodox shul was ever located there.[31] Despite the desire of several parents to hold Hebrew school classes in the Irvington district during the late 1920s and 1930s, it was rarely possible to attract an enrollment large enough to justify the expense.[32] The adults were apparently willing to bend their orthodoxy and take streetcars to attend Shaarei Torah or Neveh Tzedek, while the children commuted to the B'nai B'rith center for recreation or the Neighborhood House for Hebrew school.

Table 20. *Residential Trajectory, Shattuck and Failing School Families, 1920s*

Residential Trajectory 1920–1930	Shattuck School		Failing School	
	Male Head of Household & Widows	Other Male & Female*	Male Head of Household & Widows	Other Male & Female*
Remained in Home	20	32	22	46
Moved in district	27	51	21	43
Moved in South	5	6	0	0
Moved to Shattuck area	0	2	20	27
Moved to Northwest	4	5	4	8
Moved to East	18	23	17	32
Total	75	119	84	156
(Not in city directory)	(27)		(23)	

*Only those present in 1930 were tabulated

The general pattern of family stability, institutional support, and continual migration within the district or to nearby areas of East Portland, however, was marred by many cases of personal tragedy and family dissolution. The minutes for the 1920s of the Jewish Shelter Home at 975 South

26. Jewish Shelter Home, South Portland, ca. 1919

Corbett Street at the southern end of the Failing School district record a full range of social pathology. Divorce, desertion, mental collapse, and institutionalization appeared among the adults, while children expressed their traumas in withdrawal, chronic bed wedding, broken health, and poor performance in school.[33] The home seems initially to have been a special undertaking of Mrs. Jeannette Meier, who, on her eighty-first birthday in 1924, paid the remainder of its mortgage.[34] Board meetings were often held in the office of her son, Julius, at the Meier and Frank store, where he or his partner, Aaron Frank, often presided. When the home joined the Jewish Welfare Federation in 1924, authority was vested in a board, with Julius Meier as president. A mixture of wealthy women like Mrs. Arthur Goldsmith and Miss Eda Jacobs, as well as women of successful Eastern European families like Mrs. Nathan Weinstein and Mrs. Enkelis, also served.[35]

The home was administered with a mixture of paternalism and very professional welfare techniques. Operating on a limited budget, it depended for general maintenance on the volunteer services of men like Israel Dautoff, Lip Shank, and Max Turtledove, all of whom had successful businesses in South Portland. Mrs. Gaulda Jermuloske Hahn recalls that her parents looked with charitable pity on the children of the home, "a kind of feeling of the Yiddish *Tzadakah* (charity) that somehow those children needed to be taken care of."[36] After 1924, cases were screened for admittance by a professional social worker provided by the Welfare Federation, and routine medical services were provided by a group of four Jewish doctors on a rotating basis. The home was designed to hold ten to twelve children for short terms, but because many were from broken homes and contests for custody raised legal problems, the length of their stay was unpredictable. Indeed, several remained there for five years or more. The home could obtain legal custody of children and even placed some for adoption, though it was never considered an orphanage like the large regional institutions established in San Francisco, Cleveland, and Atlanta.[37] Mrs. Julia Swett dealt constantly with the juvenile court in custody matters, and had to provide a shrewd assessment of the personalities of fathers and mothers who were desperate to provide a home for their children despite the death or mental breakdown of spouses and the chronic lack of income.

The members of the board expressed several ideological dilemmas, which circumscribed the treatment the children received during the 1920s. They desired to raise the children entrusted to them in a Jewish atmosphere, but they also believed that, where possible, children should be reared in a family setting. Children were usually enrolled in the Hebrew school at Neighborhood House and were sent to Chanukah parties and Passover seders in nearby homes whenever possible. Neighborhood residents would occasionally take the children to the movie theaters, many of which were owned by Jews, and candy, apples, clothing, eyeglasses, and a piano were provided by Jewish housewives and merchants. But the board could never find a Jewish woman willing to reside in the home as matron, and they urged one another to visit to provide a "Jewish touch."[38] Because most board members believed that rural living would impose a needed discipline on particularly recalcitrant children, several were placed on farms even though the owners were gentiles. While trying to have parents assume responsibility for the children as soon as possible, Julia Swett and Mrs. Toba Narod, who reported on daily activities at the home, had to weigh individual cases carefully before relinquishing custody of the children. One father, raised in the San Francisco Jewish orphanage, felt the shelter home would provide better care for his son than he could; another father, however, met his child on the way to school and took him away to California. In several cases relatives anxious to adopt children were enjoined by parents or by Mrs. Swett because they seemed too domineering.

The records of the Jewish Shelter Home hardly allow for a statistical assesment of the degree of family breakdown among immigrants, but they provide an important balance to the romantic memories of children from successful families. In place of broad cultural tensions between generations that scholars like Oscar Handlin have emphasized, and the smooth transition to white-collar status that statistical analysis implies, the shelter home cases illustrate how poverty, cultural differences, and the primitive state of psychiatry led to more acute breakdown. Several young widows resorted to suicide; one separated couple placed their children for adoption and then regretted their decision; an unmarried teenage girl did the same. The strict control that one Sephardic family tried to exercise over a daughter led to her mental collapse, confinement in the state asylum at Salem, and the placement of her children in the shelter home. In this case, the state psychiatrist could provide only a general diagnosis of "a peculiar psychopathic case," which was aggravated by her contact with her parents. Her desperate letters to her children were withheld from them on the psychiatrist's advice, though Mrs. Swett interpreted their contents to the children.[39] The poverty of one musician led to a divorce and a decade-long effort to establish a household which Mrs. Swett—and the juvenile court—might find suitable. In several cases children were diagnosed as retarded, though their subsequent school records indicated that they were only suffering severe withdrawal because of desertion. In other cases women who had remarried had to be threatened with court action before they removed their children from the home to their new households. Most commonly, however, children were placed in the home by young widowers, widows, or separated parents, who were temporarily ill, too poor, or too overwrought to maintain a household, and who had no local relatives to assist them. The parents often paid a fee to the home for the child's room and board; rates were set by negotiation and depended on what each parent could afford.

Although immigrant benevolent societies provided security and fulfilled a sense of civic duty for many people, they could not meet the most severe traumas induced by migration and resettlement. Families with multiple problems, like the death of a spouse, unstable income, and little or no assistance from relatives, had to turn to the shelter home. There were tensions between grandparents with strict views of child rearing and their more lenient children; and parents who expected their children to care for themselves, much as they might have done on the streets of an Eastern European town, were at odds with modern theories of child nurture held by social workers and pediatricians. To arbitrate such conflicts the shelter home board enlisted the aid of a new public agency, the juvenile court, and the new expertise of social work and psychiatry. At the same time, though, it tried to conform to a residual sense that a "Jewish atmosphere," defined largely by ritual celebration, should surround the nurture of its wards. But the records indicate that social adjustment was in many cases far more difficult than the leadership wished to admit. Gaulda Jermuloske Hahn, who attended Failing School with shelter home children, recalls the unsettled effects on them. "There was a feeling of being together and yet there were underlying hostilities too. . . . There is a definite feeling, almost a way about the children, how they used to feel years ago [when] you didn't tell a child that they [sic] were adopted."[40]

II

Max Simon, born in Warsaw in 1898 and brought to Portland at age ten, retained a very clear recollection of the social strata within Portland Jewry at the time. He recalled three distinct groups: the wealthy of German descent; the immigrants of South Portland; and an intermediate group of whose social origins he could not be precise.[41] The latter group, no doubt, included some of those whose children attended the Shattuck School and who chose to move to the East Side. It also included men like Moses Barde, Isaac and Zack Swett, and Leo and Joseph Ricen, who by 1920 had moved to the Northwest or to new East Side neighborhoods. Some had switched their allegiance from Shaarai Torah to Neveh Tzedek, while others belonged to Ahavai Shalom. Many of these men had arrived in Portland prior to 1900 and had never lived in South Portland, while others chose to move from the immigrant district and changed their institutional allegiance when doing so. They provided the basis for a new middle class, which promoted mobility rather than isolation, and entrepreneurship rather than craftsmanship and the culture of *kashrut*. While supporting Zionism and Hebrew schooling, they also brought a new professionalism to community welfare and political consciousness.

In October 1910, a group of about sixty men met in the vestry room of Beth Israel to buy shares in a building association, which would acquire a site and erect a structure to serve as a communal center.[42] The building association was to be independent of the B'nai B'rith lodges, which would, however, purchase shares, and it would pass out of existence after the structure had been completed. What was designed as a temporary organization, however, actually addressed a subtle and permanent condition of the perpetually mobile middle class. Prior B'nai B'rith lodges had fulfilled traditional welfare needs or celebrated the status of a small elite. The B'nai B'rith Building Association, however, provided the institutional setting in which a new community ideology could be defined and a new leadership group could coalesce. A close examination of the men who contributed to the association indicates how people intent on improving their social status and augmenting community services came to be organized into a cohesive social body. An examination of the association's activities and the responses of its leaders to the crises faced by American Jewry during World War I indicate how a new ideology of cultural pluralism came to succeed the

27. Moyer Clothing Company, Ben Selling proprietor, ca. 1920 (Courtesy Oregon
Historical Society)

religious liberalism of the German elite and the separatism and orthodoxy of
the East European immigrants. The succession of leadership within the
unified B'nai B'rith lodge during the 1920s both symbolized and promoted an
ethnic respectability for what would otherwise have been a scattered Jewish
middle class. Initially, the B'nai B'rith Building Association had leadership
from a prestigious contingent of merchants and professionals from Beth
Israel, like Ben Selling, Sig Sichel, Dr. J. J. Rosenberg, Dr. Aaron Tilzer, and
Rabbi Jonah Wise. But its membership consisted of men of Polish and
Russian birth as well as of German descent. Indeed, eight of the fifteen
members of the original board of directors, men like Isaac Swett, Joseph
Shemansky, John Dellar, Alex E. Miller, and D. N. Mosessohn, were
members of Ahavai Shalom, and all except Miller had been born in Eastern
Europe.[43] The association actually consisted of two groups, those who
subscribed initially in 1910, and a slightly large group who subscribed to a
second call for funds between 1912 and 1914. The profiles of the two groups
are substantially the same, though there are a few important distinctions.
Even though the latter group of eighty-two men had a slightly higher median
age, only 40 percent could be located in the 1900 manuscript census, whereas
70 percent of the sixty-four men in the initial group were listed. The earlier

28. Ben Selling breaking ground for Sephardic Temple Ahavath Achim, ca. 1930;
   epitome of communal philanthropy

group, then, consisted of most of the members with significant longevity and
prestige in Portland. But it also contained a substantially higher percentage
of men born in Eastern Europe than did the latter group, which contained
many sons of the earliest Eastern European immigrants, including a few who
had been born in North Dakota.

The similarities, however, far outweighed the differences. Both groups,
for example, had a mean age from ten to fourteen years older that had been
true of nineteenth-century B'nai B'rith lodges, because the purpose of the
association was to erect a permanent social center for a stable mercantile
community rather than to provide mutual benefit services for newly married
men. Men were invited to join not on the basis of age or place of birth, but
because of their ability to contribute. The stated purpose of the Association,
to promote a feeling of fellowship and civic responsibility, was similar to that
of prior B'nai B'rith lodges and of the fraternal orders like the Masons and
Elks. But the association also saw itself as a community center that would
sponsor Jewish cultural endeavors and would become the focal institution for
social, recreational, and even political events.[44]

The residential pattern and trajectory of members seems to have
influenced the location of the building and provides an important clue to

their social interests, especially compared to those of people residing in South Portland. All sites considered for the B'nai B'rith building lay along the streetcar route to the northwest residential district, to which so many of the members of the association were then migrating. Like most new residential districts, the Northwest lacked recreational facilities and large buildings suitable for social gatherings, so a site between the area of employment in the central business district and the area of residence would be ideal. Immediately after its organization the board of directors acquired a property on 13th Street between Main and Jefferson, which it sold in 1913 to the *Turn Verein* for a $10,000 profit.[45] After considering several other sites, including a preferred location with a building at 13th and Yamhill, the board settled on a lot on 13th Street between Market and Mill, for which it paid only $14,000. The architect, Jacob Dautoff, submitted a plan in March 1914, and by October the building had been completed.[46] Since the turn of the century, men who were to join the association had preferred to reside on the gently sloping hills of the northwest district, and the B'nai B'rith building was erected at the height of their migration to that area. Of the seventy-nine members of the association who could be found in the 1900 manuscript census, only six lived in South Portland, and by 1910 three of them had moved away. In 1900, the majority of the subscribers lived either within or west of the Shattuck School area. The next largest contingent, slightly over 20 percent, already lived in the Northwest. By 1910, about half of those who had lived on the fringes of the central business district had moved to the Northwest, where over 40 percent of the group now resided. Most of the others changed residence in an area around the Park blocks. In a group of eighty-two men who had belonged to the building association and who in 1920 were members of a reorganized and unified B'nai B'rith lodge, 42 percent lived in the Northwest, 28 percent remained in the area around the Park blocks, and 27 percent had participated in a still newer migration to East Portland. Even this latter group, however, was connected by streetcar with the B'nai B'rith building.

The activities located in the building represented an effort by the board of directors to provide a center for all strata in the Jewish community. But the

Table 21. B'nai B'rith Building Association Members, Residential Trajectory, 1910–1920

Residential Trajectory 1910–1920	1910 Residence				New Members, 1911–1916 Residence, 1920	No.
	Central	South	Northwest	East		
Remained in home	3	0	7	1		
Moved within district	5	1	8	2		
Moved to Central		0	2	1	Central	12
Moved to South	0		0	0	South	3
Moved to Northwest	5	4		0	Northwest	9
Moved to East	7	4	0		East	8

activities they themselves sponsored catered to an upwardly mobile middle class. The board rented space to the Rose City Lodge, the South Portland Benevolent Association, and a Portland Free Hebrew School, which was shortly reorganized and located in Neighborhood House. In addition, a contingent of Sephardic Jews, who had emigrated from the Isle of Rhodes and from the Sea of Marmara area and settled initially in Seattle, rented the main hall for High Holiday services. Most of the Sephardim worked in or owned small fish and vegetable markets on Yamhill Street, and lived on the fringes of the central business district rather than in South Portland, so the B'nai B'rith building was convenient for them. But the board placed primary interest on recreation for the members and their children. They opened a gymnasium and had a shower bath and a pool with an instructor ten years before Neighborhood House was able to provide one for South Portland.[47] In addition to the high-school fraternities and athletic teams, the building also sponsored dramatic societies and a symphony orchestra. It did not house the mechanisms of rehabilitation, like medical and dental clinics, Americanization classes, or instruction in cooking and sewing, for which Neighborhood House was noted. When families and young people joined the community center they were no longer in need of comprehensive guidance; instead, they were expected to express interests, which the center would try to meet. Mollie Blumenthal, the daughter of a Latvian immigrant who peddled rugs for Joseph Shemanski, found her recreation at Neighborhood House, and saw the difference between herself and the B'nai B'rith group rather starkly. To her they were "the ritzier Jews,"[48] though in fact they were merely the new middle class.

The members of the building association were also the major promoters of Zionism in Portland. But Zionism, in Portland as across the country, was only the most pointedly ideological element in a larger effort to unify the Jewish community. Portland was too far removed from the major population centers to be strongly affected by the abortive American Jewish Congress movement, led by Stephen Wise, Louis Brandeis, and others. But in Portland as in the larger centers, a middle class, primarily of Eastern European origins and desirous of leading a community, had also emerged. When war broke out in Europe in 1914, two circumstances allowed this middle class to find its cause. First, much of the fighting on the Eastern Front left many Jews as refugees in need of sustenance. Second, the world Zionist leadership, looking for a neutral country for its headquarters, transferred its central agency to the United States. Zionist projects already existed in Palestine, and Chaim Weizmann in London lobbied for a Jewish homeland with the British Foreign Office. But major fund raising for war relief and Zionist projects occurred in the United States. The Zionist movement sent the young social philosopher Horace M. Kallen on a speaking tour of the West Coast in August 1915, and

29. Cantor Abraham Rosencrantz, Congregation Ahavai Shalom, and choir, ca.
1920

he reported to Stephen Wise that the prospects for fund raising in Portland
were good. Isaac Swett, David Solis Cohen, and Mose Mosessohn provided
local leadership, and Kallen assured Wise "that you left there rich ground,
which has fallen fallow since your departure, but which is capable of yielding
rich fruit to the cause at the hands of a good husbandman."[49] In November
1915, Wise did visit Portland, where he spoke at the B'nai B'rith building in
behalf of Zionism and the congress movement. He was warmly welcomed.
But ideological issues were not intensely debated on the West Coast, as
Marvin Lowenthal, a close friend of Kallen and Wise, quickly discovered.[50]
Instead, support for Zionism had to be subsumed under a general effort to
provide Jewish war relief and to unify both the welfare and fraternal activities
within the community.

Spurred by Wise's visit, men like Ben Selling, Nathan Strauss (the new
president of Fleischner–Mayer dry goods store), and Joseph Shemansky tried
to create a unified community so that funds for war relief and local welfare
could be more easily raised. Given their ability to increase support for the
new B'nai B'rith building, they chose the lodge as the vehicle for community
mobilization. By late 1918, they had convinced the two existing lodges to
coalesce, and they recruited hundreds of new members, including large

30. Rabbi Jonah Wise (Temple Beth Israel), and young Jacob Weinstein, B'Nai B'rith
     camp, ca. 1920s

contingents from all of the synagogues and even several dozen from the
Sephardic congregation. In   January 1919, at a large meeting, Joseph
Shemansky was elected president of the new lodge, and in his speech he
emphasized above all the need to continue recruiting.[51] As Table 22 indicates, among the seven hundred members were five of his own employees and
over a dozen employees of both Meier and Frank and Fleischner–Mayer. By
1922, with almost one thousand members, the consolidated Lodge 65 was
reputedly the largest on the Pacific Coast and produced three presidents of
the District Grand Lodge, including David Solis Cohen and Rabbi Jonah
Wise.[52] The same leaders also formed a Portland Committee on Relief of
Jewish War Sufferers in September 1919. Selling told Rabbi Joseph Krauskopf
that he had personally contributed $5,000 to Jewish war relief in 1919 and
would do the same in 1920. By then Rabbi Wise had also expressed special
interest on behalf of the community to participate in the support of Jewish
war orphans.[53] From this effort to consolidate communal loyalties and to
rationalize fund raising came a welfare federation.

   While the dislocation of war highlighted the need for communal
consolidation, the great mobility of the 1920s generated intensive cultural
insecurities throughout the country. Even in Portland, where industrial

Table 22. *Major Employers and Employees in Oregon Lodge 65, 1920–1921*

Name of Firm	Owners as Members	Employees as Members
Meier & Frank, dept. store	5	12
Lipman–Wolfe, dept. store	4	6
Fleischner–Mayer, wholesale dry goods	4	14
M. Seller, crockery importers	3	7
Simon's store, dry goods	2	6
N. & S. Weinstein, clothing	2	5
Eastern Outfitting (Jos. Shemanski)	1	5
Ben Selling & Co., clothing	1	4
Goodman Bros., shoes	4	1

production and immigrant districts were never extensive, xenophobic tensions led many people to demand cultural conformity. Initially men like Selling, Shemansky, and Rabbi Jonah Wise, the son of Isaac Mayer Wise and the successor of Stephen Wise at Beth Israel, joined the patriotic fervor. Wise in particular denigrated the Yiddish language and Jewish residential clustering as symbols of degradation. He and his colleagues saw the consolidated lodge as the best setting in which immigrant members could be Americanized. At meetings members were urged to become citizens, and the lodge fully endorsed the drive by the new patriotic order, the American Legion, for federal subsidies for Americanization classes in the public schools.[54] Rabbi Wise hoped that Jews would become fully integrated into civic life, and he used his appointment as district grand orator in 1921 to bring this message to lodges along the Pacific Coast. Wise was also appointed by Governor Olcott in 1920 to a five-man commission to beautify the highways, and in 1923 he was appointed to a three-man Oregon Board of Higher Curriculum. He was also approached by the University of Oregon to teach a course on Jewish history, and he lectured on various controversial subjects, including evolution, at nonsectarian gatherings around the state.[55]

The patriotic fervor of the early 1920s, however, assumed anti-Semitic overtones in 1922 with the emergence of the Ku Klux Klan. The Klan of the 1920s focused the confusion of small merchants and farmers at alleged threats to small-scale social life and local autonomy. With strong ties to the Scottish Rite Masons in Portland, the Klan depicted the Catholic Church as a foreign and authoritarian institution intent on subverting the free conscience of Protestant society. Rabbi Wise quickly perceived that the state-wide Klan was directed from Portland by unscrupulous men with political ambitions. Writing to a friend in San Francisco, he noted "The Klan here is more political than anything else and is trying to put certain men in office with a view to pushing its animosities against Catholics particularly and very likely against the Jews."[56] Men like Fred Gifford and John J. Jeffreys of the Klan hierarchy promoted a ballot initiative requiring that all children attend the public schools. Klan members also expressed revulsion at violations of the

Volstead Act and saw relationships between Catholic criticism of prohibition, visible increases in public intoxication, and the irresponsible use of the decade's most vital symbol of modernity, the automobile. The Klan never explained how the church was related either to alcohol abuse or speeding Model Ts and Pierce Arrows. Klan rhetoric, however, emphasized interlocking conspiracies and argued that control of the school curriculum by a Protestant majority would curtail cultural diversity and halt social disintegration.[57]

Still another issue that illustrates the economic and social dislocation of the decade and the moral ambiguities of democracy highlighted the political campaign of 1922: the demand by farmers and small businessmen for lower taxes. In some rural areas, insurgents, often with Klan backing, demanded new tax formulas, which would fall more heavily on Portland distributors.[58] Their farmer constituents wanted the federal government to build new roads so that they might modernize their marketing operations, but they resented state regulatory agencies whose staffs were paid from increased local taxes. Rabbi Wise ignored the complex social tensions represented by the taxation issue, but it came to light in Portland when a local Jew, Jesse Winburn, became the campaign manager for the Klan's candidate for governor. Wise and Ben Selling wrote to Louis Marshall, who in his youth, had known the Winburn family, urging him to intercede. Winburn told Marshall, however, that Wise and Selling had badly misrepresented him and misunderstood the campaign. He opposed the Klan and the public school initiative, he told Marshall, but he supported the proposed tax formula, which would fall more heavily on merchants like Selling. His candidate, he argued, supported the interests of farmers, small businessmen, and even "poor Jews," whereas Wise and Selling spoke for a propertied elite. Marshall doubted the authenticity of Winburn's response, and like Wise and Selling saw the Klan exclusively as a threat to religious freedom and civil liberties.[59] The dramatic growth of the local economy, however, had challenged local authority and unleashed resentments, of which animosity against wealthy Jews was a very small part. Although the school initiative passed, the United States Supreme Court declared it unconstitutional in 1925. The Klan disintegrated as a political agent in Portland by 1926, though it retained its social functions as a lodge in some small Oregon towns into the 1930s.[60]

Young men growing up in Portland during the 1920s recall the Klan as an arrogant group of bullies, but they claim to have encountered little anti-Semitism themselves. Several who attended graduate school in Chicago or law school at Columbia University in New York said they first encountered discrimination there.[61] Nevertheless, the Council of Jewish Women investigated discrimination in high-school fraternities, and the fraternities at the University of Oregon in Eugene seem not to have admitted Jews. Men like

Max S. Hirsch, a nephew of Jeanette Meier, carried on business with many gentile firms and resented exclusion from the University Club and the Arlington Club, where many major business transactions were consummated. As his son Harold recalled, "My father felt much more keenly about this than I do. He was a fairly prominent man in business circles in Portland and many of the men with whom he sat on city-wide committees belonged to the University Club. Several times, when meetings were scheduled at the University Club, my father refused to go because the Club didn't take Jews. The meetings were changed to a spot less embarrassing." And Judge Gus Solomon later reiterated that these clubs provided the setting where much important business was transacted. [62]

As the pioneer German families declined in size and as their descendants moved away, the successful Jews of Eastern European origins were not recognized as part of the city's social elite. Jews had been almost 20 percent of the San Francisco social elite in the 1880s, and 8 percent in Portland in 1891; but by 1930 Jewish households were less than 5 percent of those listed in the *Portland Blue Book and Social Register*. [63] The guardians of the pioneer heritage, surviving in a world where unfamiliar faces were achieving economic and professional prominence, recast status distinctions to satisfy their own insecurities. The editors of the *Social Register* assured their subscribers in

31. Governor Julius Meier

1930 that neither wealth nor birth into old families would insure inclusion. "Our committee on admissions makes the choice, and the public is not entitled to know how these decisions are arrived at and it is unfair to ask,"[64] the editors announced. The German Jewish pioneers had expected social divisions and had founded parallel institutions, which had become part of the city's heritage. But the descendants of Eastern European Jews, despite superior educations, had matured in a society where class lines were already established and prejudices had congealed. They had to define their status within their own ethnic community or in professional circles. Without an elite club of their own, they perceived in social exclusion a violation of their citizenship rights. This conflict between social convention and their sense of status deprivation would not be resolved until the civil-rights movement of the 1950s and 1960s.[65]

To combat anti-Semitic tensions, the B'nai B'rith Lodge, conforming to national patterns and blessed by 1916 with legal talent, instituted an anti-defamation committee. In conjunction with the Council of Jewish Women, the committee now investigated anti-Semitic jokes in local newspapers and on the vaudeville stage. While Rabbi Wise felt that the regional committee lacked a policy and failed to criticize the Klan strongly enough, in Portland

32. Meier & Frank main store, completed in 1920s (Courtesy Oregon Historical Society)

the committee obtained apologies for occasional anti-Semitic slurs.[66] During the Klan scare, however, both Ahavai Shalom and Beth Israel were victimized by arson. The perpetrators were never apprehended, apparently, though neither congregation seems to have pressed the police for intensive investigations. Ahavai Shalom simply repaired its building, and Beth Israel used the insurance to erect a brick structure, which remains one of Portland's architectural gems.[67]

Despite the prominence of the Klan and increased social exclusivity in the 1920s, Jews were not precluded from seeking high public office. In 1930 a proponent of public ownership of electric power captured the Republican gubernatorial nomination, but died before the election. The Republican state central committee replaced him with a proponent of private power. In protest, reformers nominated Julius Meier, who was easily elected governor in a write-in campaign.[68] Meier was well known in Oregon as the principal executive of the state's largest retail store, not as a spokesman or leading figure in the Jewish community, as Sol Hirsch or Ben Selling had been in a previous generation. Aside from his quiet role in the shelter home and in Beth Israel, Meier had not taken the lead in reorganizing Jewish fraternal or welfare agencies. Although his religious affiliation was well known, his pioneering lineage and advocacy of popular public issues weighed more heavily with the voters than any identification with the new middle class of entrepreneurs and professionals which the Jewish community now represented in the public mind.

The social aspirations of Portland's mobile middle-class Jews during the 1920s can be measured fairly accurately by the cultural fare provided by the B'nai B'rith Lodge. The culture of *kashrut*, which remained largely confined to the streets of South Portland and to Neighborhood House, appeared occasionally in the B'nai B'rith building in Yiddish plays. But the entertainment, like the membership, represented a professionalization of the elite activities sponsored by Lodge 416 in the 1890s. Musical performances again were the most popular, but instead of depending on the talents of wives and girl friends, professional musicians were hired to perform classical and romantic pieces at lodge meetings. The lodge also sponsored its own symphony orchestra and glee club, and a photo indicates that these groups were composed of many women and young people in addition to men.[69] The B'nai B'rith apparently did not sponsor picnics and open dances, forms of diversion so enjoyed by the residents of South Portland. Instead, it held formal entertainments like card parties and dances with the women's auxiliary to raise money for the lodge and for charity.

In addition to its athletic program at the center, the lodge expanded its philanthropic work by initiating a summer camp in 1923 for the youngsters of South Portland. B'nai B'rith camp was originally located in Wallula, Wash-

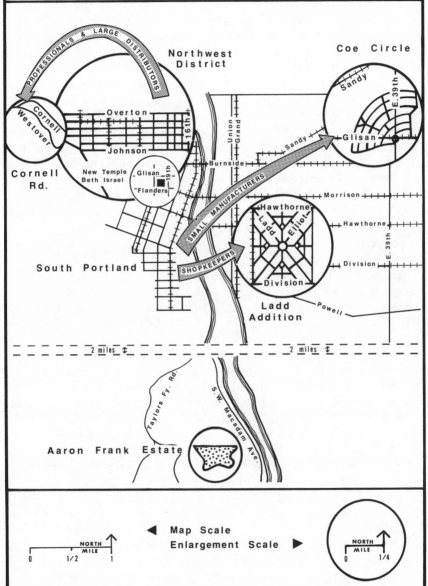

Migration of B'nai B'rith Families within Portland, Oregon, 1920's

ington, and then moved to Neskowin, Oregon. By 1928, Julius Meier's family gave acreage for a new camp site on Devil's Lake, in Oregon. Modelled after the summer camps of the YMCA and other agencies which sought to improve the health and presumably the moral perceptions of youngsters trapped in the tenements and sweat shops of eastern cities, the B'nai B'rith camp combined a simulation of "roughing it" in cabins that lacked indoor plumbing with a professional staff to supervise play. Jewish and some gentile youngsters were given "campships" to cover their expenses, and high-school boys, many with athletic skills, were hired as counselors. The cabins were erected or paid for by members of the lodge, and most of the equipment was contributed by members of the community. By the mid-1930s men like Harry Kenin, then the salaried executive director of the B'nai B'rith center, and professionals in their thirties and forties like Leo Levinson and Harry Herzog started a men's session, which quickly grew to attract over a hundred campers. Over the years, the men's week-long retreat from the bustle of the city developed a comraderie of its own.[70]

A better measure of the increasingly professional character of the membership can be seen in the entertainment which predominated at the monthly lodge meetings. Professors from Reed College, mostly non-Jews, spoke regularly on religious, political, and philosophical themes, and rabbis gave short talks on Jewish history and religion. In 1928 and 1929 a series of debates and talks focused explicitly on the work of the professional men in the organization. Several doctors spoke on the contributions of Jews to modern medicine, and Adelbert G. Bettman discussed his work as a plastic surgeon. Lawyers debated the merits of "The Old Prison System," and still another discussed his work on a local crime study commission. Rabbis new to Portland in the late 1920s, Henry Berkowitz of Temple Beth Israel and Herbert Parzen of Ahavai Shalom, spoke on behalf of Zionism and settlement work in Palestine and provided a liaison between the lodge and the local Zionist organization. A debate on the topic, "Does Modern Judaism Satisfy the Spiritual Needs of the Modern Jew?" featured the two rabbis in the affirmative and the lawyer Harry Kenin (the lodge's new executive director) and his law partner Irwin Fulop in the negative. Although the lodge rarely allowed discussion of partisan political issues, just before the gubernatorial election in November 1930, the four candidates—including Julius Meier, who was a member of the lodge—were invited to speak.[71]

The middle-class status of the B'nai B'rith members can be even more clearly discerned when its activities and membership patterns are compared with those of the Council of Jewish Women. During the 1920s the council continued to pursue the issues of nurture and social welfare, which elite women had presumed to be their province for a generation. As such issues became appropriate for political action, however, the council, through its legislative committee, drew the members more closely into a discussion of proposed social reform legislation. As Otis Graham has suggested, a male elite initiated the major political reforms of the progressive era, but an elite with conspicuous female representation promoted the major social reforms left in abeyance at the national level until addressed by the New Deal.[72] The Council of Jewish Women, in the 1920s as in previous decades, followed the lead of gentile women's clubs in taking stands on issues like separate citizenship for married women and other matters that might redefine the political relationship between the sexes.[73] But in matters that affected a clientele for which it felt special responsibility, like Americanization classes, kindergartens, and health clinics for residents of South Portland, they lobbied actively at the state legislature and at the city hall.

While the council retained certain matriarchal traditions through its dinners at the Concordia Club and its "lady bountiful" attitude toward Neighborhood House, it also endorsed a full range of humanitarian issues which the B'nai B'rith never considered. Indeed, as elite women became civically active by promoting traditional nurturing functions, they became more politically daring than middle-class men.[75] The council discussed pending state legislation on child labor, pensions for elderly widows, and clinics to control venereal disease. It also supported promotion of women to administrative posts in the school district and in juvenile courts. In addition to lobbying for increased welfare support for the indigent, the women supported a conference to control narcotics, and by 1932 they endorsed a reform of the federal criminal code so that information on birth control could be sent through the United States mail.[74] Following the lead of liberal women's groups across the country, the council also endorsed national political crusades to outlaw the submarine and poison gas in war, to have the United States join the World Court, and to support disarmament.

Whereas the B'nai B'rith raised funds for national Jewish causes, the council contributed more concretely to local Jewish educational and welfare needs. Because the Jewish Welfare Federation concluded that the Jewish community could not afford to erect and maintain a hospital of its own, the council donated $5,000 to St. Vincent's Hospital to endow a bed so that indigent Jewish women would always be able to receive treatment. A visiting committee of the council reported that the bed was in continual use from the mid-1920s on.[76] In addition, through the sale of a locally produced cookbook (a traditional nurture function), $1,000 was raised to initiate a scholarship loan fund (a means of social mobility) in 1923. The fund provided loans of about $100 each to many Jewish women, and by the end of the decade at least one male student had also been assisted. The council had contributed small amounts to a similar fund initiated almost two decades before by the Portland Women's Club, which aided needy college students from all segments of Portland society.[77] But with a much larger proportion of local Jewish young people attending college in the 1920s, the council began its own fund. By the end of the decade several thousand dollars had been lent and the council sought additional funds.

An analysis of the council's membership further demonstrates the elite character suggested by its selection of issues. Not only did women like Ida Loewenberg, Ella Hirsch, Julia Swett, Salome Bernstein, and Blanche Blumauer continue to provide leadership, but the rank and file were drawn almost exclusively from Beth Israel and Ahavai Shalom. No membership list for the 1920s is extant, but the number of members remained remarkably consistent at about four hundred to five hundred. In any given year about 350 women had paid dues.[78] In addition, 135 women who joined between 1921 and 1925 are noted in the minutes, and their pattern of persistence in the city and in particular neighborhoods further illustrates the social status of the group. The great majority, when they joined the lodge, lived either in the Northwest or on the East Side. By 1930, 81 percent remained in the city, and of those women about 70 percent remained in the same homes as when they joined the council. Of the others, five had moved from the Northwest to the East Side, but most remained in the district in which they had resided when they joined. This remarkable pattern of residential persistence suggests not social stagnation, but prior acquisition of very desirable housing. The persistence was reinforced by over a dozen members who were widows in 1920 or who were widowed during the decade and who preferred to remain in their home or in nearby apartments.

Table 23. *Council of Jewish Women, Residential Trajectory of New Members, 1921–1930*

Residential Trajectory, 1921–1930	Residence When Joining, 1921–1925				
	Central	Northwest	East	South	Southwest Terrs.
Remained in Home	10	29	31	0	5
Remained in District	1	13	5	1	0
Moved to Central		1	0	0	0
Moved to Northwest	1		0	0	0
Moved to East Portland	0	5		0	0
Moved to South Portland	0	1	0		0
Moved to suburban town	0	1	0	0	0
Moved to Southwest Terraces	0	3	1	0	
Left Portland	5	11	9	1	0

Unlike the Council of Jewish Women, the B'nai B'rith sustained a disastrous decline in membership after 1925. While the community itself gradually shrank from about 10,000 in 1926 to about 7,100 in 1946,[79] the lodge lost over half its membership between 1925 and 1931. Tensions within the lodge that led to such a drastic decline are hard to detect, but comments in the minutes suggest that the majority received little satisfaction from the events planned by the men who had assumed control during the decade. On the surface the leadership seemed to remain intact, except for men who died, like David Solis Cohen, or who left the city, like Rabbi Jonah Wise. A few members tried to reinvigorate the religious side of the lodge's work by emphasizing support for Hillel House at Reed College and at the University of California at Berkeley, and by planning an extensive series of ten-minute talks on Jewish history.[80] As membership dipped from about eight hundred in 1927 to six hundred in 1929, the leadership became alarmed. Rather than seeking broad social or cultural reasons for the decline, the officers assumed that more energetic recruitment might attract new members. In July 1928, an executive committee was formed to handle routine business, to approve proposals of the various permanent committees, and to assume responsibility for the moribund membership committee. As part of the campaign to attract new members, Ben Selling and the very personable Rabbi Berkowitz presided over a meeting of twenty-five businessmen in December 1929, to induce them to join. None of these tactics, however, reversed the decline, and when the opening meeting in September 1930 drew only nineteen members, the leadership responded to a request for a change in format.[81] Under the direction of the advertising agent Robert Smith, the debates and ten-minute talks on Jewish history were dropped, and speeches by college professors were sharply curtailed. Instead, door prizes were offered, vaudeville acts were engaged, and more card parties were planned. An extensive telephone solicitation to attract rank and file rather than simply a business elite pushed attendance to over two hundred at some meetings.[82]

Despite the onset of the Depression, which clearly prevented some retired members from meeting dues and fees, the lodge did little to make membership easier. The proposal made by the attorney Sam B. Weinstein to raise the initiation fee from $10 to $25 was tabled,[83] but the executive secretary, Ralph Herzog—who was also a law partner of Harry Kenin—refused to accommodate the needs of men with declining incomes. He felt he had been hired to balance the books rather than to make special arrangements for those down on their luck. In May 1930, for example, Jacob L. Asher, the president of a collection agency, complained that his friend Julius Sax, who had donated generously to the lodge in the past, had been expelled because he could no longer pay dues. "Mr. Sax feels very much hurt over the attitude of the administration as he is alone, without a home, and with very few friends, and the B'nai B'rith meetings were his only source of pleasure." Asher suggested that Sax's arrears in dues be forgiven and that he be reinstated, though required to pay dues in the future. Herzog did not relent, though, and Sax seems to have left Portland within the year. As Herzog explained to another older lodge member, the jeweler Ben Backman, he had accepted the position of executive secretary in January 1930, "to expedite . . . the business of the lodge and to conduct the secretary office in a

33. Officers of the B'nai B'rith Lodge No. 65, 1923–24: standing left to right: Sam B. Weinstein, Arthur Goldsmith, Si Cohen, Abe Asher, Julius Cohen, David Robinson, unidentified, Ben Selling, Alex Weinstein, Anselm Boskowitz, Abe Arbitman, Nathan Strauss, George Rubinstein; seated, left Alex E. Miller, Abe Rosenstein

business-like and efficient manner." Not until January 1933 did a discussion at an executive committee meeting lead to the consensus that every effort should be made to assist old members to retain their place in the lodge.[84]

An examination of the men who assumed leadership in the lodge during the decade should suggest why total membership may have declined. At the beginning of the decade a patriarchal business elite who employed dozens of lodge members dominated the lodge as well as other welfare organizations. Even after Joseph Shemansky retired as president in January 1920, the majority of the nine officers and five trustees were in merchandizing, especially the clothing industry, and only three were professional or semiprofessionals. The prominence in the lodge of clothing merchants encouraged their employees to join so that they might continue affiliations made on the job in the more relaxed fraternal setting. By 1930, however, professionals had come to dominte the lodge. Of the nineteen different men who served during 1929 and 1930 as officers, ten were professionals, including five lawyers. Five officers were still in the clothing industry, including Abe Arbitman, the

34. The elegance of New Temple Beth Israel, completed in 1929

manager of Joseph Shemansky's New York Outfitting Store, who had also been an officer in 1920, and who was now on the board of trustees. But the daily control of the lodge through the executive committee was exercised by lawyers. The ascendancy of men like Harry Kenin, Ralph Herzog, David Robinson, and Sam B. Weinstein brought efficiency and a more expert grasp of civic affairs to the lodge. Indeed, it was a view of civic activism similar to that espoused by the leadership of the Council of Jewish Women. But these professionals were far removed in their view of proper lodge functions from the leadership of 1920 or from the older rank and file. For example, several former presidents, reminiscing at a lodge meeting on 1 February 1927, emphasized changes in activities at meetings. They noted that sick benefits and discussion of the health of members as well as polkas had been replaced by broadly educational work and by entertainment that reflected "American" values ranging from patriotic programs to renditions of the "Black Bottom."[85] The change was not entirely comfortable.

The lodge provided the setting for identifying new spokesmen for Portland Jewry during the 1920s, but its membership patterns reflected rather than shaped the community's social structure. To demonstrate how the lodge promoted new leadership but still failed to create a cohesive community, we must first measure the shifting patterns of membership. In most studies of social status, change in occupation, place of residence, and ownership of real property are used as indicators, because they constitute major life choices for male residents of modern cities. Studies of American Jewish communities, however, show that few Jews were unskilled workers, and in commercial cities relatively few were skilled workers either.[86] Instead, the move from young white-collar employee to middle-aged proprietor and homeowner became the measure of improved status. Studies of Providence, Rhode Island, and of the London suburb of Edgware, both undertaken in the 1960s, show a strong correlation between place of birth, age, and occupation of head of household for different neighborhoods, with the social profiles varying substantially between neighborhoods. Lloyd Gartner and Albert Vorspan's study of Los Angeles suggests the same neighborhood distinctions in the 1930s.[87] Similar patterns have been traced for Portland; they will be utilized to demonstrate how changes in the class structure and geographical distribution of the community compare with shifts in lodge membership. Cultural distinctions between men of Eastern European, German, and even Turkish origins remained, and will also be taken into account.[88]

In 1920, the disparate strata of the Jewish community temporarily coalesced into a single institution; lodge members provided a composite of the occupational profiles of the lodges that had existed at the turn of the century, and included some who had been assisted by the IRO and many of the Sephardim who had arrived via Seattle. The great expansion of Portland Jewry since 1900 led to an increase in the numbers in trade (especially stores serving the city's working class), a shift from crafts and peddling to storekeeping, the appearance of proprietors and salesmen of new products—related especially to office equipment and automobiles—and the beginning of a professional class. But lodge members in 1920 were distributed through the same occupational categories and in about the same proportions as they had been in 1900. As Table 24 indicates, Jews constituted an intense occupational cluster compared to employed males in the city as a whole. The modest shift between 1910 and 1920 of jobs for males from transportation to manufacturing and clerical work included a few Jews. A few junk businesses were gradually transformed to steel foundries, a few men opened small hat, tent, and clothing "factories," and expanding businesses hired bookkeepers and accountants. But the majority of Jews were already in trade, and even the handful in "service" were primarily owners of cleaning and dying shops or of movie theaters.

Shifts in occupational categories of lodge members during the 1920s indicate some changes in the Jewish community's occupational structure and specify the changing social composition of the lodge. Skilled workers, who as late as 1900 had included harness makers, tinners, glaziers, and semiskilled

Table 24. *Occupational Profiles, Portland Males and B'nai B'rith Members, 1910–1930*

	Portland 1910		Portland 1920		Portland 1930		B.B. 1920		New B.B. 1926–1930	
	No.	%	No.	%	No.	%	No.	%	No.	%
Population 10 yrs and older	105,473		111,545		130,976		957		188	
All employed	91,344	100.0	92,320	100.0	105,711	100.0	916	100.0	170	100.0
Agriculture	3,191	3.5	4,320	4.7	2,154	2.0	0	0.0	0	0.0
Extrac minerals	523	0.6	331	0.4	271	0.3	0	0.0	0	0.0
Mfc. & mechan.	36,613	40.1	39,002	42.2	39,169	37.1	152	16.6	26	15.3
Transp. & communica	13,860	15.2	10,959	11.9	12,908	12.2	20	2.2	2	1.2
Trade	17,638	19.3	16,703	18.1	23,217	22.0	605	66.0	87	51.2
Public service	1,646	1.8	2,192	2.4	2,630	2.5	11	1.2	0	0.0
Prof., semi-prof.	4,614	5.0	5,332	5.8	7,072	6.7	87	9.5	44	25.9
Domestic & service	7,439	8.1	5,672	6.1	7,106	6.7	21	2.3	7	4.1
Clerical	5,820	6.4	7,591	8.2	8,912	8.4	20	2.2	4	2.4
No occupation							48		16	
Students							3		2	

men like teamsters, masseurs, and bartenders, had disappeared, though a few Sephardic immigrants had become bootblacks. By 1920, the skilled workers were almost exclusively tailors, cutters, printers, and butchers. During the decade, as Table 25 indicates, the skilled workers showed a high propensity to leave the city, or, if remaining, to withdraw from the lodge. In addition, skilled workers constituted less than 5 percent of new members during the decade. Employees in the various retail and wholesale stores also had a high propensity to leave Portland and a propensity about average for total lodge membership to withdraw if remaining in the city. The propensity of such employees to join the lodge during the decade was also less than it had been.

Table 25. B'nai B'rith Members, 1920: Residential Trajectory, by Occupation

Occupational Category	Remained Portland remained B.B.	Remained Portland Left B.B.	Left Portland by 1930	Died by 1930*	Total, 1920
Retail, wholesale, clothing mfg.	154	129	81	45	409
Independent agent	18	16	4	4	42
Employee	53	55	80	9	197
Mfg. (not clothing)	17	9	4	5	35
Professional	29	24	7	10	70
Semi-Professional	20	10	3	3	36
Service	17	14	10	2	43
Skilled	14	31	18	6	69
Other	4	4	6	1	15
No Occupation	6	17	10	15	48
Totals	332 (34.4%)	309 (32.1%)	223 (23.1%)	100 (10.4)	964

*SOURCE: Decennial Death Lists, Vital Statistics Section, Health Division, Oregon Department of Human Resources, Portland

The professions saw the most significant increase in Jewish employment during the decade, though the trend seems to have begun in the 1910s. Until World War I Jews were only slightly overrepresented in the professions for the city as a whole. And as was true in cities like Atlanta at the same time,[89] they only gradually moved into the traditional professions of law and medicine. The sons of the wealthy German store owners through the 1900s had generally been absorbed after high school in expanding family businesses, and with very small families in the second generation, the grandsons often found themselves as employees in large firms like Meier and Frank, Fleischner--Mayer, M. Seller, or Lowengarts. During the 1920s, however, over one-quarter of the new lodge members were professionals, and added to this should be four druggists whom the federal census classified as "tradesmen." Many of these men were sons of early Eastern European immigrants—Ricens, Weinsteins, Robinsons, Swetts, and Mosessohns—whose occupational status eclipsed that of most of the grandsons of the German pioneers. By the end of the decade, over 16 percent of lodge members were professionals, which was double their representation in the lodge of 1920, and over twice the percentage of professionals in the local labor force. In addition, the professionals had a very low propensity to leave the city or to withdraw from the lodge. Lawyers and insurance agents, among whom were many sons of Eastern European immigrants, showed the highest propensity of all occupations to retain lodge membership through the decade.

Indeed, the process of occupational succession and shifting communal leadership corresponds in many ways with the process of occupational mobility across generations presented by Clyde and Sally Griffen for skilled German and unskilled Irish workers in late-nineteenth-century Poughkeepsie, New York. The German immigrants as blacksmiths, cabinet makers, tailors, and cigar makers had far higher skills than did the Irish laborers, and they enjoyed higher income and persistence. Their sons, however, inherited a stake in obsolescing trades, whose decline in Germany had led their fathers to emigrate in the first place. The Irish, not committed to a secure though obsolescing niche, sought whatever opportunities they could find, and by the end of their careers were more likely than the second-generation Germans to have higher-paying and higher-status white-collar jobs.[90] For Portland Jews, the sons of the Germans inherited successful businesses, which allowed them to acquire greater sophistication but not different marketing skills than those possessed by their fathers. The sons of Eastern Europeans, where family income or perseverance allowed, shifted to professional skills, which enhanced their career prospects and also provided them with the expertise to address the legal, political, and welfare issues that would face the community over the next several decades. Although the sons of Portland's German Jewish entrepreneurs did not fade, as did many sons of Poughkeepsie's German craftsmen, they were often eclipsed in status by sons of Eastern Europeans.

Although the professionals who changed the content of lodge meetings may have induced men of lower status to withdraw, patterns of mobility affecting all Americans accentuated the effects of whatever programs the leadership developed. Sociologists have found that men of lower occupational status have been less likely to join voluntary associations than men of higher status, and that men experiencing occupational success have been far more likely to retain membership than those experiencing stagnation.[91] Correlating social ascent with membership in specific types of voluntary associations, especially ethnic lodges, is difficult, because cultural traditions as well as social status may influence patterns of affiliation. Nevertheless, during the 1920s a sifting process illuminated the more subtle status distinctions among the Jews in a manner similar to that identified by sociologists for more clearly stratified occupational groups.

By the 1920s Portland had become not only larger, but a more mature regional metropolis. For the first time, its adult sex ratio had become virtually evenly balanced,[92] its farm lands were being developed into subdivisions, and a marked increase in trade implied opportunities specifically for Jews. While the persistence rate for the city as a whole has not been computed, that for the B'nai B'rith members was quite high when compared with other populations that have been studied. Omitting the 100 members known to have died and those who could not be found in city directories, of 864 men, 641 (74.1 percent) remained in the city from 1920 to 1930. Such a high persistence rate was unusual even for entrepreneurs and professionals in nineteenth- and early-twentieth-century American cities, and probably reflects the intensive employment network of Portland Jewry. Very few Jews were employed by gentiles, even by large corporations, and less than ten lodge members were employed by any branch of government. For Portland's Jews, not only career success, but support through ethnic business ties reinforced job security in an expanding sector of the local economy and increased the probability that Jews would remain in town to retain lodge membership.

As with other ethnic groups, however, Jews in lower-status jobs had a higher propensity to leave town; if they remained, they had a higher propensity to withdraw from the lodge. For some occupations, unusual circumstances may have led to a higher "outmigration" rate. Federal employees virtually disappeared, in part because the United States Railroad Commission, which had directed all rail service during World War I, was abolished, and the army was rapidly demobilized. Jews employed by those agencies generally left town. Theater managers also left in large numbers, possibly because of the consolidation of ownership and the manipulation of movie distribution by the Hollywood studios.[93] But the more common pattern was for skilled workers and clerks to leave in large numbers, whereas most employers and professionals remained. To illustrate how general influences for mobility—like the coincidence of youth and low-status employment—affected Portland Jewry (and lodge membership), a ratio can be computed for each occupation of those who left town to those who died during the decade. In lieu of exact data, such a ratio suggests the relative age of persons in specific occupations. As might be expected, the ratio was high (nine to one) for employees, and low (two to one) for entrepreneurs. Clearly, mobility patterns common to most Americans predisposed men of a lower occupational strata not only to withdraw from the lodge but to leave town. An understanding of such patterns might have induced lodge leadership to try to reverse this trend, though no evidence in the minutes suggests they would have done so.

A correlation of the distribution of property ownership with the propensity to retain lodge membership, to relinquish membership, or to leave Portland, corresponds with similar correlations for occupations. First, the *percentage* of Jewish men owning property in 1920 had not increased dramatically since 1870. While the B'nai B'rith members who could be identified through city directories in 1920 were 7 times as numerous as all Jewish men listed in the 1870 federal manuscript census, there were only 8.5 times as many men who owned real property. Owners of real estate were the most stable element in the Jewish population in the expanding city of the 1920s, yet ownership had increased from only 29 percent in 1870 to 35 percent in 1920. While many B'nai B'rith members were young employees still living with their parents, Jews in overwhelming numbers were not staking out a neighborhood and sinking the bulk of their capital in homes, as were, for example, men of Italian, Polish, or Slovakian descent in eastern industrial cities. Nor were they investing widely in real estate. Of those who remained in Portland through 1930, only 6.5 percent owned more than two pieces of property. Like their predecessors of the 1870s, Jewish men of the 1920s saw other ways of investing their capital.[94]

Among the lodge members, of course, there were great variations in the percentage of home ownership according to occupation and persistence in the lodge and in the city. As Table 26 demonstrates, in most occupational categories men who remained in the lodge through 1930 were far more likely to own homes than men who resigned from the lodge or who left Portland. This was particularly true among small merchants, professionals, and employ-

Table 26. *Property Ownership, 1920, by Occupation and Institutional Trajectory*

Occupational Category	Remained B.B. through 1930		Remained Portland, left B.B. by 1930		Left Portland by 1930	
	No.	% of all men in category	No.	% of all men in category	No.	% of all men in category
Retail, wholesale, clothing mfg.	73	50.7	48	41.4	16	25.8
Other mfg.	11	55.0	2	20.0	5	50.0
Employee	25	35.2	15	17.9	9	10.3
Professional	14	53.8	5	22.7	4	44.4
Semi-Prof., govt.	3	42.8	3	50.0	2	25.0
Independent agent	11	47.8	3	27.3	6	42.9
Service	5	55.5	4	28.6	3	18.8
Skilled	1	12.5	10	34.5	6	35.3
Second hand goods, junk	7	70.0	8	46.6	1	20.0
Other	0	0.0	1	20.0	0	0.0
No occupation	2	25.0	7	41.2	5	33.3
Totals	152	(46.2)	106	(32.2)	57	(23.4)

ees, three of the four most important occupational categories. Among categories like skilled workers and owners of second-hand stores—men with low social status though not necessarily low income—the great majority left the lodge, even though their propensity to own real property was about average for the lodge. But in general, home ownership correlated closely with proprietorship or professional status, and with a high propensity to remain in the city.

While information on the age of members is not available, the implication certainly is that property ownership was closely correlated with middle age. Middle age, in turn, represented a point in the life cycle when occupations were being stabilized, a niche in the community was being established, and homes were being acquired to house growing families. It has frequently been demonstrated that property ownership is highly correlated with the propensity to remain in a city. However, not property ownership itself, but a stage in the life cycle that predisposed men of mercantile background to acquire property, promoted such high persistence.

Changes in the occupational profile of the lodge and relatively high propensity toward home ownership among those who persisted signify its rising status. Changes in residence by individual members help explain the significance of retaining or relinquishing affiliation. To interpret why men might choose to leave the lodge, one might hypothesize most simply that those who joined enthusiastically in 1920–1921 may have moved from southwest Portland during the decade and found attendance at meetings too inconvenient to be worth retaining membership. Correlations between simple patterns of intracity migration and persistence in the lodge, however, do not confirm this hypothesis. Instead, as Table 27 indicates, men moving to the East Side had only a slightly greater propensity to withdraw from the lodge compared to those who remained on the West Side, while of those few who moved to the West Side, a large majority withdrew from the lodge.

Table 27. *Intracity Migration of Lodge Members by Propensity To Retain Affiliation 1920–1930*

	Living on West Side, 1920–1921				
Trajectory, 1920–30	Remain Lodge, 1930		Left Lodge by 1930		Total
	No.	% of categ.	No.	% of categ.	No.
Remain in structure	70	61.8	43	38.2	113
Move on West Side	123	58.3	88	41.7	211
Move to East Side	74	50.7	72	49.3	146
	Living on East Side, 1920–1921				
Trajectory, 1920–30	Remain Lodge, 1930		Left Lodge by 1930		Total
	No.	% of categ.	No.	% of categ.	No.
Remain in structure	30	49.1	31	50.9	61
Move to West Side	6	37.5	10	62.5	16
Move on East Side	35	35.3	63	64.7	98

More important than simple proximity to the lodge building, however, is the social status that specific moves symbolized. For example, data for persons living on the East and West Sides in 1920 show that those who remained in the same homes or on the same street were far more likely to retain lodge membership than persons who moved longer distances. In many cases, of course, those men who remained in their homes were husbands of members of the Council of Jewish Women; they held high occupational status and had found pleasant homes even before the city's major residential expansion of the 1920s. Furthermore, no significant correlation between occupational status and propensity to change residence can be found. People of high and low status were on the move to new housing of varying prices. If men remaining in the same homes had been stagnant, as some scholars have suggested, they might have saved money by resigning lodge membership. Clearly the opposite occurred, suggesting that those desiring stability in housing desired stability in social contacts even though lodge activities and leadership were changing.[95]

For those who changed residence, correlations can easily be demonstrated between moves to high-status neighborhoods and propensity to retain lodge membership. Migration within the West Side, for example, consisted in part of professionals and wealthy merchants with a high propensity to remain in the lodge who moved from older middle-class neighborhoods to high-status areas in the West Hills. A few, like Aaron Frank, Julius Meier, and Edward Ehrman, built elaborate country estates. Another stream of migration on the West Side consisted of tailors, clerks, and retail store owners, with a general propensity to withdraw from the lodge, who moved from the Failing School area to the Shattuck School area, or people changing residence within the latter area. Much of the migration across the Willamette River to the East Side consisted of small shopkeepers and new professionals who had succeeded in business and who chose to move to new subdivisions. Men with expanding incomes, but only middling status within the Jewish community, about half retained lodge affiliation after the move. Compared to the merchants who remained on the West Side, they showed diminished loyalty to the lodge.

A few examples of neighborhoods from which lodge members were moving and others in which they were resettling should illustrate how status differentiation correlated with propensity to retain lodge membership and how Jewish social cohesiveness became diluted. Not only were men of differing occupational statuses acquiring housing farther removed from one another, but they were settling in areas that held smaller proportions of Jews than those in which they had previously lived. An area from which lodge members were steadily moving consisted of six parallel streets in northwest Portland running east and west, from Johnson on the south to Overton on

35. Elliott Street, Ladd Addition, first housing alternative to immigrant district in 1920s

the north. It constitutes the middle third of a pleasant residential area to which young couples had been moving since the mid-1890s. At the southern end the residential blocks emerge from an industrial area at 16th Street and run west to 25th Street, while toward the north they run to 27th Street. The blocks between 16th and 19th streets, however, are very short, and except for an apartment house on Lovejoy Street between 16th and 17th streets, they held very few structures in 1930. These blocks, therefore, will be excluded from the sample. Although the migration of the 1920s for Jews was generally out of the area, enough people remained and enough moved only short distances into the hills to persuade Beth Israel to erect its new building in the late 1920s just below this region on the block bounded by 19th, 20th, Flanders, and Glisan streets.

In 1920, the thirty-eight blocks in the region contained 105 B'nai B'rith members. Many lived in two- or three-story apartment houses, with thirteen clustered in the American apartment house, which still stands on the northeast corner of 21st and Johnson streets. Other families lived in wood frame single homes, and a few affluent merchants, like Aaron and Lloyd Frank and Dr. Leo Ricen, lived in large stone or brick homes on the blocks

36. Laurelhurst: middle class housing in East Portland, 1920s

beyond 25th Street, which sloped up toward the "Heights," where Julius Meier had built a home. During the 1920s, Jewish migration was substantial, led by the thirteen residents of the American apartment house. By 1930, four had died, four had left Portland, and the others had moved elsewhere. Only one identifiable Jew, a widow, now resided in the building. On Lovejoy Street, nine of the twenty B'nai B'rith members in 1920 were apartment dwellers or boarders; during the decade three died, three left the city, and two (both clothing salesmen) moved to the East Side. The ninth, a stockbroker who retained lodge membership, moved a few blocks to an apartment on Glisan Street. The eleven residents of single homes also moved by 1930. None died, but four left Portland, and only three retained lodge membership.

For the region, the pattern of residential dispersal according to occupational status conforms to the general pattern for the lodge, and to patterns established by the residents of South Portland. Of the eighty-six men who survived through the decade, forty-seven (55 percent) either remained in their homes or moved a short distance within the district, though seventeen joined the migration to the East Side. Of those who remained in the same homes, two-thirds either owned businesses or were professionals, and the employees were primarily with the old German firms like Meier and Frank and Flieschner–Mayer. Those who left Portland or who moved to the East Side were predominantly owners of small businesses or employees in such businesses. By 1930, Jewish homeowners and a greatly diminished number of apartment dwellers lived on all six streets, as well as on the numbered cross-streets, but Jews were clearly a retreating minority. Of the 896 heads of household living on the named streets in the region in 1930, only 81 were Jews, a number smaller than lodge members alone residing there ten years previously. In 1930 Jews were only 5 percent of apartment dwellers, but over 27 percent of the 116 homeowners. Like the immigrants in South Portland, they represented an aging group who had found the housing they desired. Although the quality of their homes and presumably their wealth was far greater than the Jews of South Portland, they too were being left behind by the most successful, who were moving to the various "heights" and "terraces," and by the younger merchants, who were acquiring homes in East Portland.

A brief examination of three neighborhoods to which lodge members were moving, with correlations for occupations and persistence in the lodge, further illustrates the increased class dispersal of the Jewish community and of lodge members. Two of the three neighborhoods were on the East Side, and all remain structurally intact today. All had distinctive charms, which suggests that people choosing to settle there saw them as attractive alternatives to their prior places of residence. Given the large number of gentiles among whom Jews were resettling, the choices for the move involved at least some consideration of personal comfort over the more intense neighborliness of the Shattuck School area, from which most of the migrants came.

The first neighborhood was built on the W. S. Ladd Addition, across the Willamette River from the Shattuck School area, to which it was accessible via the Hawthorne Street bridge. The area was first settled by Italian truck farmers, and in 1918 Sam Simonetto, a young Italian-born contractor, began to build single homes.[96] The development lay east of a wholesale marketing and warehousing district, and was shielded from the general grid pattern of city streets by unique street platting. In the center of the approximately one-mile-square district lay a small park, from which four streets radiated like spokes. They were in turn intersected at acute angles by very short streets, so that from the air the district appeared like an octagon enclosed in a square formed by the surrounding main thoroughfares of Hawthorne on the north, Division on the south, East 12th Street on the west, and East 20th Street on the east. The layout secured the district from through traffic even though the two major diagonal streets, Ladd and Elliott, were quite wide. The houses, each built to order, were set back on the lots, and they would be shaded when the hardwood trees planted by the curbs grew to maturity. During the 1920s, six members of the B'nai B'rith settled here, primarily on Ladd and Elliott streets. To them the single family residences, wide front lawns, and circular park must have seemed a handsome and orderly change. However, they resided among an overwhelming preponderance of gentiles: only 7 of the 152 heads of household on Ladd and Elliott streets were Jewish. Of the 6 who had been lodge members in 1920, only 2 remained in the lodge in 1930.

The second neighborhood was located about a mile and a half north and east of the first, above Coe Circle at the intersection of northeast Glisan and East 39th streets. It consists of five parallel streets which successively intersect Flanders and then Glisan east of 32nd Street, and then curl northward up a slight hill, veering sharply to the east. They then parallel Glisan and intersect 39th Street. Here the developer followed the contours of the rising slope to set this area off from the surrounding grid. The curling street patterns protect this area from through traffic, and make it the most desirable location in the vicinity. In contrast to the Ladd Addition, the majority of the houses on these blocks were quite large and occupied most of the lot. In addition, in 1930, over 77 percent owned their homes as opposed to only 60 percent for residents of the streets studied in the Ladd Addition. Three members of the B'nai B'rith lived in these attractive houses in 1920, and as the district was built up during the decade, they were joined by nine others. Two of the newcomers moved in from elsewhere on the East Side, and the others came from Southwest Portland. If occupation provides some measure of income, then the residents of this district were better off than those in the Ladd Addition. Eight of the twelve were wholesalers and suppliers, rather than retailers, and a ninth was the dentist Harry Labby. In addition, residents of this district had a greater propensity to remain in the lodge. Six of the twelve, including two of the initial three residents, remained in the lodge through 1930, a proportion about average for lodge members moving to the East Side. But this district, like the Ladd Addition, was overwhelmingly non-Jewish. The twelve B'nai B'rith members constituted the total of Jewish heads of household scattered among 350 non-Jewish families. With a move to this district the break with a traditional cultural setting was practically complete.

The third residential area consisted of streets carved into the West Hills, especially Westover Road, curving northwest and uphill from 22nd and Burnside streets, and Cornell Road, curving similarly from 26th and Lovejoy streets. The houses were set above and below street level, so that each provided a vista of the Willamette River and East Portland. The large size and distinctive architecture of each house and the curving streets make this district still among the most charming in the city. Seven lodge members already owned homes there in 1920, and nine moved in during the decade. By 1930, two residents had died, but fourteen remained. They included six executives of large firms like Mason Ehrman (wholesale grocers), Lowengart Millinary Supplies, and the Oldsmobile Company of Oregon, as well as four lawyers. The persistence rate of 79 percent for lodge membership was much higher than for the other districts, and the attorneys Sidney Teiser, Arthur Goldsmith, Otto Kraemer, and Barnett Goldstein headed lodge committees or spoke at meetings and set the social tone. But these men, while constituting an elite enclave removed from the majority of lodge members, also resided in an overwhelmingly non-Jewish region. On the two streets noted above, Jews were only 17 percent of the heads of household, and their proportion diminished on the smaller side streets. By 1930, except for those who remained in South Portland, Jews were scattering over the city, with some moderate clustering on the East Side. Rather than moving into new Jewish subdivisions as in New York, Philadelphia, and Cleveland,[97] Jews were resettling among gentiles of similar class standing and propensity to own homes. The Jewish social elite along Westover and Cornell roads was not only more physically removed and occupationally distant from the Jewish majority, but they could observe an ethnic community undergoing dispersal.

Aside from noting the ideological leadership provided by rabbis like Jonah Wise and Herbert Parzen, little has been said about the relationship between synagogue and lodge affiliation. Data for synagogue membership, especially for orthodox shuls, is not available in sufficient quantity or for the appropriate dates to allow for a systematic evaluation. Furthermore, many people belonged to more than one synagogue, often an orthodox shul like Shaarei Torah and a conservative synagogue like Ahavai Shalom. Many others participated actively in Beth Israel while retaining membership in Ahavai Shalom. Nevertheless, synagogues like Beth Israel, Neveh Tzedek, and Linath Hatzedek did represent different strata, or at least different tendencies, in local Jewish society, ranging from the descendants of old German families and the most self-consciously mobile Polish immigrants, to the most recent Eastern European and Sephardic families. A correlation of available synagogue membership data with lodge membership and with the patterns of member persistence in the lodge largely confirms the general pattern of proprietors and professionals remaining and employees and craftsmen leaving. To this general pattern, however, one important addition must be made. Even for orthodox Linath Hatzedek and Sephardic Ahavath Achim, a small contingent of entrepreneurs and synagogue officers remained in the lodge. The spokesmen for the poorer and newer elements in the community saw in the lodge a communal forum in which they should participate even though they might not exercise the same leadership in it as they did in their synagogues. A brief assessment of synagogue data will more precisely illustrate these patterns.

For Beth Israel no membership list for the 1920s exists to provide a precise correlation with membership in the lodge. Nevertheless, men like Rabbi Jonah Wise and Rabbi Henry Berkowitz, as well as laymen like Ben

Selling, Julius Meier, Charles F. Berg, Lawrence Selling, and Joseph She-mansky played such prominent roles in the lodge that the views of Beth Israel were well represented. Still, by the end of the decade the wealthy mer-chants—the Flieschner, Hirsch, Frank, and Wolfe families—were not as active as they had been. To a large extent they retreated into synagogue fund raising and socializing in their new country homes. The strongest influence within the lodge was probably supplied by the members of Ahavai Shalom. Of the 295 male members of the synagogue residing in Portland in 1920, two-thirds belonged to the lodge,[98] and 70 percent remained in the city through the decade. By 1930, almost 45 percent of the initial contingent still belonged to the lodge, a persistence rate about 10 percent higher than for lodge membership as a whole. Furthermore, Ahavai Shalom members seem to have led the migration to the Irvington section of East Portland, where the city's middle class was generally resettling. Nineteen members of the syna-gogue resided there in 1920, and seventeen of them remained through 1930. They were joined during the decade by 21 other members, moving either from the Shattuck School area or from the Northwest. In addition, many of them were manufacturers, with heavy capital investment in the city and strong propensity to remain. They included many of the ladies cloak and suit makers, and several who manufactured mattresses, store fixtures, or trunks, in addition to Jack Barde of Barde Iron and Steel, and Harry Wolf of the Alaska Junk Company. Although these men did not participate as actively in lodge programs as did the lawyers' contingent, they represented the core of the community's upwardly mobile middle class, and they provided steady finan-cial support through the depression.

Members of Neveh Tzedek had a generally high propensity to retain lodge membership, but those who moved to the more prosperous neighbor-hoods had an even greater propensity than those who remained in the Shattuck School area near the synagogue. Of the twenty-two prominent members in 1930, fourteen had belonged to the lodge in 1920, and nine had retained membership through the decade.[99] Of these nine, seven moved either to the Northwest or to Irvington, whereas two of the three who withdrew continued to reside in South Portland. Members of Linath Hatze-dek and Ahavath Achim had a much higher propensity to withdraw from the lodge than did members of Ahavai Shalom and Neveh Tzedek. Those who did retain lodge membership were among the more prominent members of their congregations. Of the 114 members of Linath Hatzedek between 1914 and 1916, only 38 are identifiable as B'nai B'rith members in 1920.[100] Of these, three could not be located in city directories and three died during the decade. Of the remaining thirty-two, only nine retained lodge affiliation through 1930, and these included manufacturers of hats, fixtures, and cooperage, as well as the owner of an army–navy surplus store. Seventeen synagogue members remained in Portland but left the lodge. These were primarily owners of small watch-repair, kosher meat, and junk stores. The six who left Portland were primarily skilled workers.

For the twenty-one identifiable Sephardim in the lodge in 1920, the correlation between retention of membership with occupation and status in the synagogue is much the same.[101] Of the seven who left Portland during the decade, all had owned or clerked in small fruit stores or shoeshine stands. Of the five who remained in the B'nai B'rith through 1930, three—Isaac Hassan, Ben Babani, and Ezra Menashe—were the most successful merchants and in the 1930s each became president of Ahavath Achim. The Sephardim who remained in Portland, however, did not join the general pattern of Jewish migration, but remained near their businesses around Yamhill Street. Their synagogue, built in the 1930s with the financial assistance of Ben Selling, was erected at 3rd and Sherman streets, in South Portland, at a time when most younger Jews were leaving the area.

In the 1920s, Portland's B'nai B'rith Lodge actively shaped a new leadership class rather than simply reflecting changes in the community's social structure. It provided the setting in which a new professional elite could coalesce to inherit leadership from the older merchants. Nor is there any indication that the pressure to become "American" led the new leaders to see their role in the ethnic lodge as less important than their roles in other voluntary associations. The most vocal members of the younger generation— including Laurence Selling (son of Ben), Leo Ricen, David Robinson, Sam B. Weinstein, Harry Kenin, and Rabbis Jonah Wise, Henry Berkowitz, and Herbert Parzen—utilized their membership to attempt to redirect communal thought. Within the lodge they tried to educate the Jewish community to contemporary issues and to professional standards. As men with modern educations, they sought to revitalize Jewish cultural identification by fusing an ideology of civic participation to traditional religious loyalties. However, they could not influence structural changes within the group because they had no employees to recruit and no means beyond the lodge to create a sense of social solidarity. Instead, they emphasized issues that enhanced their own professional status and evoked a sense of ethnic loyalty to mask the community's new stratification. Far from coalescing because institutions were joined through a loose federation,[102] the community became restratified as the German elite shrank in size and withdrew to their homes, golf club, and synagogue, the middle class resettled in East Portland, and the less successful immigrants became isolated in South Portland.

Like so many ethnic enclaves, Portland Jewry had been held together by an intensive employment network, which did not so much break down as diversify during the 1920s. As an especially secure enclave with high rates of persistence, it also retained a large measure of cultural tradition. Indeed, conflicts within the B'nai B'rith illustrate very well the special tensions between social mobility and cultural continuity that successful ethnic enclaves have encountered in many industrial societies. Whereas the Council of Jewish Women avoided this problem by maintaining a largely elite membership and changed little in size or leadership during the decade, the B'nai B'rith tried to include all social strata, but became the organ of a new professional elite. For Jews in middle-sized cities, the tensions of modernization may well have been expressed in just such dilemmas as the predictable and selective sorting of membership through voluntary associations. How such a socially dispersed community would respond to the special pressures of nation-wide economic depression and the rise of the unprecedented Nazi threat to Jewry will be the subject of the concluding chapter.

5. An Entrenched Middle Class and a Politicized Ethnicity 1930—1945

The Great Depression of the 1930s, which brought such suffering to the American working class, turned Portland's Jewish enclave in upon itself. Many Jewish families experienced severe declines in income, but prolonged unemployment seems not to have affected very many. Instead, the selective sorting by age and occupation, which was noticeable in the 1920s, persisted. Residential clustering on the East Side and in the West Hills continued, and home ownership increased to a remarkable degree. Indeed, the depression seems to have induced Jewish proprietors and young professionals to acquire property while lowering the birth rate. In the meantime, the older and poorer residents of South Portland became increasingly isolated. Their own children were moving to the East Side, while in South Portland itself gasoline stations and warehouses replaced some residential structures, and many others were left vacant.

Very little historical literature exists with which to compare the experiences of Portland Jewry during the Depression. Aside from a recent study of New York's Irish, German, Italian, and Jewish communities during the 1930s, and several studies of Black communities, most historical accounts of ethnic groups terminate with the onset of economic collapse.[1] Still, a few points should be noted. In contrast to middle-class Blacks in many cities, who found themselves trapped in deteriorating areas by restrictions on their choice of alternate housing, Portland's Jewish middle class seems to have had access to any housing it could afford. The majority of New York Jews clustered in apartments, but in Portland, Jewish families generally resided in single family homes, as did the majority of gentile families. Like New York Jewry, Portland's Jewish middle class regrouped in definite neighborhoods, but unlike Jews in Washington Heights or the Grand Concourse, they were heavily outnumbered by non-Jewish neighbors. Perhaps for that reason, combined with the economic decline that coincided with the large-scale move to suburban Irvington, Portland's Jews did not invest heavily in new institutions in their new neighborhoods. While New York's second-generation Jews also demonstrated substantial upward occupational mobility, so few Portland Jews had been blue-collar workers that the second generation simply improved on the white-collar experiences of their fathers and mothers. The measure of their improved status came in the heightened expression of stability, the acquisition of homes.[2]

Whereas Jewish families in past generations had promoted modernization, they now provided security by safeguarding the achievements of prior decades. Despite the seperation of generations by the migration of young families to Irvington, mutual support across the generations continued. Communal welfare organizations and religious institutions were all based on support of families rather than individuals. And the most dramatic political issue of the decade—the need to rescue German Jewry—required that one family sponsor another, that family ties either be reknit or at least simulated.

Perhaps most important, the political turmoil initiated by Hitler's Germany also prepared the local Jewish community for institutional and ideological changes that would continue for the next forty years. While many institutional responses to demographic changes would have occurred without the Third Reich's attack on Jews, an aggressive local reaction helped bring segments of the community together when they were physically and socially drifting apart. Synagogues may have explored and rejected mergers because of irresolvable differences in liturgy and financial and status concerns; but men and women found unity of purpose through welfare and political activities. Their common identity as Jews came to depend not on religious faith nor even on similar middle-class life styles, but on ethnic loyalties dramatized by civic activism. The rise of international anti-Semitism, however remote from Portland, brought the old German elite, which had been absorbed in meeting the financial exigencies of its temple, and the East European middle class, which had been acquiring housing in Irvington, into a loose coalition. The B'nai B'rith, through its anti-defamation committee, came to publicize anti-Semitism in Germany as well as closer to home. Local German Jews, who had not participated actively in the lodge for over a decade, were then contacted by national German Jewish leaders to direct the placement locally of German emigres. Committees from virtually all of the local Jewish organizations, including youth groups, were convened to assist in the placement effort, and coordinating committees included descendants of German and Eastern European Jews. Local Zionists joined the coalition by arguing that only a rebuilt Palestine could provide a refuge for the victims of Hitler's pogrom. Even local fund raisers like Harry Mittleman, a contractor and the moving force behind enlarging the B'nai B'rith center, actively worked to obtain affidavits for German refugees, as well as supporting the Zionist message through the Portland Hebrew School. As suburban home owners and secular liberals, Portland Jews of German and Eastern European descent defined their heritage as community service, a defense of civil liberties, and cultural instruction for their children. Social patterns begun in prosperity persisted through depression, and political activism created in response to anti-Semitism became a tradition that guided the community through the next generation and beyond.

I

The Depression of the 1930s created serious dislocations in the lives of many of Portland's Jews. Jerome Berg recalls that his father, despite efforts to attract additional patronage, lost all three of the movie houses that he had worked for over a decade to acquire:

> During the Depression, it was hard to fill the theater because it was difficult for many families to raise the five or ten cents for admission. We used a company store method of giving away bags of groceries to those who were lucky enough to have their tickets drawn. . . . We also gave a certain number of dishes away each night. . . . The idea, of course, was to make the patrons come back, because those who hadn't won a dish one night might win on the next night. We tried all kinds of incentives to increase the size of our audiences, but eventually Dad got wiped out."[3]

By 1940 Berg himself was listed in the city directory as a "salesman." Harold Hirsch, the initiator of the White Stag line of sportswear, returned from England, where he was attending Oxford University when the Depression struck, to assist his father in the Hirsch–Weis textile manufacturing business. He recalls especially selling bedding to Portland's "sporting houses" because "they always paid in cash. . . . I learned a lot about a new kind of selling, calling on them. You took cash wherever you could get it." To conserve money, he and his father "used to walk eleven blocks to the 'Buttermilk Corner' and eleven blocks back again because there, for a nickel, we could get all the buttermilk we could drink. . . . For another seven cents we could get a salami or bologna sandwich on rye to eat with our buttermilk and that was our lunch." His father's business, like many others and like both Beth Israel and Ahavai Shalom, was able to meet its debts by getting extensions on loans from E. B. McNaughton of the First National Bank, who seemed to have a special faith in Jewish clients.[4] Many other men, like Alex Goldstein, who owned a furniture store, and David Solis Cohen, Jr., lost their businesses. Some left town, and others, like Joseph Gass, went to work as agents for insurance companies.[5]

Men and women growing up in Portland during the Depression, most of whom were American-born children of immigrants, recalled that their families had diminished incomes, but that their own careers were not seriously deflected. Several young lawyers found employment with new government agencies,[6] and young doctors were also able to initiate practices. Still younger persons, like Gaulda Jermuloske and Freda Gass, managed to work their way through Reed College with the financial assistance of brothers and sisters. Most women took brief business courses after high school and found work as stenographers and bookkeepers. Unmarried graduates of the local normal school could also find employment in the public schools, because in Oregon married women were not eligible to teach school during the Depression, under the assumption that their husbands would be working and the policy decision that families were not entitled to two incomes. Gaulda Jermuloske's brothers apparently showed little academic aptitude and went to work for their father's hide business, while she went to college. Because of the acute shortage of social workers, she was able to obtain a fellowship to attend graduate school at the University of Southern California and soon found work in her profession. Freda Gass's brother, Dave, financed his college education by teaching at the Portland Hebrew School. Though he earned Phi Beta Kappa honors, he took five years to graduate because of his heavy work schedule. Her older brother Oscar, who had been a Rhodes scholar, found employment in Washington, D.C., in a federal agency, and by the time Miss Gass entered Reed, Oscar was able to send money home to assist her. "Each one of us helped the other along the way," she recalled. "My sister Lil was working at the time (prior to her marriage), and she too put in her earnings so that the family could get along."[7]

The individual recollections—that Jewish families suffered diminished income but not continual unemployment—is largely verified by other sources. Because Jews in Portland were so heavily concentrated in white-collar work, their unemployment level was no doubt much lower than the 13.5 percent found in 1937 for New York, where over 25 percent of Jewish workers were in manufacturing.[8] A list of eight hundred men and a few women hired by the city of Portland on a daily basis for general maintenance during the first week of January 1931 showed no more than two or three who may have been Jewish. Industrial employment in Portland fell by almost 37 percent between 1929 and 1931, according to the Chamber of Commerce, yet on a list of almost fourteen hundred men hired by the city for the first week of June 1931, no more than half a dozen could have been Jewish. As the Depression deepened during the first week of 1933, and before the federal government assumed responsibility for emergency relief, the city hired almost four thousand men to maintain the parks and provide other services. Among them were about a dozen men who were probably Jewish. They included Max

Rosumny, Emanuel Hirschman, and Ben Krause, none of whom had had occupations listed in the city directories for several years. Others were Eugene Rosencrantz, a student, and Max Calof, a driver, each living with his parents; Arthur Nussbaum, a meat cutter; and Jacob Calof, who had no listed occupation.[9] But Jews were very sparsely represented on these lists. Harold Wendel of Lipman, Wolfe and Company department store was a member of the Chamber of Commerce's six-man committee on unemployment,[10] yet he never emphasized the need for white-collar jobs either to the chamber or within the Jewish community. Mrs. Miriam Sandrow, widow of Ahavai Shalom's rabbi during the mid-1930s and herself a professionally trained social worker, was employed by a federal relief agency during those years, but does not recall any Jewish applicants. She recalled:

> Coming from the apple lines, protest parades, [and] ragged, haggard-faced hordes of the Northeast to Portland in 1933 was like arriving on another planet.

> Most of those receiving government relief seemed to have been transients. Indeed, supplying their physical needs with food and cheap clothing may even have improved business for many small groceries and low-priced clothing stores. . . . Vegetable gardens seemed to sprout in back yards everywhere, and some of the surplus was sold to local groceries to meet the needs of the transients receiving government subsidies.[11]

Membership data from the B'nai and B'rith for the 1930s, samples drawn from areas of conspicuous Jewish settlement in 1940, and a population survey taken by Portland's Federated Jewish Societies in 1947, all show that trends of mobility begun in the 1920s continued during the Depression, though at different rates. They generally corroborate the findings of Stephen Thernstrom for Boston's white-collar workers and employers of the 1930s, whose careers were delayed but not permanently disrupted.[12] The use of B'nai B'rith membership data for the 1930s may not at first seem as representative as such data for the previous decade, because so many younger and poorer members had left the organization during the 1920s. But because of the aging of the immigrant generation during the Depression (and their decline as a proportion of the population), the formation of new families by their American-born children (and the smaller size of such families), and the recruitment of many new members by the lodge in the late 1930s to join the anti-defamation struggle, the social characteristics of lodge members by 1940 were more representative than numbers alone would suggest. To provide a fuller picture of the Jewish community, however, samples have been drawn from the various neighborhoods—including South Portland—to complement the B'nai B'rith data.

Perhaps the most conspicuous social and demographic trends established by B'nai B'rith members and other Jewish families during the 1930s were the acquisition of homes on a much wider scale and the dramatic lowering of the birth rate. Of the 179 lodge members who had joined between 1926 and 1930, 133 remained in Portland through 1940. The persistence rate of almost 75 percent was about the same as for the 1920s, but because the calculations do not exclude those who died, a smaller proportion of adult males seems to have left during the Depression than during the preceding era of prosperity. Even so, employees were again substantially more likely to leave than proprietors, manufacturers, or professionals. More important than the relative patterns of intercity migration for different occupational groups, however, was the propensity of those who remained to acquire homes. In 1930, only 37 percent of lodge members owned a home,[13] and men who left town during the 1930s were far less likely to have owned a home and far more likely to have resided in an apartment in 1930 than were those who remained through the decade. Despite the Depression, men who owned homes were generally able to retain them, and many other men were able to become home owners. As Table 28 indicates, among the fifty-four men who owned homes in 1930 and who remained in Portland through 1940, thirty-eight still owned homes. Among the fifty-nine who had not owned homes in 1930 and who remained through 1940, thirty had managed to acquire one. Almost all who acquired homes were professionals and proprietors, though a few were salesmen.

Table 28. *Home Ownership, B'nai B'rith Members, 1930–1940*

Status, 1940	Status, 1930						Total
	Owned home		Not owner		Apt., hotel		
	No.	%	No.	%	No.	%	No.
Owned home	38	57.5	30	35.7	8	27.6	76
Not owner	12	18.2	27	32.1	3	10.3	42
Remained in apt.					10	34.5	10
Moved to apt.	4	6.1	2	2.4			6
Left Portland	12	18.2	25	29.8	8	27.6	45
Total	66	100.0	84	100.0	29	100.0	179

New Members, 1940		
Status	No.	%
Owned home	180	50.8
Not owner	109	30.8
Apt. or hotel	65	18.4
Total	354	100.0

Among the 354 new lodge members in 1940, 51 percent owned their homes. As in the late 1920s, men joining the lodge were over twice as likely to be proprietors, professionals and manufacturers as they were to be employees. And as Table 29 shows, the owners and professionals were far more likely to own their homes than were the managers and salesmen, almost a quarter of whom resided in apartments. Furthermore, employment data collected by the Federated Jewish Societies in 1947 suggests that among local Jews the proportion of employees had declined since the 1920s,[14] thus heightening the representativeness of lodge members within the Jewish community. And data collected for South Portland, where many older immigrants who never joined the lodge resided, generally corroborates the substantial increase in Jewish home ownership during the Depression. Indeed, the data suggest that the economic insecurity of the 1930s led men and women starting families to invest in property, and also led older immigrants with small businesses who were approaching retirement to acquire property as security for their old age. The new amortized FHA mortgages no doubt aided this process.

Table 29. *Home Ownership By Occupation, B'nai B'rith Members, 1930–1940*

					Inter-city Mobility, Members, 1930			
	Remained in Portland				Left Portland		New Members, 1940	
Occupation	Owned home		Did not own home		Owned home	Did not own home	Owned home	Did not own home
	1930	1940	1930	1940	1930	1930	1940	1940
Proprietor	21	23	22	20	4	8	68	30
Professional	15	26	19	8	3	6	25	30
Manufacturer	3	5	5	3	2	2	24	12
Manager	1	4	7	4	0	6	11	23
Sales, clerk	7	8	9	8	1	5	15	32
Semi-prof., agent	4	2	1	3	0	1	14	17
Service	2	3	5	4	2	2	2	5
Skilled work	5	4	0	1	0	2	6	3
No occupation	2	2	4	4	1	2	15	12
Total	60	77	72	55	13	36	180	174

A more detailed analysis of the migration around the city of B'nai B'rith members and of other Jews, combined with information on the geographical distribution of the population by age, and data on birth rates, will further explain how Portland Jewry became an entrenched mercantile and professional enclave separated by generation rather than by land of origin. B'nai B'rith members in 1940 represented about 20 percent of the adult male Jewish population. The lodge was heavily over-represented by middle-aged home-owners from Irvington, somewhat over-represented by slightly younger home owners from areas in the Southeast, and under-represented by older men residing in the Shattuck and Failing school areas. Nevertheless, the migration and settlement patterns of its members and their acquisition of homes paralleled patterns that the community as a whole shared. As Table 30 suggests, of the older contingent of B'nai B'rith members who remained in the lodge throughout the decade, the great majority remained in their homes or within the district where they resided in 1930. The largest proportion already lived on the East Side, and during the decade ten more members moved there. The second largest contingent had resided in the unstable area on the west and south fringes of the central business district, and among them 43 percent moved out of the city. Others from wealthier families moved into the West Hills. Of those residing in the Northwest, the majority remained in the district, as did the majority of the small contingent residing in South Portland. Of the over 350 new members in 1940, 53 percent lived on the East Side, and almost 12 percent resided in the West Hills or in farther suburbs, areas to which more and more of the population would move in the 1950s. Less than 8 percent resided in South Portland, a little over 12 percent in the Shattuck School area, and about 15 percent in the Northwest.

Table 30. *Neighborhood Mobility, B'nai B'rith Members, 1930–1940*

Residential Trajectory 1930–1940	Residence, 1930				
	Central	South	Northwest	East	West Hills, suburbs
Remained in home, apt.	5	4	14	17	1
Remained in region	5	3	7	30	2
Moved to Central	x	0	3	2	0
Moved to South	0	x	0	2	0
Moved to Northwest	4	0	x	1	0
Moved to East	3	1	6	x	0
Moved to West Hills, suburbs	7	2	3	4	x
Left Portland or died	18	2	5	18	0

	New Members, 1940, Residence, 1940				
	Central	South	Northwest	East	West Hills, suburbs
	44	28	53	189	42

Despite its skewed distribution in favor of middle-aged men, the proportion of Jewish home owners in the B'nai B'rith (53 percent) was about 7 percent less than the proportion of Jews who owned their homes in several areas of relatively heavy Jewish concentration in the 1940s. Though the percentage of home ownership by Jews was not higher than for their gentile neighbors in most middle-class regions, in some areas they provided exceptional stability. As Table 31 shows, in Irvington, where Jews were over 7.5 percent of the heads of households, 65.8 percent were home owners; among the non-Jews, 68 percent were owners. Although few Jews clustered on particular blocks, Jewish families were scattered from East 5th Street through East 28th Street and beyond. In the more exclusive Cornell Road area, where Jews were over 20 percent of the population, and in the neighborhood around

East 39th and Glisan streets, where they were only 3.3 percent of the population, over 90 percent of the small contingents of Jewish men owned their own homes. The proportion was over 20 percent higher than for their gentile neighbors. Even in South Portland, among almost two hundred Jewish heads of households, 52 percent owned their homes in 1940. Despite the relatively low rate of ownership compared to Jews in other districts, the proportion of Jewish home owners was almost exactly the same as for the contingent of 139 Italian heads of household who shared the neighborhood. The two immigrant groups combined constituted 44 percent of the district's heads of household, but 60 percent of its home owners. The Depression, then, did not prevent young Jewish proprietors and professionals residing in Irvington from buying homes, did not deprive well-to-do Jews along Cornell Road of their homes, and convinced many immigrants, Italians as well as Jews, to buy small properties in the area where they had resided most of their lives.

Table 31. *Jewish and Non-Jewish Heads of Household Residing in Homes, 1940*

Neighborhood	Total heads hshld	Property owners		Jewish heads hshld	Jewish Property owners		Italian heads hshld	Italian Property owners	
		No.	% hds hshld		No.	% Jewish hds hshld		No.	% Italian hds hshld
Irvington 1: (E.7th–E.15th)	986	596	60.4	90	52	57.8			
Irvington 2: (E.16th–E.28th)	1166	872	74.8	71	54	76.1			
E.39th & Glisan	394	298	76.0	13	12	92.3			
Cornell–Westover	81	61	75.3	17	16	94.1			
South Portland	764	296	38.7	198	103	52.0	139	75	54.0

The movement to home ownership was not a sudden departure, but represented an intensified trend. Most of the elite German Jews had owned their homes, though some—like Ben Selling as a newly married man in the 1880s—attached little significance to living in his own home compared to residing with his parents.[15] But just as the young married couples of the 1890s moved to the new residential neighborhood in the Northwest, so the young married couples of the 1920s and the 1930s moved to Irvington. The real contrast should be made with skilled industrial workers, who combined their capital through building and loan associations to acquire homes close to their places of employment. Whether they were predominantly factory workers of German or Irish descent escaping from the paternalism of George Pullman's model community, or Polish workers who had always been left to their own devices for shelter, the desire for property ownership was strong.[16] The Jewish entrepreneurs and professionals, however, had anticipated geographic mobility within a family rather than a communal context. Once having found a locale secure from the encroachments of commercial or industrial sprawl, they put their savings into homes. They did not, however, invest in institutions that might secure the neighborhood as an ethnic enclave.

For the Jews, and perhaps for other segments of the population, the Depression marked the era during which the elderly were being separated from their middle-aged children and grandchildren.[17] The limited representation of South Portland's residents in the B'nai B'rith in 1940 suggests the social and geographical separation of the middle-aged from the elderly (with a few conspicuous exceptions), and the Jewish population census of 1947 provides extensive statistical verification. As Table 32 indicates, data gathered for South Portland shows that exactly one-third of the men and women were age fifty or over, compared with only 23 percent in Irvington and 16 percent in the Southeast in that age category. Although South Portland was not nearly so under-represented in the 25-to-49 age category, many of these men and women must have been childless, because only 17 percent of the population there was under age 18. In Irvington, the proportion of children was 25 percent, whereas in the Southeast it was over 30 percent. Although the Failing School in the 1930s still had a far higher percentage of Jewish children than did any other grammar school,[18] over twice as many Jewish children by 1947 were scattered through the larger Irvington district. As the oral histories suggest, children of the immigrants were still being reared in South Portland during the Depression. But their older brothers and sisters and the American-born children of the Polish Jews who provided the base for Ahavai Shalom now resided in Irvington and the Southeast.

Table 32. *Jewish Population, Portland, Oregon, 1947*

Age Distribution by Regions

Age Groupings*	Irvington		Southeast		Northwest		Central, South	
	No.	% of Total	No.	% of Total	No.	% of Total	No.	% of Total
0–17	542	25.0	136	30.7	148	15.6	256	16.6
25–49	823	38.0	215	48.5	291	30.7	542	35.2
50 & over	499	23.0	71	16.0	267	28.2	510	33.1

*The 18–24 age grouping has been omitted because they are often the most mobile and most likely to be out of town at college. In 1947 they were also the most likely—among the men—to be in the Armed Forces.

The changing birth-rate between the mid-1920s and 1946 further suggests how decisions about family and housing were related and helps explain some of the unusual demands placed on communal institutions during the Depression. The 1947 community census indicates population for some specific ages and for some groups of ages, so the impact of the

Depression can only be approximated. But quite clearly, men and women had decided to limit their family size at the same time that they decided to invest in home ownership. For persons residing in the districts where Jews had most heavily settled, districts which held over 70 percent of the Jewish population, there were approximately 102 children per year for those between ages 16 and 20, all born prior to the Depression. For ages 6 to 15, born between 1931 and 1940, there were only approximately 56 per year. Since the population's mobility from the city had decreased during the Depression, one can reasonably assume that this group of youngsters from elementary through early high school provides a fair representation of the Jewish children actually born in Portland during those years. For the city as a whole, births fell from 5,222 in 1925, to 3,676 in 1930, and by 1934 had climbed back to 4,108. The same trend of drastic decline in 1930-31 and gradual recovery was true nationally,[19] but the proportionate decline in Jewish births seems to have been far greater. For the war years and 1946, despite the separation of men and women because of military service, the birth rate among Jews had already risen to almost 65 per year, and children under one year of age in the selected districts numbered 77.

The rather high birth rate for the late 1920s also helps explain the increased enrollment at the congregational Sunday Schools and the Portland Hebrew School from the mid-1930s through World War II. Children born between 1926 and 1930 would have begun to enroll in Jewish religious schools between about 1935 and 1940, just when the schools, despite the Depression, experienced dramatic increases in enrollment. Payment of tuition was generally voluntary, so that attendance would not necessarily have detracted from family income. Boys attending the Hebrew school in the afternoons could not work as newsboys or messengers and might indirectly lessen potential family income. But twenty years after the height of immigration, despite the Depression, parents seem not to have worried about such sources of family income. If a residual concern about apportioning education among children of diminished family income was registered, it may have been expressed in sex discrimination: Whereas about half the graduates of the Hebrew school in the 1920s were young women, during the Depression they were only about one-third of the graduates.[20] Parents, nevertheless, seemed anxious to have their children attend some form of religious school. By the late 1930s the Sunday schools of Beth Israel and of Ahavai Shalom were overwhelmed with students. The Hebrew school sponsored a branch at Ahavai Shalom and a larger, if less financially stable, one in Irvington.[21] Since the latter lacked a religious building which could provide rent-free facilities, the parents had difficulty raising sufficient funding for a stable operation. Nevertheless, a combination of the "baby boom" of the late 1920s, a continuing interest by parents, and the reputation of Beth Israel's

Sunday school and the Portland Hebrew School for competent instruction led to substantial community investment in education even during the Depression.

II

With the Jewish community continuing to separate by income and generation during the Depression, cohesive action to combat unemployment is hard to detect. The only conspicuous effort to supplement family income came from the Council of Jewish Women. Between 1930 and 1932 both the national and local organizations suffered a decline in membership, loss of revenues and increased demand from the members most active in settlement work for the organization to confront unemployment more directly. Locally, council membership fell from 406 paid in April 1930, to 353 paid in April 1931, and to 328 in April 1932.[22] To sustain membership, the executive board recommended that dues be lowered, a proposal which was acceptable in part because the national office was cutting staff to lower its overhead costs. In November 1930, Dr. Viola May Coe, chair of the City Federation of Women's Clubs, had addressed the council to ask for support of a plan to provide jobs for the unemployed, and Mrs. Arthur Senders of the council then headed a new committee on vocational guidance and employment. In late 1931, the council went on record supporting Senator Robert Wagner's bill calling for government aid to the unemployed, and just over two months later the executive board heard a detailed report from Mrs. Senders on a local Chamber of Commerce survey of unemployment. To supplement Jewish family income the council initiated an Opportunity Bake Shop in November 1931, though the records of its sales seem to date from June 1932.[23]

The records of the bake shop board of directors indicate a rather small operation supervised in a maternal way by the wives and daughters of the well-to-do for the less fortunate Eastern European women. Certainly compared to the thousands whom the city employed each week, the work of the bake shop board was never designed to provide substantial employment. The work itself, of course, was traditional for females, and the supervision mixed noblesse oblige with a concern for efficiency. When the small building in which baking was performed needed painting or when a fan had to be installed, Mrs. James Rosenfeld, Mrs. William Ehreman, or Mrs. Isadore Lang would volunteer the services of their chauffeurs for the labor. And as Mrs. Swett reported on the women being employed, "Each case was the story of prevention of enrollment on the relief lists through the meager wages earned at the shop."[24]

Yet the operation of the shop suggests how women who were accustomed neither to hardship nor to business management developed a sense of expertise and real responsibility toward people whom the city and the Chamber of Commerce totally ignored. The chamber leadership assumed not only that the Depression would quickly end, but that only industrial workers should be the object of employment efforts. Their meetings with employers included almost exclusively representatives of heavy industry; they totally excluded women. At best, they suggested that the newspapers encourage housewives to hire persons to perform "odd jobs."[25]

The council, however, understood that poor families usually relied on female employment, and they established the bake shop to supplement family rather than individual income. The shop was initially located in a small annex next to the B'nai B'rith building, but when the lodge planned an expansion late in the decade the shop was moved to the garage of the Jewish Shelter Home, which the council also helped supervise. Both locations were close to the apartments and homes in which the workers lived. In November 1934, the shop did about $350 in business, and by December 1935, that had risen to almost $500. Later in the decade, monthly sales dipped to about $350, though during the Christmas, Chanukah, and Passover seasons they increased again.[26] Receipts for 1936 were over $3,100, with baking having been suspended for the summer, when the demand for products generally diminished. Mrs. Goldsmith, the supervisor, was paid $10.00 a week, a sum later increased to $12.50.[27] The bakers, of course, received much less, sometimes no more than $5.00 a month for two or three days labor a week. Women were called in as the demand for the product increased, though bakers occasionally worked around the clock. With the increase in sales late in the decade, wages were increased slightly, and by early 1939, Mrs. Minnie Cody, the new manager, was hired at $60 a month.[28] Sporadic figures on the number of women employed suggests that perhaps eight to ten worked at the same time, though at different tasks or perhaps during different shifts. In the first quarter of 1938, seventeen women worked at the shop, and during the year twenty-four different women were hired.

The shop was intended to provide employment, but it also manufactured products which the management wished to induce the public to consume. Problems of marketing, cost-cutting, and management came to be considered equally with spreading employment among those in need. Most of the members of the executive board hoped to make the operation profitable, so they explored various avenues for advertising, distributing, and varying the goods. After a delivery boy at $1.00 a day was deemed too expensive, volunteers distributed the products to stores and to social events. To expedite management and production, the board even hired an efficiency expert briefly.[29] In addition, they held the traditional card parties and other events to subsidize operations. The major products were noodles and caramels, which could be stored. Occasionally women baked bagels, strudel, or cookies, but most perishable items like coffee cake and rolls were produced in conjunction with meetings of the council or of other women's organization, where the sale of a guaranteed quantity would prevent waste. At one point Miss Rose Goodman was asked to follow the society columns of the local newspapers to induce people giving affairs to order baked goods from the shop.[30]

The members of the executive board could not predict how long the Depression might last, but unlike their male counterparts at the Chamber of Commerce they prepared for a lengthy siege. Perhaps their experience with Neighborhood House made them more realistic in assessing social distress. By 1937 they considered permanent remodelling of the Shelter Home garage and the opening of a retail outlet in a location closer to a business district. For the first time, the bake shop showed a profit in December 1938, and January 1939.[31] Salaries were raised slightly and plans made to expand operations. By the end of 1940, advertising had increased, members were contacting other organizations on a regular basis to supply pastries for meetings, and wages had increased to over $2,200 for the year, up from $1,900 the year before. The steady improvement in the financial operation of the shop, however, was an ominous sign for an operation designed to relieve unemployment. By May 1941, Miss Jacobs reported that so few women were requesting or accepting work that it would not be possible to continue operations. Women who had developed expertise in organizing a business, and who had finally developed a profitable venture now found that its welfare purpose was no longer needed. With some consternation and regret they disposed of the equipment and ceased operations.[32]

The minutes of the bake shop board of directors provide a fascinating view of how upper-middle-class women learned to cope with the economic distress of others, but they say little about the women who were assisted. However, a report prepared for the board by a social worker on the sixteen women who were employed in the shop in 1941 does suggest the kind of person who sought financial assistance. It indicates especially how family ties remained the basic means for coping with economic hardships and how the women saw in the strengthening of those ties the major alternative to support by the community. Most women employed at the bake shop seem to have been elderly, to have been living in South Portland, and to have had occasional support from sons and daughters either living with them or in Seattle or California. The bake shop work had helped to tide them over when family financing failed. A few, like Mrs. Rose Swerdlick, Mrs. Anna Coll, and Mrs. Fannie Tinkelman, were widows who for a time needed bake shop work for support. Mrs. Swerdlick was the widow of Louis, a furniture worker, who had apparently been assisted to come to Portland many years before by the Industrial Removal Office.[33] She lived in 1941 with three sons, none of whom was listed as employed in the city directory. Mrs. Tinkelman had also been assisted to come to Portland by the IRO, and had been living with a son and two daughters, all of whom, however, were employed. Claire was an assistant buyer at Lipman, Wolfe; Mitzi, an inspector at Meier and Frank; and Isadore, an elevator operator at Jennings Furniture. In early 1941, Mrs. Tinkelman sold her home on Southwest 5th Street, which she and her husband had owned for many years, and moved away to live with another daughter in Seattle.[34] In this case, as in several described in oral histories, the family—with the financial resource of the Jewish department stores as a base—had sustained itself through the Depression. Other women, like Mrs. Yetta Kahn, Mrs. Becky Klonoff, and Mrs. Gladys Fisher, were married to peddlers whose incomes were meager and sporadic. Most, however, also had small second-hand stores, and with the economic upswing with the opening of defense plants in late 1940 and 1941, the social worker felt that the women would be able to support themselves without the bake shop work. A residual group of women, however, were truly dependent. Mrs. Rose Calof lived with her aged parents and her small daughter, and had no other income. Possibly her male relatives were the Calofs who had appeared on the city rolls of those given emergency employment in 1933. Mrs. Esther Wallace supported herself from housework and the bake shop earnings, and Elizabeth Kreider seemed completely dependent on bake shop employment.[35] In these cases, reliable family attachments were missing, and the individuals could not benefit from the economic surge as the American economy prepared for war.

If the bake shop demonstrated how well-to-do women adapted traditional charity and how poorer women sustained themselves until family support networks could be reknit, the synagogues illustrate how families tried to deal with a residual sense of communal responsibility. By the late 1920s, Beth Israel and Ahavai Shalom were not so much institutions of different social classes as symbols of different social tendencies. Beth Israel in the early 1920s began to accept men of Polish and Russian descent as members, though its board was still dominated by men of German descent. It provided some Eastern Europeans not only with symbolic recognition of their social ascent, but with real opportunities to participate in community-wide activities. By contrast, Ahavai Shalom remained a provincial institution that lacked outside contacts and a sense of religious direction. Alex E. Miller, the president of Ahavai Shalom in 1920 and again in 1925, joined Beth Israel in 1923, as did young David Robinson. By 1924, Nathan Bialkin and M. L. Holzman of Ahavai Shalom had also joined the temple, and by 1929 ambitious young lawyers like Harry Kenin and Irwin Fulop and the contractor Harry Mittleman had done the same. By 1930, Joseph Shemanski was elected president of the temple, though he served for only one term.[36] Men usually retained membership in Ahavai Shalom, whose dues were only $30.00 a year plus seats for the High Holidays,[37] but they saw in Beth Israel a communal representation of their own move to an integrated and modern life.

Ahavai Shalom, perhaps because many of its most ambitious members chose to affiliate with Beth Israel and to pay its dues of at least $60.00 a year, faced continual financial crisis even during the prosperous 1920s. It had difficulty paying $5,000 a year to its rabbis when Jonah Wise and then Henry Berkowitz at Beth Israel were receiving $10,000 to $12,000.[38] It had no plans to improve its building, enlarge its religious school, or attract young people. Ambitious young rabbis like N. B. Kreuger, Morris Teshnor, and Elliott M. Burstein stayed from one to three years during the 1920s before accepting pulpits in larger cities. As Alex E. Miller candidly stated in his presidential address in 1925, "We were very fortunate to have had the opportunity to release Rabbi Teshnor from his contract, for had he remained, our financial condition would have been greatly impaired."[39] Yet, Miller noted, a synagogue without a spiritual leader could not endure, and the congregation had to increase its income. By 1928 President Sam Swirsky noted that the congregation was on much sounder financial footing, largely because of a bequest from the will of Abraham Wildman, which enabled it to meet a mortgage payment and to collect interest from an investment to pay for religious school teachers. But the annual budget was only a few thousand dollars higher than the $10,000 it had been in 1921.[40] The addition of Herbert Parzen as rabbi in 1928 brought a scholar and future luminary of Conservative Judaism to the pulpit. But the new members were largely an older group of merchants and clothing manufacturers who lacked interest in wider civic activities.

Most indicative of the contrast between the two institutions were their respective reactions to the fire that each experienced in late 1923. Ahavai Shalom, already feeling it could undertake no major reconstruction, secured a $10,000 loan from E. B. McNaughton of the First National Bank, and with the insurance repaired the old building. Rabbi Kreuger urged the congregation to erect a much larger building, and he supported a possible merger with Neveh Tzedek to create a center of Conservative Judaism. When the prospective merger fell through and the congregation voted not to expand its building, Rabbi Kreuger amplified his discontent and resigned.[41] Undeterred, men like Sam Swirsky, Nathan Weinstein, Abe Asher, and the Sisterhood proceeded to raise money to meet the mortgage while lamenting the decline in membership and the weakness of the religious school.

When Beth Israel confronted the devastation of its building, two factions quarrelled over how to rebuild. A minority, led by the older merchants like Ben Selling and especially by former mayor Joseph Simon, accepted Rabbi Wise's insistence that a much larger edifice be erected, but they preferred to remain on the old site. The congregation had just raised

$80,000 in pledges to complete a school building adjacent to the temple, and to abandon the new structure would lead to a severe financial loss. Younger members, however, argued that the neighborhood itself was deteriorating and would soon be dominated by apartments, grocery stores, and even garages, which would detract from the appearance of the proposed temple and the decorum of religious services. In his reply Simon revealed a generational conflict over the proper relationship between the elite and the city which set him apart from his younger colleagues. He had lived since the 1860s in the core area with married relatives, was quite accustomed to sharing living, working, and worship space with varied peoples and structures, and like older members of Ahavai Shalom looked on the downtown areas as the natural location for a communal center. On three different occasions Simon forced the congregation to vote on the choice of a site.[42]

Although the first vote resulted in a tie, Simon was finally bested by the only member of the congregation whose wealth and prestige could have prevailed against him, Julius Meier. Meier, a far younger man, lived on Willamette Heights overlooking the Northwest district and was building a country estate on the Columbia River. He argued that the old site did not warrant the investment of the amount of money the congregation could raise to erect a structure commensurate with its ambitions. By September 1926, Meier had convinced the executive board to acquire another site, and in a new vote Simon's motion to remain on West 12th Street was defeated, 89 to 24. Instead, the board acquired most of a square block between Flanders and Glisan in the Northwest for $65,000, and proceeded to raise $300,000 to begin construction of a building. Falling somewhat short of their goal, they borrowed $150,000 from the First National Bank, which was to be paid back with interest over the next twelve years.[43]

The new membership, many of whom lived in the Northwest or on the spacious residential blocks of Irvington, was impressed by the elaborate architectural renderings of Ralph Herzog and others, and was willing to invest in a residential area. For them Beth Israel's new location would celebrate their own escape from the "congestion" of the central city and would fulfill their desire to contribute equally with gentiles to civic beauty. As Meier—whose growing retail sales provided as good a measure as that of any businessman of Portland's prosperity—attested, the city had grown from less than 50,000 when the old Beth Israel was erected to over 300,000 by 1924. For him and his supporters, the Jewish community must maintain its civic prestige by responding to this growth as effectively as other segments of the city's population.[44] The debt, which represented less than a third of the cost of acquiring the site and constructing the temple, hardly seemed consequential in the heady prosperity of the mid-1920s. Within five years, however, it would have serious consequences for the congregation and for the families who had pledged to pay it.

When the Depression descended on the community, Ahavai Shalom and Beth Israel were under different kinds of pressure and reacted differently. Regrettably, the minutes of Ahavai Shalom for 1928 through 1933 are missing, so one can at best interpolate patterns of response. Nevertheless, one is struck primarily by the continuity in activities and policy from the late 1920s through the late 1930s, compared with the sense of crisis at Beth Israel. With low dues, salaries, and budgets, and with very limited communal ambitions and contacts, Ahavai Shalom seemed most concerned with raising small amounts of money to meet current demands. Membership, which had reached 277 in 1923 under Rabbi Kreuger, had fallen to 169 in 1928, after several rabbis had come and gone in a brief period. Yet by 1935 it had declined only slightly to 152. A drive led by Rabbi Sandrow increased membership to 180 by January 1936. Under his successor, Charles Sydney, several other families joined, so that almost 200 families belonged by the end of the decade.[45]

Beth Israel was not much larger than Ahavai Shalom in the early 1920s, and when Rabbi Jonah Wise left to accept the pulpit of the Central Synagogue in New York in May 1925, membership was at about 250. The new building and a drive to pay off the mortgage yielded 367 members by 1928.[46] Rabbi Henry Berkowitz's warm personality was particularly attractive to young people, so that families remained in the congregation, and the religious school rapidly expanded even during the Depression. Enrollment in the religious school reached 360 by November 1934, at a time when enrollment at Ahavai Shalom's school was about 150 and enrollment at the Portland Hebrew School was about 180. Dues at Beth Israel were assessed by a committee, which set $60 a year as the minimum and levied fees that might reach as high as an additional $700 a year for wealthy members like Julius Meier, Max S. Hirsch, and Harold Wendel. Although elderly Ignatz Lowengart argued that the Depression had not brought hardship to individual members; many families chose to withdraw, and most requested substantial reductions in their assesments. Membership fell to 251 in January 1934, and by the end of the decade had declined to 230. A congregation that had been over twice as large as Ahavai Shalom in the late 1920s was now only slightly larger, and on the surface, at least, far less solvent.[47]

At Ahavai Shalom the Sisterhood held social events to raise funds for the mortgage payments and to accumulate cash to acquire the adjacent lot on which a religious school building was contemplated. The process took the entire decade, with the mortgage being refinanced several times, yet never exceeding $5,000. The rabbi's salary fluctuated between $3,000 and $4,000 annually, while the salaries of the religious-school teachers were paid in part from tutition fees but largely from the interest on the bequest from the Wildman fund.[48] While officers like Sam Swirsky, J. J. Shecter, and Mrs. Nathan Weinstein might take pride in their relative solvency, their major innovation during the decade was to introduce a form of junior membership for unmarried people under age 35 and to accomodate the demographic changes which produced an enlarged clientele for the religious school. Mrs. Sandrow, the product of a graduate program in social work, recalls that her most interesting experiences during the mid-1930s were with men like Roscoe Nelson, John Beer, a young lawyer from a wealthy New Orleans family who had married a local girl of Eastern European descent, and the Kenins, persons who were primarily affiliated with Beth Israel and who had contacts with local liberal causes.[49]

At Beth Israel, despite the continual state of financial crisis, the magnitude of fund-raising and continuing contacts with outside institutions created a more dramatic atmosphere. Because fees were so much higher, even men like Max S. Hirsch, Lloyd Frank, and Julius Meier were forced to request reductions of 50 percent or more.[50] Many men of Eastern Europe descent like Michael E. Rogoway, Harry Kenin, and Irwin Fulop were forced to resign, and men like Herbert Sichel and Henry Metzger accumulated debts of over $300 on their fees. By the end of 1931, 20 percent of the members owed over $9,000 on past due accounts.[51] With such large debts, shrinking membership, and a religious-school building that could not be sold because of low property values, Julius Meier suggested in early 1932 that the congregation consider a merger with Ahavai Shalom. A meeting of the boards of the two congregations, however, led to an impasse. Ahavai Shalom's board objected to the abbreviated ritual for observing holidays then in practice in Reform temples like Beth Israel, but there were also complex financial matters pertaining to the cemetary and the charge for maintenance dues. The minimum dues at Beth Israel, of course, were double the normal charges at Ahavai Shalom, and one can well imagine the responses of the latter's board to Beth Israel's mortgage.[52] Talk of a possible merger did not arise again.

Nevertheless, a major change of mood occurred at Beth Israel in early 1935 with a report by the aged Joseph Simon on the proceeds of the new Benjamin Blumauer Fund. The fund, created by the will of Blumauer, provided generous grants totaling $75,000 to forty-one institutions, including $10,000 each to the Hebrew University, the Hebrew Benevolent Society, and the B'nai B'rith Building Association, $7,500 to the Jewish Shelter Home, and $6,000 to the Joint Distribution Committee. In addition, Simon reported, the fund would yield about $150,000 to Beth Israel, whose board would oversee annual grants, to be provided by rents from land holdings and interest from investments. Although the synagogue could not appropriate funds directly from the endowment to meet its mortgage, it could receive benefits indirectly. In 1936, for example, the Hebrew Benevolent Society, which had received $10,000 from the Blumauer will, lent $5,000 at low interest to Beth Israel to help meet mortgage payments and operating expenses. And the directors of the Blumauer Fund became the major dispensers of philanthropic grants in the community, to non-Jewish as well as Jewish organizations. Large amounts, for example, were granted to the Hebrew Union College to subsidize publication of scholarly books. Reed's Institute of International Relations received several grants through the intercession of David Robinson, who felt its work promoted toleration locally and abroad in an era of rising racial hatred, and Linnfield College also received several hundred dollars. Thousands were also donated to international Jewish causes devoted to the rescue of German refugees and to resettlement work in Palestine. Locally, grants went to clinics at the University of Oregon Medical School in which Laurence Selling participated, to the Opportunity Bake Shop to repair its facilities at the Shelter Home, and to a local scholarship fund supervised by the Council of Jewish Women.[54] The largest grant, $12,000, was made to the Jewish Community Center, which had to change its name from the B'nai B'rith Building Association in order to qualify. Because the B'nai B'rith had received a direct allocation under the Blumauer will, it could not receive subsequent grants, so the Building Association formally dissolved. It gave its assets to the new Jewish Community Center, which then applied to the Blumauer Fund. The grant enabled the Jewish Community Center to finance its extensive rebuilding program from 1937 to 1939.[55]

With the knowledge that a large sum of money existed upon which the Jewish community ultimately could draw, Beth Israel refinanced its mortgage and proceeded to revitalize its internal organization. A youth group, the Octagonal Club, was formed, and after its representative expressed the desire to a board meeting, it was given more direct access to synagogue business. Rabbi Berkowitz, David Robinson, and others were much concerned about the limited contact between the board and the membership and by the low attendance at Friday night services, and they tried various measure to increase interest. A men's luncheon club was begun, though after attracting only a small attendance it was suspended. A newsletter, which had been suspended during the early 1930s to save money, was reinstated, and the board pledged to guarantee that some of its members would attend all Friday night services.[56] Despite a failure to attract many new members, the minutes of the board for the late 1930s indicate both a general vitality in contracts with Christian churches—as had been true since the era of Stephen Wise— and a response to the plight of Jews in Germany and elsewhere. When Rabbi Berkowitz was out of town, ministers from liberal Protestant churches often took his place in the pulpit, and prominent Jews like Jacob Rader Marcus, Abba Hillel Silver, Ludwig Lewisohn, and Rabbi Abba Abrams of the American Jewish Committee appeared at the synagogue.[57] Rabbi Berkowitz's own prominence in the councils of the Union of American Hebrew Congregations also gave some luster to the congregation. In December, 1937, a Friday night service was presented on a national radio network as part of a religious broadcast series.[58] By the end of the decade concern for meeting mortgage payments, funding the religious school, and attracting more members had become less pressing, compared to support for the plight of German Jews. Herman Stocker, an emigre, spoke on the need of American Jews to renew contracts with their German relatives in order to sponsor their rescue, and Anson Boskowitz suggested that the temple itself assume responsibility for a family.[59] The board provided High Holiday seats for emigres in 1938, 1939, and 1940, and through the Blumauer Fund contributed to rescue ventures and even some resettlement work in Palestine. While the effects of the Depression on congregational finance still occupied much of the attention of the board and was reflected in low membership through the late 1930s, a more acute political consciousness had taken hold.

III

Portland Jewry had not in the past taken strong political stands. Individual Jews had formed political cliques within the merchant class and played prominent roles in Republican party politics. Organizations like the B'nai B'rith had promoted international Jewish causes and the Council of Jewish Women had lobbied in the state legislature for child welfare and other legislation. Although Stephen Wise had influenced Theodore Roosevelt's policy toward autocratic Rumania and the community had condemned Russia's pogroms, the leading voice for Jewry in the 1920s, Rabbi Jonah Wise, had warned against efforts by Jews as a community to influence American foreign policy.[60] At most the lodge and other organizations had promoted settlement work in Palestine and occasional support for local advocates of publicly owned utilities.

The crisis of the 1930s precipitated by the Nazis, however, helped politicize the Jewish community and saw an abandonment of the timid councils of Jonah Wise. The most acute and comprehensive discussion of political circumstances faced by local, national, and international Jewry occurred at meetings of the B'nai B'rith. The organization nationally was less demonstrative in response to the rise of Hitler than was the revitalized American Jewish Congress movement, and less interested in settlement work in Palestine than Mizrachi or other Zionist groups.[61] But in Portland, the absence or small size of other institutions threw the discussion of crises into the general meeting of the lodge. Leaders of other organizations, like Zack Swett, Rabbi Sandrow, and Harry Mittleman of the Zionists; David Robinson, Roscoe Nelson, and Harry Kenin, who were active in anti-defamation work; and Anson Boskowitz, who became heavily involved in sponsoring German emigres, all took their interests to lodge meetings. And national representatives of all of those groups, many drawn to Portland to request funds from the Blumauer Trust Fund, spoke at lodge meetings. In the spring of 1936, Morris Rothenberg, national president of the Zionist Organization of America, and Howard Stern of the Joint Distribution Committee, both addressed the lodge. A year later Gedalia Bublick of Mizrachi addressed the group, and Maurice Samuel spoke shortly thereafter.[62]

The new vitality of the lodge could be discerned by a dramatic growth in membership. From a figure of probably less than 300 in late 1933, membership reached 450 by April 1935, 575 in January 1936, and over 650 by January 1939.[63] Its vigorous response to anti-Semitism and new interest in political activism and Zionism was made possible by the expansion of the social class that had gradually assumed control of the organization during the 1920s. To reverse the decline that had begun in the late 1920s, the lodge in 1933 had resolved that the retention of older members was more important than the recruitment of new ones. In several cases debts to the lodge were forgiven, and older members were allowed to retain membership if they made token payment of dues. By 1937, the lodge resolved that men with twenty-five years of affiliation would not be required to pay dues if they could not afford to do so.[64] But more important, as the sons of the Eastern European immigrants became more entrenched as home owners in Irvington, they became more susceptible to recruitment by men of the same social background, like David Robinson, Harry Mittleman, Ben Medofsky, Sam B. Weinstein, and other leaders in the lodge. Though it is difficult to prove, it would appear that they brought to the lodge a view of Jewry that was more ethnic than religious. The Portland Hebrew School in the 1930s was the city's strongest single proponent of an ethnic view of the Jewish community, and virtually every graduate had adult relatives in the lodge by 1940.[65] Its principal through the 1950s, H. I. Chernichowsky, spoke at lodge meetings and became a member late in the 1930s. Although the definition of Jews as an ethnic people was heavily promoted by anti-Semites, who saw Jews as a "race," ethnicity as a concept also supported the drive for unity across class and affiliational lines that the lodge itself conducted. In addition, ethnicity as a concept also justified political action in defense of Jews as a permanent cultural minority rather than as a mere aggregate of people who shared a religious preference.

The increase in lodge membership during the 1930s corresponded not only with increased anti-Semitism in Germany and in the United States, but with the steady increase in home ownership, especially in Irvington and the Southeast. Because almost two-thirds of the new members of the lodge during the decade settled in these areas, and because the leadership lamented several times that the descendants of the old German families did not belong to or were not active in the lodge, it seems fair to conclude that the lodge attracted men similar to the leadership group. The new men were not employees of the leaders, as had often been the case in the early 1920s,[66] but were simply less prosperous or less civicly active independent proprietors, professionals, and manufacturers, who, under prodding, were willing to join an organization which itself was responding to a political crisis. Although one should not discount the importance of the building program promoted by Harry Mittleman and supported by the grants from the Blumauer Fund, the growth of the lodge in the face of membership losses at Beth Israel and only small gains at Ahavai Shalom is impressive. And whatever the motive of individuals for joining, the expansion of anti-defamation and pro-Zionist work in the lodge as the decade wore on indicates growing Jewish middle-class support for aggressive group politics.

From the moment when Hitler seized power in Germany in March 1933, the local lodge was appraised of anti-Semitic policies. The national chairman of the Anti-Defamation Committee sent a memo on conditions in Germany, and Colonel Charles Robertson of the United States Intelligence Service gave a lengthy talk on Hiter[67]—the first of many the lodge would hear through 1941. Robertson argued that drastic measures were necessary, but he cautioned that Jews themselves should select their actions carefully so as not to jeopardize those remaining in Germany. Even more important, lodge secretary Ben Medofsky's brother Morris, who had changed his surname to Meadows, was secretary to the United States ambassador to Germany under Herbert Hoover and sent back intimate information through uncensored diplomatic channels.[68] By the end of the decade he had settled in Portland and joined the lodge. Rabbi Berkowitz gave reports at the lodge's biweekly board meetings and at the monthly general meetings on anti-Semitism in Germany, many outside speakers were brought in, and by 10 May 1933, a lengthy discussion that included Alex E. Miller, Harry Mittleman, Milton Tarlow, Nathan Weinstein, Harry Kenin, Harry Gevurtz, Anson Boskowitz, Dr. I. H. Chernichowsky, and others explored all sides of the question.[69] Policy decisions were made, which led to a vigilance committee to boycott German goods, support for the Joint Distribution Committee, and a request to President Roosevelt to condemn anti-Semitism in Germany. Over the next several years the lodge supported a boycott by the United States of the 1936 Olympics in Berlin, criticized the national B'nai B'rith for failing to support the World Jewish Congress, and sent several protests to the President and the State Department against the growing horrors in Germany.[70] Interpreting Zionist activity as a means for rescuing German Jews, the lodge protested vigorously in October 1938, when the British initimated that they might revoke the Balfour Declaration. Although elected officials and candidates for office were consistently denied permission to speak at meetings, at the height of the election campaign in 1940 a debate on the presidential race was held. Young Richard Neuberger, who had formerly opposed American participation in European affairs, now vigorously supported Franklin D. Roosevelt and his obviously pro-British and anti-fascist policies.[71]

Protests against Hitler's policies were matched by scrutiny of local anti-Semitic outbursts. As in prior decades, however, the nature and extent of anti-Semitism in Portland and in the Pacific Northwest is hard to gauge. A recent study of ethnic relations in New York during the Depression demonstrates how the Nazi movement centered there, gaining its greatest support from recent German immigrants, while most of the older German fraternal orders eventually condemned Hitler. The source of anti-Semitic tensions in New York has been attributed to extensive Nazi propaganda and to the depressed economic conditions which made upwardly mobile Jewish teachers and other public employees, as well as small businessmen, the rivals of already established Irish white-collar workers and German store keepers. Violence against Jews occurred in areas where they were mixed among Irish and German populations. In Portland, however, the Jews, the Irish, and the Germans were too small a proportion of the population to dominate neighborhoods (except for the elderly Jews and Italians in South Portland) or to see one another as direct rivals. Instead, David Robinson had speakers like Judge Samuel Stern describe anti-Semitic rhetoric in Seattle, while he promoted inter-faith meetings at public institutions, brotherhood activities, and funding for international relations work at Reed College.[72] Speakers at the lodge were just as often discussing brotherhood work as describing examples of anti-Semitism.

The minutes of lodge meetings where Robinson, Sam Weinstein, and others discussed local examples of anti-Semitism are laconic, and Mrs. Miriam Sandrow recalls that Robinson seemed "fanatical" in his search for local instances. Oral histories do suggest vestiges of social exclusion. Gus Solomon initiated a law practice with young Leo Levenson and Irwin Goodman because none could find employment with established gentile firms. Dr. Max Simon, president of the Oregon Academy of Opthalmology and Otolaryngology, found that he could gain admittance to specific social clubs only during meetings of the professional organization.[73] Nevertheless, the rhetoric that fueled the Brown Shirts in larger eastern cities had only minor echoes in Portland. Richard Neuberger, then a reporter for the *Oregonian*, was shaken by what he heard when attending a meeting of the local America First Committee in September 1941. He had staunchly supported organizations and political figures that had opposed a military build-up during the late 1930s, and he had considered himself a principled pacifist who shared certain views with the America Firsters. Writing to a number of friends, including the secretary to Senator Burton K. Wheeler, he noted:

> I attended an America First meeting here last night. I am sure you would have been as disgusted as I was. The chairman denounced "the Eppsteins and Wetsteins trying to get us into war." There was much denunciation of immigrants and refugees "who change their names, and their noses, too," and each mention of Roosevelt and Churchill was assiduously booed, although not references to Hiter.

One of the main speakers, Neuberger added, was a Chief Red Cloud, "a renegade Indian who has praised the Nazis for years and been quoted so in the press." In response to one letter, Oswald Garrison Villard ruefully told Neuberger, "I am distressed by what you write as to the American First meeting. Anti-Semitism will rise steadily as we get into the war and will be one of its curses."[74] While Neuberger's general assessment of President Roosevelt's popularity in the Pacific Northwest suggests that the America Firsters were a distinct minority, the combination of anti-Semitic rhetoric and stubborn social discrimination seemed magnified against the worsening world situation.

The growing desperation of German Jews was most dramatically brought home to Portland Jewry initially through the appearance of persons who had recently returned from Europe and then by the arrival of emigrés. In November 1935, Morris Levitin of Seattle Lodge described his recent experiences in Russia, Poland, and Germany; in June 1936, the District Grand Lodge of Germany informed the Portland Lodge that Herman Lowengart would shortly arrive; and in October 1937, a B'nai B'rith member from Frankfort-am-Main described his experiences. The B'nai B'rith nationally assessed each member annually $1 for German relief, and discussion of how to raise the assessment as well as continual reports on German affairs occurred at most lodge meetings.[75] Perhaps the best way to recapture how German repression was brought home to Portland Jewry is to refer to the reminiscences of Kurt Schlesinger. A prominent lawyer in Berlin when Hitler came to power, Schlesinger managed to come to America in March 1939, and to find his way to Portland three months later. He had an introduction to Max S. Hirsch, chairman of the local emigre society, and with Sidney Teiser, he went around the state to persuade smaller Jewish communities to pledge to accept responsibility for subsequent immigrant families. His story was told to many groups and helped to recreate the ring of terror closing around German Jewry.

Because Schlesinger had been a volunteer veteran of World War I, the Nazis has allowed him to practice law after most other Jews had been forbidden to do so. His contacts with government bureaucrats and the deepening crisis led him to become a liaison man between the official Federal Association of German Jews and the various government ministries. Just prior to the burning of the synagogues and the mass arrests of November 9 and 10, 1938, friends in the ministries had warned him to leave Berlin. Another Chrisian friend had arranged for a house in the Berlin suburbs where he could hide. Schlesinger recalled:

> I found my way to a little house at the end of the road. I rang the door bell and the door opened. The first thing I saw was a coat rack in the hall and on it hung a Nazi uniform with the swastika and arm band and the Nazi hat. You can imagine my feelings. I didn't understand. I knew that the lady who had sent me to this address was beyond reproach, but here I was faced with this uniform. Next I saw in the doorway a middle aged woman and her husband, who was blind. They welcomed me in. It turned out that the uniform belonged to their son who was a member of the S.A. . . . [But] the people asked me in and I found a family of warm understanding, with a desire to help.

When Schlesinger was finally able to contact his wife, two weeks later, she took the train to a nearby station, where the son wearing the S.A. uniform met her and accompanied her to the house. A Jewish friend who had preceded Schlesinger to America in 1938 was finally able to get a man in Los Angeles with the same surname to provide an affidavit, and Kurt Schlesinger and his family escaped to the United States.[76] The German government, however, confiscated 97 percent of his assets, as they did for all emigrés, so the Schlesingers had to begin in America with nothing but their skills and the good will of the local Jewish communities. This kind of rescue, while recreating in America the chilling atmosphere of Nazi Germany, also made the lodge's emigre committee, composed of men of German ancestry like Julius Asheim and Anson Boskowitz, feel that their mission was not hopeless.

The actual work of resettling emigrés fell to the committee on emigres formally organized in August 1936, by Max S. Hirsch. He had been contacted by a National Coordinating Committee which had begun taking responsibility for resettling refugees when they arrived in New York in 1934. The Portland group was part of a larger network of West Coast committees located in Los Angeles, San Francisco, and Seattle. To assist him, Hirsch turned to members of his synagogue who had additional institutional contacts, like Sam B. Weinstein and David Robinsin,[77] and to Mrs. Julia Swett, who had succeeded her late husband as executive secretary of the Federated Jewish Societies. Initially, the committee members tried to obtain affidavits for the trickle of men and women referred to them by the National Coordinating Committee. The affidavit required a local person to pledge financial sustenance for the emigre, though the committee assumed that community agencies would provide money and goods should any persons not be able to support themselves. The committee then tried to find employment for those who actually arrived in Portland. Several emigrés stayed in Portland only briefly before jobs were found for them in Seattle or elsewhere, while others for whom no suitable jobs could be found were returned to San Francisco.

By early 1937, however, the number of emigrés desiring placement in Portland had increased, and Hirsch realized that the local committee would need permanent financing and more systematic organization. The Blumauer Fund provided an initial grant of $1,500, and subsequently the Jewish Welfare Federation provided several thousand dollars annually to allow the committee to keep permanent files, to provide emergency support for emigrés who lacked local families, and to sponsor field work by the committee. A loan from the Hebrew Benevolent Society in 1940 helped meet emergency expenses.[78] By March 1939, the committee had processed 344 cases, procured 157 affidavits, and placed 66 families in or near Portland. When Dr. S. C. Kohs of the National Coordinating Committee visited Portland in May 1939, the local committee agreed to place twenty-four families during the next year.[79] To facilitate placement, Sidney Teiser travelled to southern and eastern Oregon, where small committees in towns like Salem, Eugene, Medford, Pendleton, Bend, and even Walla Walla, Washington, agreed to accept responsibility for a total of thirty-five families. Though these towns often could not find employment for families whom they had pledged to place, thus creating an unemployment problem in Portland, several dozen families eventually resettled there.[80]

The placement of the emigrés had some resemblance to the last group of immigrants to be sent to Portland, those sponsored by the Industrial Removal Office between 1906 and 1917. Like the IRO migrants, the emigrés usually lacked money and definite employment prospects, and needed shelter and some social contacts to feel part of the new community. But apart from these very general consequences of forced migration, the emigrés were unique among Jewish arrivals in Portland and probably in all other Western cities because of their exceptional skills and their isolation from extended family support. Among the cases discussed in detail at committee meetings, several were young men and women seeking work as clerks, seamstresses, or janitors until they could find educational or employment opportunities. Some were placed with relatives, and others found homes with local Jewish families. But the great majority of the emigrés were either professionals or experienced managerial personnel. Several of the latter were placed with Meier and Frank; Lipman, Wolfe; or Eastern Outfitting, though in a period of high American unemployment the committee was careful to follow the national policy and not to displace American workers to make way for emigrés.[81] The committee and the emigrés themselves hoped that the latter could reestablish broken careers in their professions, but professional organizations, fearful of an influx of emigrés who might threaten their livelihood, required that the newcomers demonstrate their expertise in extraordinary ways. Musicians, of course, were required to join a union at their port of entry, usually New York. Dentists were required to enroll for further training, medical doctors not only had to pass an examination, but to take special graduate courses and to register for an internship, virtually all of which, the committee learned, were reserved for graduates of the University of Oregon Medical School.[82] The lawyers had been trained in Roman law, and their formal education had not prepared them for the English common law or for Oregon statutes.[83] Most of these men simply sought other work. Through some skilled lobbying the committee helped defeat a bill in the legislature that would have prevented all emigrés from practicing law, medicine, or dentistry.[84] Unlike the IRO migrants, then, the emigrés did not simply find less skilled work temporarily; in many cases they had to abandon careers or attempt to initiate new ones.

The problems of social adjustment were even more complex, and the committee found its responsibilities more comprehensive than those of the local agents of the IRO thirty years before. While Ben Selling and Sig Sichel evaluated employment opportunities and reunited families, the committee had to provide immediate economic necessities and establish a communal context for men and women who were initially alone. Perhaps because the emigrés were German Jews accepting the sponsorship of descendants of German Jews they were socialized within the communal network of the elite—at least initially. Not only were they provided with High Holiday seats at Beth Israel, but most resided close to the synagogue. Unlike the IRO migrants, none of the emigrés seems to have resided in South Portland, the former immigrant district. Instead, a check of the nineteen emigré families listed in the city directory in 1940 shows that some resided in the Southeast, a few just south of the central business district, but most in the Northwest near Beth Israel. A large group had been placed at the Cecelia Apartments at 2186 Glisan Street, just two blocks from the temple.[85] "The Cecelia," Kurt Schlesinger recalled, was "modest but clean." With so many people arriving without the paraphernalia for starting a home and without local relatives to assist them, the committee formed subgroups to acclimate the newcomers. A group headed by a Mrs. Bischoff met the emigrés at the train station and took them to their apartment, for which the committee paid. "The Committee," Schlesinger again noted, "showed great consideration in furnishing the apartment, in stocking the pantry with all that was needed and in having a hospitality committee show us around."[86]

The specific services provided by the committee were also similar to those that had been made available through Neighborhood House to the IRO migrants. Classes were initiated in English, as were lectures on American government and politics. But the experiences of uprooting and resettlement, and the effort to find suitable employment in a new land suffering from depression and regulation of the professional job market, created common bonds among the immigrants. By January 1940, the emigres themselves had organized, and, with the assistance of Julius Zell and John Beer (a relative of David Robinson's), they divided into two discussion groups which might utilize their comraderie to develop English language skills. John H. Miller, an emigré who had spent a year in Florida running a grocery store before resettling in Portland in 1941, recalls that these discussion groups continued through and beyond the war years. They became a permanent means for the emigrés to acknowledge their ordeal and to celebrate their achievements as a distinct segment of the local community. Many civic officials addressed them in the years after the war, and the emigrés were especially proud of the work they had done and the jobs they had created for Portlanders.[87]

Employment, of course, remained the single greatest necessity for a secure life. As Julius Zell noted in a report on his work to the committee, as an immigrant himself in New York many years before he had been assisted by the Emigrant Aid Society, and he realized that "gainful occupation is the most important need."[88] Although Kurt Schlesinger does not consider the matter in his recollections, the anxieties engendered by having to leave a distinguished career as an attorney and to seek whatever work was available in a distant land must have been acute. In most families women as well as men had to seek work, and often women were easier to place in menial jobs than the husbands, who remained unemployable. Indeed, the committee was surprised at the willingness of people whom they considered too old to work to seek employment to support themselves. Members of the committee initially made contacts among their friends, like Harold Wendel, Aaron Frank, and Sanford Brandt of Gevurtz Furniture Company, to place people, and then each member took formal responsibility for a specific emigre. By 1940 all of the local Jewish organizations were convened, and each pledged to provide a committee to keep in touch with the emigre committee in seeking job opportunities.[89] Several of the emigré women were hired directly at the Opportunity Bake Shop. Most important, the committee secured from the Hebrew Benevolent Association and the Jewish Welfare Federation grants to make loans that would tide individuals over until they could find work or gain admittance to schools. Others, like Kurt Schlesinger, were sent to E. B. McNaughton of the First National Bank for loans to start a small business.

In 1938 a group from Germany calling itself the *Israelitische Gemeinde* contacted Max S. Hirsch about starting a cooperative farm in southern Oregon. A professor from Oregon State College was consulted, and after deciding that the families, only one of whom had had experience as farmers, should own separate plots rather than holding the land in common, a site was located near Grants Pass. Sanford Brandt spent several days there examining possible locations, but when the price of the land was increased in March 1939, the project fell through. By 1940, however, a Cedarbrook Dairy Farm was begun with a loan of several thousand dollars from the committee. As more capital was needed, the committee forgave 75 percent of its loan so that the farm could borow $3,000 from the Jewish Agricultural Society.[90]

The inquiries about farming and the Cedarbrook Dairy were some-what unusual for the emigrés and suggest a residual pastoral desire among some Central European Jews as well as a continuing image of Oregon as the ideal location for such visions. More commonly, though, emigrés found employment as salesmen, clerks, or bookkeepers, with many eventually starting small groceries or cleaning shops. Several were also ultimately able to begin again as doctors or lawyers. Sali Oppenheimer and Alexander Levy both were able to open medical offices by 1940, Bruno Linde resumed the practice of law, and the remarkable Kurt Schlesinger, after admittedly failing as a grocery store owner by 1950, took a job with the city and worked his way through law school at night. He received his American degree in law at age sixty.[91]

Emigré work indicates not only how a process of immigration and resettlement continued through the mid-twentieth century. More impor-tantly, the specific response to the emigrés indicates that American Jewish leaders were informed on the terror against German Jewry by 1934, and that in a community remote from the eastern population centers most middle-class Jewish communal institutions were able to respond with either direct assistance or political protest. American Jews were not only being asked to contribute financially to the victims of pogroms, as had been the case before World War I. Now families were arriving in their midst without the ability to bring possessions with them or even to continue normal communication with families in Germany. The occasional concern that the National Coordinat-ing Committee was sending people who were poorly prepared for Portland's labor market or that people should be retrained in Germany before being sent to America was lost amid the growing perception that rescue itself was the primary matter. Between January and June 1940, for example, fifty-seven emigrés had arrived in Portland. Seventeen had been placed initially in other towns, two were attending schools, five were considered too old to work, and the rest had found jobs. Of the twenty-four family units received from July through September 1940, six were sent to smaller towns, and twelve were already working in Portland.[92] Without the cooperation of the B'nai B'rith and other organizations, the emigre committee could not have been so successful. Precisely this experience at coordinating local organizations to-ward a communal goal provided the basis on which similar work was undertaken with the survivors of the Shanghai community and even of Auschwitz who arrived in Portland after World War II.[93]

By the time the United States entered World War II, the Portland Jewish community had established social patterns, a welfare network, and even a political stance which defined an entrenched middle-class community. The struggle to combat both the international and local consequences of Hitler's racial violence had generated a mood of ethnic assertiveness that overcame residual class divisions. While aging immigrants in South Portland remained largely apolitical, the sons of Schnitzers, Zidells, and Rosenfelds— who became millionaire industrialists during the war—were leading the boycott of German goods during the late 1930s.[94] Lawyers of Eastern European descent like David Robinson, Sidney Teiser, and Sam B. Weinstein, while strengthening Jewish welfare and civic institutions from an earlier era, also brought ethnic issues into the political arena as a matter of right. During the war they appraised the government of alleged subversion by supporters of the Brown Shirts and by men who had bellowed their patriotism by attacking Jews. By contrast, the lodge led a massive drive to purchase war bonds and to provide facilities for troops stationed in the region. The B'nai B'rith also saw its demand for the protection of the civil rights of Jews as the basis of support of the same rights for other minorities. While hardly alone in this effort, it strongly supported a state FEPC statute when the federal law expired after the war. David Robinson, Gus Solomon, and Richard Neuberger became state leaders both for FEPC and broader civil rights legislation.[95]

The social contours of Portland Jewry by the 1940s seemed very similar to those of most other Jewish communities beyond New York. Their dispersal according to wealth and generation was very similar to that in Cleveland; Providence, Rhode Island; and even London, England, though those communities were much larger.[96] Perhaps the small size of Portland Jewry and its concentration in trade made social mobility much easier and led to its extraordinary dispersal among gentiles. Unlike in Philadelphia, Cleveland, or Los Angeles, new middle-class neighborhoods were never predominantly Jewish, and Jewish institutions were not dispersed and rebuilt in the suburbs until the 1960s. This is not to suggest an absence of ethnic cohesiveness, to which a growing B'nai B'rith, a strengthened federation, an active Council of Jewish Women, and the Hebrew school all attested. It suggests rather that in the face of external crisis a strong residue of ethnic identity could be tapped. A tradition of residential dispersal within a medium-sized city was not a deterrent to an intensive expression of ethnic loyalty.

Conclusion

The Jewish community of Portland, Oregon, has been a small contingent in the migration and resettlement of Central and Eastern European Jewry in Western Europe and the Americas. The upheavals in agriculture and the rise of factory industries which enclosed land, uprooted peasantries, and made handicraft skills gradually obsolete, sent Jewish peddlers and craftsmen in search of new clients and new livelihoods. And, as Moses Rischin has emphasized, new patterns of rationalistic thought encouraged men and women to question religious authority and to create a new sense of themselves as an "ethnic" people.[1] America provided a unique opportunity for voluntary reconstruction of ethnic communities. Martin Cohen stated perhaps most cogently the unique character of America when he argued that "In America it is the individual Jew himself who ultimately has determined his own identity. . . . The history of American Jewry is thus in a fundamental sense the story of men's reactions to the opportunity of fashioning their Jewish identity."[2] Nevertheless, networks of trade which focused on a metropolis and the aggregation of Jews of very different cultural backgrounds in new cities were common from Berlin to Paris and London, from Buenos Aires to New York and San Francisco.[3] The small Jewish community in Portland, in the far northwest corner of the United States, provided both an isolated setting where Jewish mercantile skills were needed and a liberal atmosphere where Jewish institutions were encouraged to help shape the civic order. Portland's Jews have generally appreciated the social freedoms of their city, but have ignored the similarity of their experiences to those of Jews in other middle-sized commercial towns in other parts of the United States.

In this study I have tried to link the experiences of four generations of German and Eastern European Jews in Portland to the larger patterns of social change that led to a modern middle-class Jewry throughout the Western World. I have argued that like the working classes described by E. P. Thompson, Herbert Gutman, and others, the middle class too had to create institutions and new social patterns to accomodate innovations in technology, communications, and the liberal political climate of the Western democracies.[4] An enormous cultural gap separated the master craftsmen and independent farmers—to whom Benjamin Franklin referred as men of the "middling sort"—from the store owners, lawyers, doctors, and accountants to whom twentieth-century scholars refer when they use the term "middle class." Furthermore, for Jews in particular, who were accustomed to mercantile pursuits, changes within the family were as rapid and pervasive—if not more so—as changes in the work place. Perhaps reflecting their minority status, which created a need to protect their families, Jewish women seemed reluctant in Portland to provide political leadership among elite women. But the American-born generations paralleled the gentile elite and then the middle classes in their decisions to limit family size, participate in white-collar employment, and develop vigorous and politically active voluntary associations. The Portland story demonstrates that as patriarchal forms of family and business were eroded, women often played the leading role in creating new social forms and initiating civic action to confront the consequences of lengthy migration and urban dislocations. This was not simply the professionalization of traditional nurturing functions, but the attempt by women to participate equally with men in setting the ethnic community's social and political agenda.

In this regard the records of agencies like the First Hebrew Ladies Benevolent Society, the Industrial Removal Office, the Jewish Shelter Home, and the Opportunity Bake Shop, when supplemented by data on individuals and families from public records, provide a full picture of both social dislocation and efforts by ordinary people to overcome it. On the nineteenth-century frontier, traditional forms of charity were greatly expanded to meet more comprehensive needs than in Europe, and strong-willed women accumulated administrative expertise, which they passed on to their daughters. In the early twentieth century, Eastern European Jewish women expressed responsibility for families extended through generations and over vast distances as they manipulated meager resources and appealed to the generosity of the German elite. Indeed, the consequences of family breakdown, as opposed to the upheavals of individuals, fell largely to women, a subject heretofore generally neglected in studies of immigration and community reorganization. In the most severe cases, where parental bonds were destroyed, the Jewish female elite acquired some professional skills and enlisted the aid of others to resolve the problems of poverty and even premature death. And during widespread depression, when the Jewish community itself was less affected by unemployment, elite women again tried to support familial ties among the impoverished elderly. Efforts by women to resolve the community's most severe social problems were hardly unique to Portland. Scholars, however, have rarely examined the means employed to alleviate distress and especially the relationship between changes in the family life of the elite and their efforts to organize for the assistance of others.

A number of scholars like Sidney Goldstein and Steven Hertzberg have emphasized how the occupational and residential evolution of Jewish communities has been dramatically affected by general patterns of urban expansion.[5] As Jews—like other urban dwellers—improved their occupational status, they left areas of initial immigrant settlement and followed streetcar routes and subways, and later automobile highways, to new residential districts. Deborah Moore has recreated this pattern for New York Jews who moved to the Bronx and Brooklyn during the 1920s and 1930s.[6] Moore and Jeffrey Gurock both note how in New York patterns of settlement and acculturation deviated substantially from those described by Louis Wirth in his classic study of Chicago's "ghetto."[7] Wirth emphasized initial settlement by immigrants near the city's core, with successive migration to suburban residential areas as immigrants or their children accumulated greater wealth.[8] The extraordinary density of New York's population led immigrant Jews to settle well beyond the "immigrant district" of the Lower East Side in alternate low-rent areas like East Harlem. In addition, the second generation in New York did not uniformly desert the ideals of the immigrants, but redefined orthodoxy in religion and radicalism in politics to create a renaissance of Jewish culture. In addition, Gurock notes how some German Jews cooperated with Eastern European Jews to support culturally innovative yet religiously orthodox institutions.[9]

In Portland, Jewish settlement corresponded more closely to the Wirth model and followed patterns similar to other middle-sized cities like Atlanta, Georgia, and Columbus, Ohio.[10] But settlement did not correspond to a notion of where Jews should settle or how a ghetto should be organized. Instead, Jews, like other merchants, settled where their services were most needed. Polish as well as German Jews arrived before an immigrant district ever developed in South Portland. Jewish second-hand stores and pawn shops with owners initially living nearby dotted the rooming-house district near railroad and wharving facilities, where the city's proletariat resided. Much like the Jewish merchants clustered in Polish neighborhoods in Philadelphia or Chicago in the late nineteenth and early twentieth centuries,[11] those in Portland purveyed wares as their fathers had done in small European market towns. Furthermore, in a city where immigrants never constituted a major portion of the population, districts of high density never developed. Population pressure never forced immigrants to seek residences away from South Portland, though a desire to locate elsewhere led many to seek better housing on the East Side. Because Eastern European Jews were merchants and craftsmen, their persistence rates in South Portland were much higher than for laborers, and their visibility as proprietors was far greater than their numbers suggested. Finally, the rapid intracity mobility and small size of the Jewish population never allowed the children of the Eastern European immigrants to construct ethnically intensive middle-class suburbs, as occurred, for example, in Cleveland and Philadelphia, as well as in the Bronx and Brooklyn. No doubt Portland's settlement pattern of merchants scattered among a gentile work force and resettlement in mixed suburban neighborhoods had parallels in New York; but what was incidental in the metropolis defined social relations in the smaller city.

Cooperation between German, Polish, and Russian Jews to create new institutions could be found in Portland as well as in New York. However, such efforts focused on a secular community center rather than on ideological support for neo-orthodoxy. Ben Selling's or Joseph Shemansky's donations to orthodox shuls or to the Hebrew school were individual acts of charity rather than efforts to modernize their own ideologies. The thorough integration of Portland's Polish as well as German Jews into the residential flow of the gentile middle class, and their lack of interest in creating either voting blocs or radical politics, led them away from orthodoxy and the culture associated with *kashrut*. Most Portland Jews who retained contact with the community assumed an ethnic identity that complemented their status as successful merchants. While the orthodox synagogue Shaarei Torah continues to prosper, and a small Hebrew day school is now closely affiliated with it, the craft traditions and markets associated with immigrant life had faded by the 1930s. And most prominent rabbis who held pulpits in Portland, like Stephen Wise, Jonah Wise, Herbert Parzen, and Edward Sandrow, sought larger opportunities closer to the metropolis or in it.

The relationship between Portland Jewry and the civic arena has evolved with the development of the merchant class. Even in the heyday of Joseph Simon as "boss" of the Portland Republican Party, patronage was not used to solidify a Jewish hold on an electoral district or to provide employment for the Jewish party faithful. For New York, Moses Rischin has noted how wealthy German Jewish merchants like the Seligmans helped found exclusive social and political clubs with gentiles in the 1860s, but by the late 1870s they faced proscription. The Russian immigrants in New York by the 1890s expressed their class interests through radical politics, eventually electing Meyer London to the United States House of Representatives prior to World War I.[12] In Portland, as in other Pacific Coast cities, German Jews were among the generation of merchants that founded the town; in the nineteenth century they helped create a civic order in which office holding and private voluntarism fortified social stability. As boosters of urban growth, German Jews generally were allied with the merchant elite in the Republican party, and they joined the Masonic and Elks lodges. To insure their personal welfare they created B'nai B'rith lodges and a benevolent association. While appearing prominently in the *Social Register*, they discreetly honored social conventions which seemed to mark most southern and western cities by forming a separate Concordia social club apart from their gentile peers. Anti-Semitic sentiment existed in the Pacific Northwest, though it seems rarely to have found political expression or to have impeded the careers of forceful Jewish men with political ambitions.

When Eastern European Jews arrived in the late nineteenth and early twentieth centuries, they became provisioners to the city's proletariat. Those of them who persisted and improved their income and social status, even over two or three generations, could no more have expected recognition within the pioneer elite than could Italian or Scandinavian newcomers. Instead, the *Social Register* celebrated the entrenched mercantile luminaries, while Jewish newcomers experiencing economic success organized their own institutions like the B'nai B'rith. Professionals of Eastern European origins who wished to pursue political careers did so after first establishing a base within the ethnic lodge network. Unlike in the major eastern cities, in Portland there was never a Jewish proletariat, a Jewish union movement, or a radical politics based on visions of Eastern European social democracy.

Finally, in this study I have not tried to present any grand schemes of social modernization or comprehensive reinterpretations of Jewish history. I have suggested, however, than an ethnically diverse middle class, like the working class, was reforged in America, and that the ideology of boosterism in public and private life enabled disparate elements to cooperate where necessary while remaining separate where desirable. I have also assembled data from sources which until recently have been largely neglected, to measure the impact of change on the lives of ordinary—though not working-class—men, women, and children. I have stressed repeatedly that the middle-class Jewish enclave experienced as much and as rapid fundamental change within the confines of the family as in the world of work. Changes in the lives of women and children were perhaps more comprehensive than for men, although the use of traditional cultural forms provided the personal bonds that made new roles and new ideals more palatable. And as a Jewish merchant enclave, Portland Jewry maintained loose ties to the intellectual and institutional centers of national ethnic life. But Portland Jewry also cultivated its own frontier image, which was kept alive as much by the pride of its spokesmen as by the failure of the city to generate an industrial proletariat. Portland Jewry has matured as an entrepreneurial and professional class with strong ethnic institutions in a city which has avoided the cultural tensions of the larger cities of the East and Midwest. But it has also paid a price, by losing many of its most talented sons and daughters to wider opportunities and more exciting locales elsewhere.

Appendix: Sources and Methods

Because this study has tried to recreate the experiences of Portland's Jewish community by focusing as much on individuals and families as on institutions, the search for sources has led to some unusual places. The major primary sources are listed according to archival locations, but a few comments are useful for persons contemplating similar studies of other communities. Very few letters of the elite, or community newspapers upon which so much social history has formerly depended, remain for Portland's Jewish community. Among the exceptions are the papers of Ben Selling at the Oregon Historical Society. The collection consists primarily of letter books for the mid-1880s and a few private notebooks listing assets and debits for specific years from 1890 through 1910. When supplemented by several of the oral histories, they explain how the Jewish trading network was established and maintained. The scrapbooks of Joseph Simon were excellent for tracing his political career and its relationship to those of Selling, Sig Sichel, Solomon Hirsch, and others. The Jonathan Bourne Papers in the Oregon Collection at the University of Oregon were helpful in determining the attitudes of Solomon Hirsch and a few others toward speculative investment and the experiences of Joseph Simon in Washington, D.C.

Among the rabbis, the letters of Stephen Wise at the American Jewish Historical Society at Brandeis University provide exellent documentation of his career in Portland. His candid letters to his wife and to Adolph Wolfe are especially helpful for recreating the social network among the German elite, as well as his own opinions on religious and political topics. Henry Berkowitz and Jonah Wise have both left small letter collections at the American Jewish Archives in Cincinnati, which explain their views on liberal Judaism, anti-Semitism and other topics. The David Solis Cohen Papers at the Jewish Historical Society of Oregon are disappointing. Although they contain many drafts of over eighty speeches delivered before various public bodies on secular and religious occasions, very few letters revealing Cohen's personal contacts are included. Information about Rabbi Edward Sandrow has been obtained in correspondence with his widow, Mrs. Miriam Sandrow of Woodmere, New York. Information about Rabbi Joseph Fain and the orthodox community has been obtained from his daughter, Mrs. Dorothy Fain Fisher of Los Angeles, and from numerous oral histories.

In addition to the records of various Jewish communal institutions, public sources have provided the bulk of the material. The search for data about individuals led first to the membership lists of institutions, then to the United States manuscript censuses for the reconstruction of households. Information about specific employers and mobility of individuals over decades was traced through city directories. The records of the Industrial Removal Office at the American Jewish Historical Society, catalogued by city and/or state, illustrate patterns of migration and resettlement for Eastern European Jews. For family data after 1900, membership lists for institutions like the B'nai B'rith, the Council of Jewish Women and the synagogues again provided data on individuals, which could be supplemented by information from city directories. Selected households could be partially reconstituted through the files of several public schools. The Administrative Department of the Portland Public Schools retains class lists from 1914, but lists clearly visible through xeroxing (and therefore accessible for research purposes) are available only from 1920 onwards. Data on the parents of pupils has been kept on microfilm on enrollment cards, which are held at the Oregon State Archives, in Salem. By combining names of parents, enrolled children, and additional persons with the same surname and same address listed in city directories, households could be partially reconstituted. Note that persons listed in city directories were not necessarily older siblings of the school pupils, but could have been unmarried aunts, uncles, or cousins.

To assist in the measure of mobility from 1920 to 1930 by distinguishing those who died from those who left the city, data were gathered from the decennial death lists at the Vital Statistics Section, Health Division, Oregon Department of Human Resources, in Portland. Information on real property holdings has been gathered from the 1870 federal census (the last to include this data), and for 1921 (the first year for which data are available), from the Index to Tax Rolls, Multnomah County Bureau of Assessment and Taxation. Home ownership for 1930 and 1940 was taken from city directories for those years. Prior to 1930 this information was not included in the directories.

No effort has been made to create statistically precise samples of the Portland population as a whole in given years. Instead, I have gathered data on complete sub-populations, like head of households residing on specific streets, or relied on data from other studies for comparative purposes. The 1900 federal manuscript census provided information on all Italian households in Multnomah County, and the city directories for 1930 and 1940 provided information on home ownership by heads of household listed by street address. From them I could determine home ownership for all Italians in South Portland and for all persons in the various districts where Jews were concentrated. The most useful secondary sources for mobility data on ethnic groups in other cities have been Stephen Thernstrom, *The Other Bostonians: Poverty and Progress in the American Metropolis* (Cambridge, Mass.: 1973); Howard P. Chudakoff, *Mobile Americans: Residential and Social Mobility in Omaha, 1880–1920* (New York: 1972); Peter Decker, *Fortunes and Failures: White Collar Mobility in Nineteenth Century San Francisco* (Cambridge, Mass.: 1978); Clyde and Sally Griffen, *Natives and Newcomers: The Ordering of Opportunity in Mid-Nineteenth Century Poughkeepsie* (Cambridge, Mass.: 1978); Glenna Matthews, "The Community Study: Ethnicity and Success in San Jose," *Journal of Interdisciplinary History*, 7 (1976): 305–18. For Jews in other cities, the most helpful studies were Steven Hertzberg, *Strangers within the Gate City: The Jews of Atlanta, 1845–1915* (Philadelphia: 1978); Marc Lee Raphael, *Jews and Judaism in a Mid-Western Community: Columbus, Ohio, 1840–1975* (Columbus: 1975); Mitchell Gelfand, "Jewish Economic and Residential Mobility in Early Los Angeles," *Western States Jewish Historical Quarterly*, (1979): 332–47; Sidney Goldstein and Calvin Goldscheider, *Jewish Americans, Three Generations in a Jewish Community* (Englewood Cliffs, N.J.: 1968); Deborah D. Moore, *At Home in America: Second Generation New York Jews* (New York, 1981).

The role of Jews in Portland politics can be traced in part through the City of Portland Archives, where Council Documents and Mayor's Office Papers are kept. The archives are curently on the top floor of the Oregonian Building. The Proceeding of the City Council, however, are currently stored in ledger books in the basement of the City Hall, as are records of emergency employment during the first three years of the Depression of the 1930s. Because Jews were not sufficiently concentrated to allow for an assessment of voting behavior, and because their sense of civic identity seemed to rest on participation in voluntary associations, several secondary studies have provided useful guidance to the function of such organizations. These include: Don H. Doyle, *The Social Order of a Frontier Community: Jacksonville, Illinois, 1825–1870* (Urbana, Ill.: 1978); Stuart Blumin, *The Urban Threshold: Growth and Change in a Nineteenth Century American Community* (Chicago: 1976); Paul Boyer, *Urban Masses and Social Order in America, 1820-1920* (Cambridge, Mass.: 1978); Dean R. Esslinger, *Immigrants and the City: Ethnicity and Mobility in a 19th Century Mid-Western Community* (Port Washington, N.Y.: 1975).

Much of the corroborative evidence about family ties, fondly remembered neighborhood institutions, dances, and social conventions have come from oral histories on file in transcript form at the Jewish Historical Society of Oregon at the Portland Jewish Community Center. Memories may romanticize events and confuse names and dates, but impressions of family members remain vivid, and the social ambiance of the community remains fresh over the years. In addition, relations through marriage, informal contacts for employment opportunities, differences between method of labor from factory to factory, or the impact that personalities made on segments of the public, would be almost impossible to detect without this personal testimony. Old South Portland, especially, lives in the memories of its children, and who is to say that their impressions of its nurture are less significant than its objective social conditions, which can be more easily measured?

Primary Sources

1. *United States Government Sources*
   Manuscript Census of the United States, Multnomah County, Oregon, 1860, 1870, 1880, 1900 (microfilm)

2. *State of Oregon*
   State Archives, *Salem:* Pupil Enrollment Cards, Failing and Shattuck schools, 1920, Portland Public School Records (microfilm)
   Bureau of Vital Statistics, Portland; Decennial Record of Deaths, 1920s, 1930s

3. *Multnomah County*
   Office of Assessment and Taxation: Index to Tax Rolls, 1921–1922 (microfilm)

4. *City of Portland Archives*
   Common Council Records (basement of City Hall)
   Council Documents, Mayoral Terms of Bernard Goldsmith, Philip Wasserman, Joseph Simon
   Mayor's Office Correspondence, Joseph Simon (1909–1911)

5. *Portland Public Schools*
   Administrative Department: Class Lists, Failing, Shattuck, and Couch schools, 1920

6. *Private Archives*
   American Jewish Historical Society, Brandeis University, Waltham, Mass.
      Industrial Removal Office Papers
      Stephen S. Wise Papers
   American Jewish Archives, Hebrew Union College, Cincinnati, Ohio
      Henry Berkowitz Papers
      Congregation Beth Israel, Marriage Licenses, 1884–1912, Deaths, 1876–1912

Horace M. Kallen Papers
Jonah Wise Papers
Bancroft Library, University of California, Berkeley
Edward Failing, Remembrances of His Father, Josiah (1889)
First Hebrew Congregation of Albany, Oregon, Minutes and Miscellaneous Correspondence, 1878–1924
Mark Lewis Gerstel, Memoires
Bernard Goldsmith, Interview (29 November 1889)
William Sargeant Ladd, dictation (10 July 1888)
Philip A. Marquam, dictation (22 November 1889)
Judge William Strong's Narrative and Comments (20 June 1878)
Congregation Neveh Shalom
Ahavai Shalom, Minute Books (1912–1928, 1934–1940)
Jewish Historical Society of Oregon
B'nai B'rith Building Association, Minute Books, 1910–1917
David Solis Cohen Papers
Committee on Emigres, Minute Book, August 1936–31 December 1948
Council of Jewish Women, Minute Books, 1896–1932
First Hebrew Benevolent Society, Minute Books, 1883–1920
First Hebrew Ladies Benevolent Society, Minute Books, 1874–1910
Jewish Shelter Home, Minute Book, 1921–1932
Opportunity Bake Shop, Minute Book, 1935–1941
Jewish Education Association of Portland, Minute Books, 1927–1940
Portland Hebrew School, Minute Books, 1916–1934
Oral Histories
Aiken, Miriam (22 July 1974)
Albert, Louis (7 December 1973)
Baum, Ted (   )
Berg, J. Jerome (6 March 1976)
Cohen, Freda Gass (25 April 1975)
Cohen, Moses "Scotty" (4 June 1975)
Finkelstein, David (23 April 1976)
Hahn, Gaulda Jermuloske (19 June and 17 December 1980)
Hervin, Mrs. Israel (3 May 1974)
Hirsch, Harold (7 and 26 July, 10, 11, and 13 August, and 14 December 1977; 14 March 1978)
Horenstein, Sadie (9 December 1975)
Kirshner, Hyman Morris (13 June 1974)
Labby, Manly Abraham (27 January 1975; 3 and 9 February 1976)
Levinger, Henry (13 July 1977)
Markewitz, Arthur (11 March and 10 May 1977)
Menashe, Ezra, and Joya Hanna (16 January 1975)

Miller, John H. (10 and 17 August 1976)
Policar, Harry (29 January 1975)
Rosenfeld, Miriam (15 April 1975)
Rubenstein, Flora Steinberg (9 December 1973)
Schlesinger, Kurt (16 June 1977)
Schnitzer, Morris (25 November 1977)
Sholkoff, Estelle Director (21 May 1975)
Simons, Dr. Max (7 March 1975)
Solomon, Judge Gus (14 February 1976)
Stampfer, Rabbi Joshuah (28 February 1980)
Sussman, Gilbert (1976)
Swett, Dr. William (24 February 1977)
Trachtenberg, Gladys "Laddie" (11 December 1973; 19 January and 29 August 1977)
Wax, Frohman C. (9 January 1978)
Judah Magnes Memorial Museum, Berkeley, California
B'nai B'rith Lodge 65, Minutes, 1933–1946
B'nai B'rith Lodge 314, Minutes, 1899–1904
B'nai B'rith Lodge 416, Minutes, 1891–1904
Congregation Linath Hatzedek, Minute Book and membership lists, 1914–1920
Portland Hebrew School *Observer*
Portland, Oregon, Jewish Population Census (March 1947)
Proceedings, B'nai B'rith District Grand Lodge No. 4 (selected years, 1866–1910)
Oregon Collection, University of Oregon, Eugene
Jonathan Bourne, Jr., Papers
B'nai B'rith Lodge 65 Papers, 1927–1931
Portland, Oregon, Chamber of Commerce Papers (1930s)
Otto J. Kramer Papers
Wayne Morse Papers
Richard Neuberger Papers
Portland Blue Books, 1891, 1900, 1910, 1930
Portland City Directories, 1865–1940
Scribe (1919–1925)
Westshore (1879–1890)
Oregon Historical Society, Portland
Congregation Beth Israel, records 1858–1940 (microfilm)
Photographic Archive
Ben Selling Papers
Joseph Simon Scrapbooks
Urban Archives, Temple University, Philadelphia, Pennsylvania
Rabbi Joseph Krauskopf Papers

Abbreviations

AJA	American Jewish Archives, Cincinnati, Ohio
AJH	*American Jewish History*
AJHS	American Jewish Historical Society, Waltham, Massachusetts
BL	Bancroft Library, University of California, Berkeley
CPA	City of Portland Archives, Portland, Oregon
JHSO	Jewish Historical Society of Oregon, Portland
JJS	*Jewish Journal of Sociology*
JSH	*Journal of Social History*
NS	Congregation Neveh Shalom, Portland, Oregon
NYPL	New York Public Library, 42nd Street & Fifth Avenue, New York, N.Y.
OC	Oregon Collection, University of Oregon, Eugene
OHS	Oregon Historical Society, Portland
PHR	*Pacific Historical Review*
PS	*Population Studies*
UA	Urban Archives, Paley Library, Temple University, Philadelphia, Pennsylvania
WHQ	*Western Historical Quarterly*
WJHC	Western Jewish History Center, Berkeley, California

Notes

Introduction: Social Process and Ethnic Identity, A Complex Relationship

1. Stephen Thernstrom, *The Other Bostonians: Poverty and Progress in the American Metropolis, 1880–1915* (Cambridge: 1973); Howard Chudakoff, *Mobile Americans: Residential and Social Mobility in Omaha, 1880–1920* (New York: 1972); John Bodnar, *Immigration and Industrialization: Ethnicity in an American Mill Town, 1870–1940* (Pittsburgh: 1977); Steven Hertzberg, *Strangers within the Gate City: The Jews of Atlanta, 1845–1915* (Philadelphia: 1978) are excellent examples of this literature and the most helpful for this study.

2. Herbert Gutman, *Work, Culture and Society in Industrial America* (New York: 1977); Joseph J. Barton, *Peasants and Strangers: Italians, Rumanians, and Slovaks in an American City, 1890–1950* (Cambridge: 1975); Virginia Yans McLaughlin, "Patterns of Work and Family Organization: Buffalo's Italians," *Journal of Interdisciplinary History* II (2): (1971) 299–314; idem, *Family and Community, Italian Immigrants in Buffalo, 1880–1930* (Ithaca: 1977).

3. The best effort to study a mercantile enclave historically is Peter Decker, *Fortunes and Failures: White Collar Mobility in Nineteenth Century San Francisco* (Cambridge: 1978), which includes much material on the social life of San Francisco's German Jews.

4. Two recent volumes by E. Kimbark MacColl have documented the activities of the Portland business elite. See *The Shaping of a City: Business and Politics in Portland, Oregon, 1885 to 1915* (Portland: 1976), and *The Growth of a City: Power and Politics in Portland, Oregon, 1915 to 1950* (Portland: 1979).

5. See the articles of Tamara K. Hareven, which present a far more complex analysis than I have summarized here, particularly, "The Family Cycle in Historical Perspective: A Proposal for a Developmental Approach," in Jean Cuisenier, ed., *The Family Life Cycle in European Societies* (The Hague & Paris: 1977), 340–48; and, "Family Time and Historical Time," in Alice S. Rossi et al., eds., *The Family* (New York: 1978), 57–68.

6. See particularly, Bodnar, *Immigration and Industrialization*, 142–49; Victor Greene, *For God and Country: The Rise of Polish and Lithuanian Consciousness in America* (Madison: 1975), 29–30, 34–35, 51–52; Barton, *Peasants and Strangers*, 13, 99–104.

7. See the suggestive comments, however, in Greene, *For God and Country*, 53–55; Barton, *Peasants and Strangers*, 70–75.

8. Don H. Doyle, *The Social Order of a Frontier Community, Jacksonville, Illinois, 1825–70* (Urbana: 1978), 13–15, and passim; Dean R. Esslinger, *Immigrants and the City: Ethnicity and Mobility in a 19th Century Mid-Western Community* (Port Washington: 1975), 28, 107–111; Peter R. Decker, *Fortunes and Failures: White Collar Mobility in Nineteenth Century San Francisco* (Cambridge, Mass.: 1978), 107–115.

9. Jonathan Mesinger, "The Jewish Community in Syracuse, 1850–1880: The Growth and Structure of an Urban Ethnic Region," Ph.D. diss., Syracuse University, 1977; Stephen Mostov, "A Sociological Portrait of German Jewish Immigrants in Boston: 1845–61, *AJS Review*, III (1978): 142–47; Marc Lee Raphael, *Jews and Judaism in a Midwestern Community: Columbus, Ohio, 1840–1975* (Columbus, 1979).

10. William Bowen, *The Willamette Valley: Migration and Settlement on the Oregon Frontier* (Seattle: 1978).

11. Glenna Matthews, "The Community Study: Ethnicity and Success in San Jose," *Journal of Interdisciplinary History*, VII (1976): 305–18.

1. Ethnicity, Mobility, and Class: The Origins of a Jewish Social Structure, 1855–1900.

1. "Judge William Strong's Narrative and Comments, June 20, 1878," manuscript, Bancroft Library, U.C., Berkeley, 14, 21; William A. Bowen, *The Willamette Valley, Migration and Settlement on the Oregon Frontier* (Seattle: 1978), 61; John M. Faragher, *Women and Men on the Overland Trail* (New Haven: 1979), 7–11.

2. Paul M. Merriam, "Portland, Oregon, 1840–1890: A Social and Economic History," Ph.D. diss., U. of Oregon (1971), 20–22, 232, 285–87, 298–309; E. Kimbark MacColl, *The Shaping of a City: Business and Politics in Portland, Oregon, 1885–1915* (Portland: 1976), 45; Bowen, *Willamette Valley*, 89; Ben Selling to Uncle (?), 29 April 1883, Ben Selling Papers, Oregon Historical Society, Portland, Oregon.

3. MacColl, *Shaping of a City*, 3–5, 17–37.

4. Physical segregation of the Chinese and their function as laborers appears most dramatically in the United States manuscript censuses of 1870 and 1880, where several thousand Chinese, almost all males, are listed consecutively as roomers in boarding houses. See also Lawrence Larsen, *The Urban West at the End of the Frontier* (Lawrence, Kansas: 1978), 21–26. Violence is noted in Ben Selling to "Bennie," 23 March 1886, Selling Papers.

5. Wolfgang Kollman and Peter Marschalk, "German Emigration to the United States," in *Perspectives in American History*, VII (1973): 526.

6. Mack Walker, *German Home Towns: Community, State and General Estate, 1648–1871* (Ithaca: 1971), 6, 18, 52, 76, 81, 87, 104, 140; Marc Lee Raphael, *Jews and Judaism in a Midwestern Community: Columbus, Ohio, 1840–1975* (Columbus: 1979), 16.

7. Mack Walker, *Germany and the Emigration, 1816–1885* (Cambridge: 1964), 52, 158.

8. "Bernard Goldsmith," interview, Portland, Oregon, 29 November 1889, p. 2, BL.

9. Jonathan S. Mesinger, "Peddlers and Merchants: The Geography of Work in a Nineteenth Century Jewish Community," Discussion Paper Series, No. 38, Department of Geography, Syracuse University (October, 1977), 7–10; Steven Hertzberg, *Strangers within the Gate City: The Jews of Atlanta, 1845–1915* (Philadelphia: 1978), 18–19; Raphael, *Jews and Judaism*, 35–46; Bill Williams, *The Making of Manchester Jewry, 1740–1875* (New York: 1976), 113–19, notes decline of rural peddling by the 1840s.

10. Bowen, *Willamette Valley*, 23.

11. "Chain migration" is stressed in Josef J. Barton, *Peasants and Strangers: Italians, Rumanians, Slovaks in an American City, 1890–1950* (Cambridge, Mass.: 1975), 6, 22.

12. "Bernard Goldsmith," 3–5, 8; "Gladys 'Laddie' Trachtenberg," interview, 11 December 1973; 19 January and 29 August 1977, p. 3, Oral History Project, Jewish Historical Society of Oregon.

13. "Henry Failing," interview, 1888, p. 2, BL.

14. "William Sargent Ladd," dictation, 10 July 1888, pp. 10–11, 17, 20, BL.

15. Herbert Gutman, *Work, Culture and Society in Industrializing America* (New York: 1976), 43.

16. "Bernard Goldsmith," p. 2; " 'Laddie' Trachtenberg," p. 3.

17. Joseph Gaston, *Portland, Oregon, Its History and Builders* (Portland: 1911), 163, 258; Chester P. Higby, *The Religious Policy of the Bavarian Government during the Napoleonic Period* (New York: 1919), 316.

18. Mark Lewis Gerstle, "Memoirs," (microfilm), p. 9, BL.

19. Walker, *German Home Towns*, 87; Lee M. Friedman, "The Problems of Nineteenth Century Jewish Peddlers," *American Jewish Historical Quarterly*, XLIV (September 1954): 1-7.

20. David Gerber, "Ethnics, Enterprise and Middle Class Formation: Using the Dun and Bradstreet Collection for Research in Ethnic History," *Immigration History Newsletter*, XII (May 1980): 5.

21. Gaston, *Portland, Oregon*, II, 234-35, and biographies of Jacob Fleischner, Samuel Rosenblatt, Sig Sichel, Solomon Hirsch, Edward E. Cohen, Nathan Loeb, and Moses Seller. See also Robert E. Levinson, *The Jews in the California Gold Rush* (New York: 1978), 132-33; William G. Robbins, "Opportunity and Persistence in the Pacific Northwest: A Quantitative Study of Early Roseburg, Oregon," *PHR*, XXXIX (1970): 279-96; "Harold Hirsch," interview, 7 & 26 July 1977, p. 1.

22. Levinson, *The Jews in the California Gold Rush*, 124-26, 130-31.

23. "Sylvan Durkheimer," interview, 3 March 1975, 3-6.

24. Ben Selling to Gus Winckler, 31 January 1883; Selling to Dear Uncle, March 1883; Selling to B. Scheeline, 14 April 1883; Selling to Winckler, 9 August, September 1, 1883; Selling to Julius Prechet, 22 May, 1886, Selling Papers.

25. Ben Selling to Alex Sinsheimer, 3 October 1883; Selling to Messrs Alexander and Fagilo, 3 October 1883; Selling to Messrs Rothchild and Bean, 4 October 1883; Selling to "Friend Mose," 20 March 1886; Selling to Sinsheimer, 20 March 1886; Selling to Uncle (S.F.), 4 July 1886; Selling to Sarah, 24 August 1886; Selling to Alex Sinsheimer, 20 December 1886, Selling Papers.

26. Ben Selling to B. Scheeline, 14 April 1883, Selling Papers.

27. United States Census of Manufacturers, manuscript, Multnomah County, Oregon, 1880. For the change of Fishel and Roberts to A. Roberts, clothier, see *Westshore* (April 1882), 79. See also "Minutes", First Hebrew Ladies Benevolent Society of Portland, Oregon, 26 February 1882, JHSO; Peter Decker, *Fortunes and Failures: White Collar Mobility in Nineteenth Century San Francisco* (Cambridge: 1978), 187; Glenn Porter and Harold C. Livesay, *Merchants and Manufacturers, Studies in the Changing Structure of Nineteenth Century Marketing* (Baltimore, 1971), 8-12. The *Westshore* (September 1879), 281.

28. Ben Selling to Uncle (S.F.) 4 July 1886, Selling Papers.

29. Ben Selling to David M. Bressler, 16 April and 12 May 1908, Portland, Oregon Agents File, Industrial Removal Office Papers, American Jewish Historical Society, Brandeis University.

30. Margaret Walsh, "Industrial Opportunities on the Urban Frontier: 'Rags to Riches and Milwaukee Clothing Manufacturers, 1840-1880," *Wisconsin Magazine of History*, LV (1974), 178-88; Stuart E. Rosenberg, *The Jewish Community in Rochester, 1843–1925* (New York: 1954), 119-25.

31. Data derived from United States Census of Manufacturers, manuscript, Multnomah County, Oregon, 1880; United States Manuscript Census of Population Multnomah County, 1900, and city directories; *Westshore* (April 1879), 121.

32. United States Census of Population, Manuscript, Multnomah County, Oregon, 1880 & 1900, for households of Isaac and Ralph Jacobs. See also, *Westshore* (July 1887), 198; (May 1879), 132. Homes of the Jacobs brothers appear in *Westshore* (June 1882), 106.

33. Julius J. Nodel, *The Ties Between: A Century of Judaism on America's Last Frontier* (Portland: 3 December 1959), 72; "Laddie Trachtenberg," p. 4; "Judge Deady in Relation to B. Goldsmith," 1889, p. 4, Bancroft Library; Jeff W. Hayes, *Looking Backward at Portland: Tales of the Early 80s* (Portland 1911), 66; Solomon Hirsch to Jonathan Bourne, Jr., 18 August 1895, Joseph Simon to Bourne, 22 October 1889, Jonathan Bourne Jr., Papers, OC; Ben Selling to W. K. Tichenor, 23 February 1883; Selling to Dear Uncle, 1 March and 19 April 1883, Selling Papers; Decker, *Fortunes and Failures*, 96-97.

34. Decker, *Fortunes and Failures*, 80-82, 238; Don H. Doyle, *The Social Order of a Frontier Community, Jacksonville, Illinois, 1825–1870* (Urbana: 1978), 101.

35. "Bernard Goldsmith," pp. 2-3; Photo of cargo for M. Seller & Co., folder #1744, neg. no. 9427, OHS.

36. On Dun & Bradstreet see Decker, *Fortunes and Failures*, 99-101; Gerber, "Ethnics, Enterprise, and Middle Class Formation," 3-5; Petition of A. Meier, 9 September 1871, City of Portland, Council Documents, 1871, City of Portland Archives.

37. Minute Book, First Hebrew Benevolent Association of Portland, Oregon, pp. 9-11, JHSO; Leon Jick, *The Americanization of the Synagogue, 1820–1870* (Hanover, N.H.: 1976), 106.

38. Doyle, *Social Order of Frontier Community*, 3-5; Edward Kantowicz, *Polish-American Politics in Chicago, 1880-1940* (Chicago: 1975), 18-28; Victor Greene, *For God and County, The Rise of Polish and Lithuanian Consciousness in America* (Madison:

1975), 34-42; Caroline Golab, *Immigrant Destinations* (Philadelphia: 1977), 153-54.

39. Cash Book, First Hebrew Benevolent Association of Portland, Oregon, 24 April 1887 notes amendment to their constitution establishing a permanent fund of $20,000. The note is signed by Philip Wasserman and Emil Franks. Minute Book, First Hebrew Benevolent Association, 16 & 20 April and 3 June 1886; 5 March and 15 December 1887; 10 May 1888; 22 January 1890. Assets are listed annually. See also Ben Selling to Henry Ackerman, 14 October 1886, Selling Papers.

40. Minute Book, First Hebrew Benevolent Association, 5 March 1890.

41. Ibid., List of Assets, 4 April 1895.

42. Congregation Beth Israel, Trustees Meeting, 3 May 1903; 5 January and 2 February 1905, microfilm, OHS. For emphasis on Oregon's healthful climate see Bowen, *Willamette Valley*, 18.

43. Minutes and Miscellaneous Correspondence of the First Hebrew Congregation of Albany, Oregon, 1878–1924, 21 July 1878; 29 April 1883; microfilm, BL, shows the same creation of a congregation for burial purposes and for religious services at some holidays. Levinson, *Jews in California Gold Rush*, 98-100; Jick, *Americanization of Synagogue*, 80.

44. Congregation Beth Israel, Trustees Meeting, 2 February 1905; Doyle, *Social Order of Frontier Community*, 12-13.

45. Minutes of Special Meeting of Congregation Beth Israel, 24 September 1865. Date on Herman Bories from United States Manuscript Census of Population, Multnomah County, 1870 & 1880; Nodel, *Ties Between*, 19-20.

46. Jick, *Americanization of Synagogue*, 39.

47. Minutes, Special Meetings, Beth Israel, 8 October 1865; 7 July and 6 October 1867.

48. Ibid., 5 November 1865; 29 April and 11 November 1866.

49. Ibid., 26 January and 13 April 1879.

50. Minutes, Board of Officers, Beth Israel, 15 January, 14 March, 13 June, and 24 September 1880.

51. Ibid., 2 August 1895; Nodel, *Ties Between*, 44.

52. Stephen S. Wise to Solomon Hirsch, 3 July 1900; Hirsch to Wise, 10 October 1900; Adolph Wolfe to Wise, 28 November 1911, Stephen S. Wise Papers, AJHS.

53. Rudolph Glanz, "The 'Bayer' and the 'Pollack' in America," *Jewish Social Studies* X (January 1955), 33-35; data on Robert Abrahamson and Mendel Cohen from the United States Manuscript Census of Population, Multnomah County, 1900.

54. Edward E. Grusd, *B'nai B'rith: The Story of a Covenant* (New York: 1966), 12, 16-17, 20-21, 27; Jacob Katz, *Jews and Freemasons in Europe, 1723–1939* (Cambridge, Mass: 1970), 164-66.

55. Doyle, *Social Order of a Frontier Community*, 179; Stuart Blumin, *The Urban Threshold: Growth and Change in a Nineteenth Century American Community* (Chicago: 1976), 181-84.

56. Grusd, *B'nai B'rith*, 41; Albert Vorspan and Lloyd Gartner, *History of the Jews in Los Angeles* (San Marino, California: 1970), 56; *Proceedings of the District Grand Lodge No. 4, 22nd annual convention, Sacramento, California, January 25–26, 1885* (San Francisco: 1885), 134-35.

57. William Toll, "Fraternalism and Community Structure on the Urban Frontier: The Jews of Portland, Oregon—A Case Study," *PHR*, XLVII (1978): 382, for detailed tables; Doyle, *Social Order of Frontier Community*, 182; Blumin, *Urban Threshold*, 177.

58. Toll, "Fraternalism and Community Structure," 383, Table 3; Merriam, "Portland, Oregon, 1840–1890," 178-80.

59. Membership list for Lodge 314 in *Proceedings, District Grand Lodge No. 4, 1885,* 155-56.

60. See also Marc Lee Raphael, "The Utilization of Local and Federal Sources for Reconstructing American Jewish Local History: The Jews of Columbus, Ohio," *AJHQ* LXV (1975): 13.

61. Mesinger, "Peddlers and Merchants," 34-48.

62. Grusd, *B'nai B'rith*, 86; *Proceedings, District Grand Lodge No, 4, 1885,* 134-35.

63. Rafael, "Jews of Columbus,", 13; Vorspan and Gartner, *Jews in Los Angeles*, 35; Hertzberg, *Strangers within the Gate City*, 152.

64. On Sabato Morais, see Henry Feingold, *Zion in America: The Jewish Experience from Colonial Times to the Present* (New York: 1974), 184, 186.

65. B'nai B'rith Lodge 416, "Minutes," 17 September 1891; 4 August 1892; 10 January 1893; North Pacific Lodge 314, "Minutes," 10 December, 1899, Western Jewish History Center, Berkeley, California.

66. Lodge 416, "Minutes," 31 May and 18 June 1891; 16 June, 1892.

67. Hayes, *Looking Backward at Portland*, 48.

68. *Portland "400" Directory, 1891* (Portland: 1887), 91.

69. Merriam, "Portland, Oregon, 1840–1890," 169; John Higham, *Send These to Me: Jews and Other Immigrants in Urban America* (New York: 1975), 183-93; Decker, *Fortunes and Failures*, 118, 232.

70. *Portland City Directory, 1879* (Portland: 1879), 47.

71. *Portland City Directory, 1887* (Portland, 1887), 91; *Portland "400" Directory, 1891,* 15-17; Ben Selling to Jake, 16 March 1886, Selling Papers.

72. *The Portland Blue Book, 1901* (Portland, 1901), 50-51; Congregation Beth Israel "Gold Book, 1887," & "Minutes, Special Meetings," 9 June 1863, Beth Israel Archives, OHS. Drawing of the new temple in *Westshore* (December 1888), 624. For a photo and discussion of Temple Emanu-EL of San Francisco's building see Fred Rosenbaum, *Architects of Reform, Congregational and Community Leadership, Emanu-EL of San Francisco, 1849-1980* (Berkeley: 1980), 29-32. Also, Jick, *Americanization of Synagogue*, 180-81.

73. Jews had not yet moved into the most exclusive section along 19th Street. See Merriam, "Portland, Oregon, 1840-1890," 179-80. On San Francisco Jewish residential clustering see Decker, *Fortunes and Failures*, 205, and Gerstle, "Memoires," 37. For the significance of streetcar construction on social class boundaries, see Sam Bass Warner, Jr., *Streetcar Suburbs: The Process of Growth in Boston, 1870-1900* (New York: 1972), 2-3, 21-29.

74. Lodge 416, Minutes, 30 July, 13 August, 17 September, and 1 and 15 October 1891.

75. Ibid., 18 April–17 October 1893; national malaise noted in Grusd, *B'nai B'rith*, 113-22.

76. William Toll, "Mobility, Fraternalism and Jewish Cultural Change Portland, 1910-1930," *AJH*, LXVIII, 4 (June 1979): 463-64.

77. *Proceedings, District Grand Lodge No. 4, 1904* (San Francisco: 1904), 36.

78. Ibid., 36; *Proceedings, District Grand Lodge No. 4, 1907* (San Francisco: 1907), 38.

79. *Proceedings, District Grand Lodge No, 4, 1906* (San Francisco: 1906), 91; Lodge 416, "Minutes," 19 April, 3 May, 6 September, and 4 October 1904.

80. Isaac Swett to Rabbi Joseph Krauskopf, 30 November 1897, Joseph Krauskopf Papers Urban Archives, Temple University (hereafter UA); David Nemerovsky to Ben Selling 21 April 1922, IRO Papers; First Ladies Hebrew Benevolent Society, "Minutes," 6 September 1898, 27 February 1900, 26 February 1901; Council of Jewish Women, "Minutes," 3 February 1904, JHSO.

81. Ahavai Shalom, "Membership List, 1921," Congregation Neveh Shalom Archives, Portland, Oregon.

82. Hays, *Looking Backward at Portland*, 33, 58, 66, 76-77.

83. Toll, "Fraternalism and Community Structure," 397; George I. Brodie to Joseph Simon, 3 July 1909, Mayor's Office Correspondence, 1909, PA.

84. *Proceedings, District Grand Lodge No, 4, 1904*, 36; *Proceedings, District Grand Lodge No. 4, 1907*, 81-83.

85. Howard Chudakoff, *Mobile Americans, Residential and Social Mobility in Omaha, 1880-1920* (New York: 1972) 70, 85-86, 91.

86. I. M. Rubinow, "Economic Conditions of the Jews in Russia," *Bulletin of the Bureau of Labor, No. 72* (Washington, Sept. 1907), 498-99, 503-04; Thomas Kessner, *The Golden Door: Italian and Jewish Immigrant Mobility in New York City, 1880-1915* (New York: 1977), 86-90, 94; Alter F. Landesman, *Brownsville; The Birth, Development and Passing of a Jewish Community in New York* (New York: 1969), 3, 101; Jeffrey S. Gurock, *When Harlem Was Jewish, 1870-1930* (New York: 1979), 27, 38-40.

87. *Proceedings, District Grand Lodge No. 4, 1904*, 119-21; *Proceedings, District Grand Lodge No. 4, 1906*, 91, 31-32; Lodge 314, "Minutes", 25 August and 8 September 1904.

88. Toll, "Mobility, Fraternalism and Jewish Cultural Change," 464.

89. The Jewish population of Portland has been derived from the manuscript census of Multnomah County for 1900. As in the use of earlier censuses, names were initially taken from Jewish institutions, and then the use of Jewish names and similar occupations, as well as physical propinquity and place of birth, led to the inclusion of many more families.

2. Jewish Women and Social Modernization, 1870-1930

1. Stephen S. Wise, *Child Versus Parents, Some Chapters on the Irrepressible Conflict in the Home* (New York: 1922), 37.

2. Tamara K. Hareven, "The Family Cycle in Historical Perspective: A Proposal for a Developmental Approach," in Jean Cuisenier, ed., *The Family Life Cycle in European Societies* (The Hague: 1977), 347; Virginia Yans McLaughlin, *Family and Community, Italian Immigrants in Buffalo, 1880-1930* (Ithaca: 1977), 18; Josef J. Barton, "Land, Labor and Community in Nueces: Czech Farmers and Mexican

Laborers in Texas, 1880-1930," in Fredrick C. Luebke, ed., *Ethnicity on the Great Plains* (Lincoln, Neb., 1980), 196-98.

3. Edward Shorter, *The Making of the Modern Family* (New York: 1975), 66-74.

4. John M. Faragher, *Women and Men on the Overland Trail* (New Haven: 1979), 110-12.

5. John E. Knodel, "Two and a Half Centuries of Demographic History in a Bavarian Village," *Population Studies*, XXV (November 1970), 365; Faragher, *Women and Men*, 40; William Bowen, *The Willamette Valley, Migration and Settlement on the Oregon Frontier* (Seattle: 1978), 23, 26, 53, 76-77; Christopher Carlson, "The Rural Family in the Nineteenth Century: A Case Study in Oregon's Willamette Valley," Ph.D. diss., University of Oregon, 1980, ch. 5.

6. "Bernard Goldsmith," dictation, Portland, Oregon, 29 November 1889, 1, BL; Beth Israel "Special Meeting," 29 April, 1866, Beth Israel Papers (microfilm), OHS.

7. Knodel, "Two and a Half Centuries," 359.

8. Ibid., 361.

9. Richard Sennett, *Families against the City, Middle Class Homes of Industrial Chicago, 1872-1890* (Cambridge, Mass.: 1970), 102-03, 106; Knodel, "Two and a Half Centuries," 361.

10. Wise, *Child versus Parent*, 82.

11. John E. Knodel, *The Decline of Fertility in Germany, 1871-1939* (Princeton: 1974), 70.

12. Shorter, *Making of Modern Family*, 67-71; Faragher, *Women and Men*, 47, 50, 57.

13. First Hebrew Ladies Benevolent Society, Minute Book. 24 May 1874, JHSO; Jacob R. Marcus, *Communal Sick Care in the German Ghetto* (Cincinnati, Ohio: 1978 ed.) 139-45.

14. First Hebrew Ladies Benevolent Society, Minute Book, 2 November 1874; 21 February and 28 November 1875; 27 November 1881; 29 November 1887; 26 November 1889.

15. "Judge Deady in Relation to B. Goldsmith," 3 December 1889, 2, BL.

16. First Hebrew Ladies Benevolent Society, Minutes, 27 August 1883; 25 August, 1884.

17. Ibid., 13 June 1875; 6 July 1879; 30 May 1893.

18. Ibid., 24 February 1885.

19. Date from Beth Israel, Minutes of Board of Officers, 11 August 1872–31 December 1873.

20. Data compiled from ibid., 18 June 1893–2 December 1895, also indicates diminished proportion of infant deaths.

21. First Hebrew Ladies Benevolent Society, Minutes, 22 August 1875; Beth Israel, Minutes of Board of Officers, 2 March 1873.

22. Common Council "Minutes", 14 July 1869, Auditor's Archives, Portland City Hall; Philip Wasserman, "Statement of the General Affairs of the Municipal Corporation, 1872," in Council Documents, 1872; "Mayor's Annual Report, 1909," p. 13; "Mayor's Annual Report, 1910," p. 4, in City of Portland Archives, Oregonian Building; Bowen, *Wilmette Valley*, 18-19.

23. Stephen S. Wise to Louise Wise, 15 October 1902, Stephen S. Wise Papers, *AJHS;* Samuel C. Ramer, "Childbirth and Culture: Midwifery in the Nineteenth Century Russian Countryside," in David L. Ransel, ed., *The Family In Imperial Russia, New Lines of Historical Research* (Urbana: 1978), 228; Yans McLoughlin, *Family and Community* 106.

24. All data derived from the Federal Manuscript Census, 1900, Multnomah County, Oregon (microfilm), *OC.*

25. First Hebrew Ladies Benevolent Society, Minutes," 25 November 1884; 24 February 1885; 24 May 1885; 27 May and 25 November 1890, 12 June 1892. By the 1890s, over $1,000 was expended annually on members and the "worthy" poor, with about 100 payments averaging $10 to $12 each.

26. Ibid., 10 and 26 May 1903; 9 May 1906; *Proceedings, District Grand Lodge No. 4, I.O.B.B. 1907* (San Francisco: 1907) 83; Temple Beth Israel, "Minutes, Board of Directors," 3 May 1906.

27. Ladies Benevolent Society, "Minutes," 11 November 1904; 30 November 1909.

28. Ibid., 28 May 1907.

29. Knodel, "Two and a Half Centuries," 360-61.

30. "Interview with Leo Adler," JHSO.

31. "Interview with Gladys 'Laddie' Trachtenberg," 11 December 1973; 19 January and 29 August 1977, pp. 15-16.

32. *Fourteenth Census of the United States, 1920, IV, Population, Occupation* (Washington: 1923), 1201.

33. Data on Anselm and Fred Boskowitz from Federal Manuscript Census, 1900, Multnomah County, Oregon, and from Portland city directories. For similar case see "Interview with Gladys Trachtenberg," p. 12.

34. Ansley J. Coale and Melvin Zelnick, *New Estimates of Fertility and Population in the United States* (Princeton: 1963), 37. See also Tamara K. Hareven and Maris A. Vinovskis, "Patterns of Childbearing in Late Nineteenth Century America: The Determinants of Marital Fertility in Five Massachusetts Towns in 1880," Hareven and Vinovskis, eds., *Family and Population in Nineteenth Century America* (Princeton: 1976), 101; Knodel, "Two and a Half Centuries," 370-71.

35. Knodel, *Decline of Fertility in Germany,* 90, 97, 136-137; Sennett, *Families against City,* 78-79. For fertility decline as only an aspect of a general reorientation of values, see Robert V. Wells, "Family History and Demographic Transition," *JSH,* 9 (Fall, 1975): 6-7.

36. William Toll, "Fraternalism and Community Structure on the Urban Frontier: The Jews of Portland, Oregon—A Case Study," *PHR,* XLVII (August 1978): 398-94.

37. Charlotte Baum, Paula Hyman, Sonya Michel, *The Jewish Woman in America* (New York: 1975), 48.

38. Council of Jewish Women, Minutes, 15 September 1899, JHSO.

39. Sennett, *Families against the City,* 53-54, 111-12.

40. Paul Boyer, *Urban Masses and Moral Order in America, 1820-1920* (Cambridge, Mass.: 1978), 132-33, 143-55, 179, 194-200.

41. Council of Jewish Women, Minutes, 29 April 1896; 14 December 1897.

42. Ibid., 3 February 1897; 5 February 1902; 4 March 1908.

43. Ibib., 2 December 1903.

44. Ibid., 1 November 1899; 8 February 1900; Stephen S. Wise to President and Board of Trustees, Beth Israel, 6 October 1899, Wise Papers.

45. Council of Jewish Women, Minutes, 8 April 1901.

46. Ibid., 4 and 6 January and 3 M ay 1905.

47. Ibid., 1 April 1903; 3 February 1904.

48. Ibid., 4 January and 1 November 1899; 6 March 1900; 2 October 1901; 13 February 1902; 6 May 1908; 2 December 1914.

49. Ibid., 29 August 1900.

50. Ibid., 6 January 1899; 19 June 1901; 5 February 1902.

51. Ibid., 2 December 1903; 5 January 1910; 4 January 1911; 7 February 1912; Joseph Teal to Joseph Simon, 30 January 1911; Simon to Teal, 31 January 1911; Teal to Simon, 1 February 1911; Mayor's Officer Papers. CPA.

52. Council of Jewish Women, Minutes, 29 September 1915; 15 May 1916.

53. Ibid., 7 March and 3 October 1906; 6 March 1907; 5 February 1908; 13 January and 3 March 1909.

54. Manly A. Labby, interview, 27 January 1975; 3 and 7 February 1976, p. 4; Moses Scotty Cohen, interview, 4 June 1975, p. 2.

55. Boyer, *Urban Masses and Moral Order*, 96-101; Council of Jewish Women, Minutes, 8 January, 26 March, and 31 December 1913.

56. Patricia Branca, "A New Perspective on Women's Work: A Comparative Typology," *JSH*, 9 (Winter 1975): 141, 144.

57. Flora S. Rubenstein, interview, 9 December 1973, pp. 6-7; data from city directories.

58. Yans McLaughlin, *Family and Community*, 186.

59. Baum, *Jewish Women in America*, 56.

60. Marc L. Raphael, *Jews and Judaism in a Mid-Western Community, Columbus, Ohio, 1840-1975* (Columbus, Ohio: 1979), 96-99; Arcadius Kahan, "Economic Opportunity and Some Pilgrims' Progress: Jewish Immigrants from Eastern Europe in the United States, 1890-1914," *Journal of Economic History*, XXXVIII (March 1978): 236-37; Yans McLaughlin, *Family and Community*, 34-35; Joseph J. Barton, *Peasants and Strangers: Italians, Rumanians and Slovaks in an American City, 1890-1950* (Cambridge, Mass.: 1975), 32-47.

61. Frederick W. Skinner, "Trends in Planning Practices, The Building of Odessa, 1794-1917," 153-55, and Michael F. Hamm, "The Breakdown of Urban Modernization: A Prelude to the Revolution of 1917," in Hamm, ed., *The City in Russian History* (Lexington, Ky.: 1976), 197.

62. Jacques Silber, "Some Demographic Characteristics of the Jewish Population in Russia at the End of the Nineteenth Century," *Jewish Social Studies*, XLII (Summer-Fall 1980), 278; Robert E. Johnson, "Family Relations and the Rural-Urban Nexus Patterns in the Hinterland of Moscow, 1880-1900," in Ransell, ed., *Family in Imperial Russia*, 268, 271.

63. J. Weinstein to David Bressler, 6 February 1905, I.R. Roberts to IRO, 20 October 1909; General Manager, IRO, to Roberts, 28 October 1909; Ben Selling to IRO, 5 September 1915; Industrial Removal Office Papers, AJHS; Manly Labby, interview, p. 3.

64. Manly A. Labby, pp. 6-9; Hyman Kirshner, interview, 23 June 1974, pp. 4-5.

65. David M. Bressler, *The Removal Work, Including Galveston* (New York: 1910), 3; John Livingston, "The Industrial Removal Office, the Galveston Project, and the Denver Jewish Community," *AJH*, LXVIII (June 1979): 442-43.

66. Rafael, *Jews and Judaism*, 146-55; Steven Hertzberg, *Strangers within the Gate City: The Jews of Atlanta, 1845-1915* (Philadelphia: 1978), 80-81; Robert Rockaway, "Ethnic Conflict in an Urban Environment: The German and Russian Jew in Detroit, 1881-1914," *AJHQ*, LX (October 1970): 133-50.

67. Ben Selling to David Bressler, 29 November 1906; 10 March and 12 May 1908; IRO Papers; First Hebrew Benevolent Society, Cash Book, pp. 177-79, JHSO.

68. Ben Selling to David Bressler, 19 September 1907; 15 July 1908; 5 and 25 August 1908, IRO Papers.

69. Ben Selling to David Bressler, 10 September and 3 December 1907; 30 April 1908, Bressler to Selling, 8 M ay 1908; Alex Grubman to Bressler, 31 October 1910; Selling to IRO, 26 June 1917, IRO Papers.

70. Ben Selling to David Bressler, 28 December 1907; 3 February 1908; Bressler to Selling, 3 July 1908; Selling to Bressler, 20 August 1908; Bressler to Selling, 2 September 1908 (quotation), Selling to Bressler, 23 September 1908, IRO Papers.

71. Gaulda Jermuloske Hahn, interview, 10 June 1980, p. 3.

72. "Fecundity of Immigrant Women," in *Reports of the Immigration Commission*, vol. 28 Senate Document No. 282, 61st Congress, 2nd session (Washington, 1911), 811-13.

73. Mrs. Miriam Sandrow to author, 13 June, 1980; Mrs. Dorothy Fain Fisher to author, 4 October 1981.

74. Data on Robisons from federal manuscript census, 1900, and from city directories. Information on Mrs. Nudelman from Ben Selling to David Bressler, 15 May 1908, IRO Papers; information on Mrs. Borenstein from Freda Gass Cohen, interview, 25 April, 1975, pp. 4-5; differences in employment between European and American-born women noted in Corinne Azen Krause, "Italian, Jewish and Slavic Grandmothers in Pittsburgh: Their Economic Roles," *Frontiers*, I (Summer 1977): 21.

75. Gaulda Jarmuloske Hahn, interview, pp. 6-8.

76. *Thirteenth Census of the United States, 1910, IV, Population, Occupation, Statistics* (Washington, 1914), 194, 206. See also Thomas Kessner and Betty Boyd Caroli, "New Immigrant Women At Work: Italians and Jews in New York City, 1880-1905," *Journal of Ethnic Studies*, V (Winter 1978): 27-28, which indicates that by 1905 Jewish women in New York City already clustered in white-collar work. See also David Katzman, *Seven Days a Week: Women and Domestic Service in Industrializing America* (New York: 1978), 49; George Masnick and Mary Jo Bane, *The Nation's Families: 1960-1990* (Cambridge, Mass.: 1980), 53.

77. Pupils from the Failing and Shattuck schools were identified from class rolls located in the School Clerk's Office, Portland, Oregon Public Schools. Parents were identified from pupil enrollment cards on microfilm, Oregon State Archives, Salem, Oregon.

78. *Thirteenth Census, IV, Population*, 202, 204, and *Fifteenth Census of the United States: 1930, Population, IV, Occupation by States* (Washington, 1933), 1362 indicates that while jobs in trade for men increased by 31.6%, those for women increased by 132% over the twenty-year period.

79. Miriam Sandrow to author, 17 December 1980; Dorothy Fain Fisher, taped interview, in possession of author.

3. *Civic Activism: The Public and Private Sources of Ethnic Identity*

1. Ben Zion Dinur, "American Jewish Historiography in the Light of Modern Jewish History," *Publications of the American Jewish Historical Society*, XLVI (March 1957): 203-4.

2. Michael R. Marrus, *The Politics of Assimiliation: A Study of the French Jewish Community at the Time of the Dreyfus Affair* (Oxford: 1971), 58, 62-3, 71-6; Bill Williams, *The Making of Manchester Jewry, 1740-1875* (New York: 1976), 53, 56, 104-05, 152, 162; V.D. Lipman, *Social History of the Jews of England, 1850-1950* (London: 1954), 37-38, 60-62.

3. Oscar Handlin, *The Uprooted*, rev. ed. (New York: 1973), 203-30.

4. Uriel Tal, *Christians and Jews in Germany: Religion, Politics and Ideology in the Second Reich, 1870-1914* (Ithaca: 1975), 33-4, 90-91, 123-34; Ismar Schorsch, *Jewish Reactions to German Anti-Semitism, 1870-1914* (New York: 1972), 5 and passim.

5. Oscar Handlin, *Boston's Immigrant's: A Study in Acculturation*, rev. ed. (New York: 1968), 76-82; Peter R. Decker, *Fortunes and Failures: White Collar Mobility in Nineteenth Century San Francisco* (Cambridge, Mass.: 1978), 166, 171.

6. Lawrence Larsen, *The Urban West at the End of the Frontier* (Lawrence, Kansas: 1978), 33; Stuart E. Rosenberg, *The Jewish Community in Rochester, 1843-1925* (New York: 1954), 12, 16, 109, 111-19; Steven Hertzberg, *Strangers within the Gate City, The Jews of Atlanta, 1845-1915* (Philadelphia: 1978), 50, 101-02, 124-25, 157-58, 167-69; Marc Lee Raphael, *Jews and Judaism in a Mid-Western City, Columbus, Ohio, 1840-1975* (Columbus, Ohio: 1979), 4, 83; Lloyd P. Gartner, *History of the Jews of Cleveland* (Cleveland: 1978), 26, 74-79.

7. John M. Faragher, *Women and Men on the Overland Trail* (New Haven: 1979), 35.

8. Daniel J. Elazar, *Community and Polity: The Organizational Dynamics of American Jewry* (Philadelphia: 1976), 56.

9. Clipping, ca. 1879, noting Joseph Simon as chairman of the Portland Fire Board and the delegate from Willamette Company No. 1, Joseph Simon Scrapbook, OHS; *Ceremony of the Presentation of the Silver Masonic Trowel to Willamette Lodge No. 2, A.F. & A.M., April 20, 1908* (pamphlet), with list of members on last two unnumbered pages, David Solis Cohen Papers, JHSO.

10. The continuation of familial politics into the 1880s is noted in E. Kimbark MacColl, *The Shaping of a City: Business and Politics in Portland, Oregon, 1885-1915* (Portland: 1976), 51-76, and passim.

11. Don Doyle, *The Social Order of a Frontier Community, Jacksonville, Illinois, 1825-70* (Urbana: 1978), 178.

12. "Bernard Goldsmith" (interview), 29 November 1889, pp. 5-6.

13. Joseph Gaston, *Portland, Oregon, Its History and Builders,* (Portland: 1911), 258-60.

14. *The Westshore* (July-August 1880), 217.

15. For alignment of Jewish stores see *The Westshore* (February 1878), p. 1; ibid., (May 1880), p. 136; Message of Mayor Goldsmith to City Council, 5 January 1870, Records, Common Council, City of Portland.

16. Records, Common Council, 8 January 1868; Council Documents, City of Portland, 30 June 1871; Beth Israel, annual meeting, 30 September 1866, Beth Israel Papers, OHS.

17. Receipts of Emil, Lowenstein & Co., and L. Goldsmith & Co., (1871), Council Document, City of Portland; Petition of Phil Cohen and others (11 August 1869); Remonstrance of H. Bories and others (24 October 1869); Petition of J. Levy (24 November 1869), petition of S. Blumauer (24 November 1869), etc., Records, Common Council, City of Portland.

18. Lyle W. Dorsett, *The Pendergast Machine* (New York: 1968), 13-14; Zane L. Miller, *Boss Cox's Cincinnati: Urban Politics in the Progressive Era* (New York: 1968), 77.

19. Records, Common Council, City of Portland, 8 January 1868; Minutes, Special Meeting, Beth Israel, 9 June 1863, Beth Israel Papers.

20. Records, Common Council, 1 July 1869; "Bernard Goldsmith," 8, 14; Joseph Simon Scrapbook, 26 April 1876.

21. Records, Common Council, City of Portland, 5 January 1870; Council Documents, 26 December 1872, City of Portland Archives.

22. Council Documents, January 1873, Message of Mayor Philip Wasserman, City of Portland Archives.

23. Ibid., January 1873.

24. Records, Common Counsil, 1 and 7 July 1869; Council Documents, 10 July 1871, City of Portland Archives.

25. Council Documents, 17 August, 1870.

26. "Bernard Goldsmith," 8-9; Records, Common Council, 29 June 1871; Council Documents, 1872, Philip Wasserman, "Statement of General Affairs of the Municipal Corporation."

27. Records, Common Council, 29 June 1871.

28. Records, Common Council, 11 August 1869.

29. "Statistical Report of the Arrests Made by the Police Force of Portland for the Year Ending December 31st 1872," in Council Documents (Box 24, Folder 13), City of Portland Archives.

30. Carl V. Harris, *Political Power in Birmingham, 1871-1921* (Knoxville: 1977), 96-99; Elliott M. Rudwick, *Race Riot at East St. Louis, July 2, 1917* (New York: 1972 ed.), 190; Larsen, *Urban West*, 69, 86. Portland's municipal finances were subdivided, with the power to raise and spend revenue vested not only in the city council but in numerous independent boards, including a school board and a water committee. See MacColl, *Shaping of a City*, 64-65; Joseph Simon to S. J. Hay (Mayor of Dallas, Texas), 31 January 1910, Mayor's Office Papers, City of Portland Archives.

31. Records, Common Council, 14 July 1869.

32. Council Documents, 11 and 21 June 1873, City of Portland Archives.

33. Council Documents, 25 June 1873, City of Portland Archives.

34. Decker, *Fortunes and Failures*, 246-48.

35. Ben Selling to "Bennie," 23 March 1886, Ben Selling Papers, OHS.

36. Data on Cohen and Bernstein obtained from the United States Manuscript Census, Multnomah County, Oregon, 1900 (microfilm), O.C. Cohen lived with the Bernsteins. On Cohen's family background, see "In Memorium Isaac N. Solis," pamphlet in D. Solis Cohen Papers.

37. Council for Jewish Women, Minutes, 12 and 22 May, and 4 November 1896; 2 March 1921; JHSO.

38. David Solis Cohen, "Our Unwelcome Sojourner, A Glance at His Condition and Surroundings," n.d.

39. Ibid.

40. See David Solis Cohen, "Talk to the Turnverein"; "Masonry and Flag Day" (ca. 1906); "Talk to Masons on Close of the Nineteenth Century"; "Talk to a Subordinate (i.e., local) Lodge of the B'nai B'rith."

41. Cohen, "Our Unwelcome Sojourner."

42. David Solis Cohen, "Talk on Yom Kippur"; "Talk on Passover."

43. "Judge Deady in Relation to B. Goldsmith," 3 December 1889, p. 2, Bancroft Library.

44. Joseph Simon Scrapbook, Election Returns, 1876, 18 June 1877; 16 April 1878; 3 June 1878; 20 April 1882.

45. MacColl, *Shaping of a City*, 60-62, for a jaundiced view of Simon as a "boss."

46. Joseph Simon Scrapbook, 4 August 1875; 26 April 1876; 18 June 1877; 17 April 1878; 20 June 1881; 2 December 1881.

47. Joseph Simon to Jonathan Bourne, Jr., 21 December 1898, Jonathan Bourne Papers, OC. Of the 392 appointees as policemen, special deputies,' firemen and laborers between January 1910 and 30 June 1911, perhaps two were Jewish. Names of appointees are recorded in Executive Board Proceedings, Common Council Record Books, Basement of City Hall. See also Jacob Rosenthal to Joseph Simon, 24 June 1910; Edward Ehrman to Simon, 24 June 1910; Mark Levy to Simon, 24 June 1910; Mayor's Office Papers, 1910, City of Portland Archives.

48. First Hebrew Ladies Benevolent Society, Trustees Meeting, 16 August 1874; Council of Jewish Women, Tenth Annual Meeting, 3 May 1905; JHSO.

49. By 1920 Joseph Simon was by far the largest Jewish property holder in Portland, with 20 parcels. By contrast Ben Selling owned only 3 parcels, as did Julius Meier. See Multnomah County, Oregon, Index to Tax Roll and Block Books, 1921-1922, pp. 550-51, County Assessor's Office. On Simon's earlier career, see Simon to Jonathan Bourne, Jr. 22 October 1889, Bourne Papers.

50. Joseph Simon Scrapbooks, 3 January 1883, indicates that Simon was the last president of the Fire Board of delegates, holding office from 1880-82.

51. Ben Selling to Leo, 25 August 1883, Selling Papers.

52. Richard Gottheil to Stephen Wise, 13 February 1901; Stephen Wise Papers, AJHS; Isaac Swett to Rabbi Joseph Krauskopf, 14 December 1897; Ben Selling to Krauskopf, 29 April 1904; Joseph Krauskopf Papers, UA.

53. John Higham, *Send These to Me: Jews and Other Immigrants in Urban America* (New York: 1975), 138-73.

54. Decker, *Fortunes and Failures*, 99; David Gerber, "Ethnics, Enterprise and Middle Class Formation: Using the Dun and Bradstreet Collection for Research in Ethnic History," *Immigration History Newsletter*, XII (1) (May 1880): 5.

55. "Harold Hirsch", interview with Shirley Tanzer, 7 and 26 July 1977; 10, 11 and 13 August 1977; 14 December 1977; 14 March 1978, p. 3-4.

56. Ben Selling to Gus Winckler, 14 and 18 November and 12 December 1883, Selling Papers. Selling's "monitoring" is described in "Interview with David Finkelstein," 12 December 1975, p. 13, JHSO.

57. Jeff W. Hayes, *Looking Backward at Portland: Tales of the Early 80s,* (Portland: 1911), 58. (pamphlet in NYPL)

58. Ben Selling to "Friend Leo," 21 May 1886; Selling to Uncle, 21 May 1886; Selling Papers.

59. Ben Selling to A. Levy, 29 May 1886, Selling Papers.

60. Ben Selling to Friend Leopold, 19 June 1886; Joseph Simon Scrapbooks, clipping ca. 1888, indicating Simon is still in state legislature.

61. Michael N. Dobkowski, *The Tarnished Dream: The Basis of American Anti-Semitism* (Westport, Conn.: 1979), passim.

62. David Solis Cohen, "Prejudice" (ca. 1902).

63. Bureau of Information and Advice, Industrial Removal Office, report on Portland Jewish Community, 6 March 1912, Industrial Removal Office Papers, AJHS.

64. MacColl, *Shaping of a City,* 73-74.

65. Joseph Simon Scrapbooks, *The Oregonian,* 22 February 1885, in OHS; David Solis Cohen, "Mitchell Republicans" (ca. 1904); Joseph Teal to Joseph Simon, 30 January 1911; Simon to Teal, 31 January 1911; Teal to Simon, 1 February 1911; Mayor's Office Papers, City of Portland; E. Kimbark MacColl, *The Growth of a City: Power and Politics in Portland, Oregon, 1915 to 1950* (Portland: 1979), 22.

66. Sig Sichel to Joseph Simon, 29 March 1910, Mayor's Office Papers.

67. Certificate of Nomination of Ben Selling, Republican candidate for United States Senate, 4 May 1912, Ben Selling Papers; Ben Selling to Jonathan Bourne, Jr., 8 April 1912, Jonathan Bourne Papers.

68. MacColl, *Growth of a City,* 14, 52.

69. David Solis Cohen, "Worker's Federation Talk"; "Women's Suffrage Talk"; "Committee of One Hundred and Fifty Talk."

70. David Solis Cohen, "Second Talk on Hanukah"; "Talk on Bible Study"; "The Tallows Candle."

71. W.E.B. DuBois, *The Philadelphia Negro: A Social Study* (Philadelphia: 1899), 385-89, 394-96.

72. David Solis Cohen, "Masonry and the Coming Century."

73. David Solis Cohen, "Talk to the Elks of Tacoma" (ca. 1902).

74. David Solis Cohen, "Talk on Installing New Rabbi at Ahavai Shalom"; "Talk on Laying Cornerstone at Beth Israel" (23 April 1888).

75. David Solis Cohen, "The Purpose of the Synagogue," *Jewish Exponent* (16 September 1904), p. 1; "Dedication of Tacoma Temple."

76. David Solis Cohen, "Is Hebrew a Dead Language?"; untitled talk on Talmud.

77. David Solis Cohen, "The New Religion"; "Talk on Installing New Rabbi at Ahavai Shalom."

78. Alexander Blackburn, First Baptist Church, to Stephen Wise, 17 April 1901, Stephen Wise Papers.

79. David Solis Cohen, "Zionism and Masonry" (ca. 1917).

80. David Solis Cohen, "Zionism and the B'nai B'rith" (ca. 1910).

81. Ben Selling to Joseph Krauskopf, 29 April 1904, Krauskopf Papers; Otto Kramer, untitled talk on Zionism, ca. 1905, Otto J. Kramer Papers, OC.

82. David Solis Cohen, "Palestine and Zionism," (ca. 1920); "Zionism and the B'nai B'rith" (ca. 1910).

83. Louis D. Brandeis, *The Jewish Problem and How To Solve It* (n.p., 1916); Horace M. Kallen, *Zionism and World Politics: A Study in History and Social Psychology* (London: 1921), 267-69, 277-79.

84. Louis J. Swichkow and Lloyd P. Gartner, *The History of the Jews of Milwaukee* (Philadelphia: 1963), 55, 64, 93-4, 106-07, 111-12, 117-19, 160-64; Steven Hertzberg, "Unsettled Jews: Geographic Mobility in a Nineteenth Century City," *AJHQ*, LXVII (December 1977), 125-39; Raphael, *Jews and Judaism*, 45-6, 88-90, 122.

85. Ben Selling to Father, 24 December 1883, Ben Selling Papers; Adolph Wolfe to Stephen Wise, 26 October 1904, Wise Papers; Gladys Laddie Trachtenberg, interview, 11 December 1973, pp. 5-7; Solomon Hirsch to Jonathan Bourne, Jr., 30 August 1897, Bourne Papers; Ben Selling to Joseph Krauskopf, 18 June 1897, Krauskopf Papers.

86. George I. Brooks to Joseph Simon, 3 July 1909, Mayor's Office Papers, CPA; MacColl, *Shaping of a City*, 196, 213; Paul Boyer, *Urban Masses and Moral Order in America, 1820-1920* (Cambridge, Mass.: 1978), 181-98.

87. Stephen Wise to Louise Wise, 28 October 1902 (quotation), October 1902, Stephen Wise Papers; *The Personal Letters of Stephen Wise*, ed. Justine Wise Polier and James Waterman Wise (Boston: 1956), 95; *Stephen S. Wise, Servant of the People*, ed. Carl Voss, (Philadelphia: 1969), Wise to Theodore Herzl, 16 May 1904.

88. David Solis Cohen, "Talk to Committee of One Hundred and Fifty"; Abigail Scott Duniway to Stephen S. Wise, 29 January 1901, Wise Papers. On Roosevelt, see Moses Rischin, *The Promised City: New York's Jews, 1870–1914* (New York: 1964 ed.) 15, 184.

89. David Solis Cohen (talk on the need for political reform); Cohen, "Address before the Consumer's Leagues," in Stephen S. Wise and D.S. Cohen, *Two Addresses before the Portland, Oregon, Branch of the National Consumer's League* (Portland: 1906), 9-16; Abigail Scott Duniway to Stephen Wise, 29 January 1901, Stephen Wise Papers.

90. Joseph Simon to Jonathan Bourne, Jr., 17 August 1897, Bourne Papers.

91. William H. Corbett to Joseph Simon, 15 June 1910; Simon to Corbett, 16 June 1910; Mayor's Office Papers, CPA; Executive Board Proceedings, 30 June 1910; 30 August 1910, CPA.

92. Ben Selling to Simon (?), 23 March 1883, Selling Papers.

93. Solomon Hirsch, Simon Blumauer, Charles Kohn (committee) to Stephen Wise, 31 July 1899; Ben Selling to Wise, 22 July 1899; Wise to Board of Trustees, Beth Israel, 3 and 6 October 1899; Solomon Hirsch to Wise, 11 November 1899, Contract of Stephen Wise for $5,000 annually, Wise Papers; Stephen Wise to Louise Waterman, 1899, in Polier and Wise, eds., *Personal Letters of Stephen Wise*.

94. Isaac Swett to Joseph Krauskopf, 30 November 1897, Krauskopf Papers.

95. Annual Report of the President (Adolph Wolfe) of Beth Israel, 29 October 1903; Wolfe to Wise, 21 June 1904, Wise Papers.

96. Resolution of B'nai B'rith Lodge 416, 27 October 1902; Stephen Wise to Leon Levy, President, International Order of B'nai B'rith, 27 June 1903, Wise Papers.

97. Abigail Scott Duniway to Stephen Wise, 29 January 1901; Wise to Louise Wise, 14 April 1902; 24 September, ? September, 10 October 1902; 1 January 1903, Wise Papers.

98. Bureau of Information and Advice, Industrial Removal Office, 6 March 1912, Report on Portland, Oregon, IRO Papers.

99. Philip Cowen [*The American Hebrew*] to Stephen Wise, 10 September 1900, Wise Papers.

100. David Bressler to Stephen Wise, 27 July 1903, Wise Papers; Ben Selling to David Bressler, 10 March 1908, IRO Papers.

101. "Statement," 1 February 1908, Ben Selling Cash Book, Selling Papers.

102. David Bressler to Ben Selling, 2 April 1906; Selling to Bressler, 7 September 1907; Sig Sichel to Bressler, 19 August 1913; Bressler to Sichel, 25 August 1913; Joseph Simon to Bressler, 16 June 1909, IRO Papers.

103. Ben Selling to David Bressler, 19 September 1907, IRO Papers. Congregation Linath Hatzedek Ledger, 1913 Membership List, includes Jacob Tonitsky, along with Swerdlichs, Jukelsons, Unkelis, and Jermuloski among other IRO assisted immigrants. On Tonitsky's religious work, see "Flora Steinberg Rubenstein," interview, 9 December 1973, p. 7, JHSO.

104. Sig Sichel to David Bressler, 19 August 1913, IRO Papers.

105. Ben Selling to David Bressler, 3 December 1907, IRO Papers; David Bressler, *The Removal Work, Including Galveston* (New York: 1910), 18; John Livingston, "The Industrial Removal Office, The Galveston Project, and the Denver Jewish Community," *AJH*, LXVIII (June 1979): 452-56.

106. Alex Grubman to David Bressler, 22 November 1910, IRO Papers.

107. Ben Selling to David Bressler, 28 September 1908, IRO Papers.

108. Hertzberg, *Strangers within the Gate City*, 78; Robert Rockaway, "Ethnic Conflict in an Urban Environment: The German and Russian Jew in Detroit, 1881-1914," *AJHQ*, LX (December 1970), 143. Of the 96 persons discussed in the correspondence between the IRO central office in New York and the agents in Portland between 1906 and 1913, only 39 could be located in Portland directories within two to five years of their appearance in the records. As Philip Cowen had assumed, persons on whom families were willing to expend money for transportation across the continent would probably try to assist the persons to stay.

109. Ben Selling to David Bressler, 28 October 1908, IRO Papers.

110. Walter Laquer, *A History of Zionism* (New York: 1972), 61-83; Irving Howe, *World of Our Fathers* (New York: 1976), 27-29.

111. Isaac Swett to Joseph Krauskopf, 30 November 1897, Krauskopf Papers; Otto J. Kraemer, untitled memorial to Isaac Swett, n.d., Kraemer Papers.

112. Data on Swett farm is taken from the United States manuscript census, Multnomah County, Oregon, 1900. See also Dr. William Swett, interview, 24 February 1977, p. 5, JHSO. Table 1.

114. Jacob Riis to Stephen Wise, 23 March 1901, Wise Papers; Stephen Wise to

113.   Table 1: Families with Children Born in North Dakota, 1884–1889

Head of House-hold	Age (1900)	Occupation (1900)	Youngest child born N.D., age (1900)	Next child Born age (1900)	Place of Birth
Brumberg, Israel	42	cloth merch	13	9	Oregon
Calof, Max	55	junk dealer	13	10	Minn.
Cohen, Samuel	37	cloth merch	11	9	Oregon
Dubiver, David	64	store kpr	11	10	Oregon
Gale, Marcus	40	cloth merch	13	none	x
Goldstein, Hyman	40	2nd hnd furn	11	9	Oregon
Goldstein, Jacob	48	2nd hnd grocer	14	6	Oregon
Levdansky, Nathan	48	trvlng slsmn	13	none	x
Nudelman, Philip	42	expressman	9	6	Oregon
Rosencrantz, Jacob	36	2nd hnd store	11	10	Oregon
Ruvensky, Louis	39	furn mfc	11	8	Oregon
Weinstein, Solomon	40	2nd hnd dlr	12	9	Minn.

See also, "Russian Jewish Farm Colony in Burleigh County, North Dakota, 1880," *Western States Jewish Historical Quarterly*, XII (1980), 38.

Louise Waterman, 1899, in *Personal Letters of Stephen Wise*.

115. "Mrs. Miriam Rosenfeld," interview, 15 April 1975, pp. 2-8, JHSO.

116. The Jewish bath house is mentioned in "Mrs. Flora Steinberg Rubenstein," interview, p. 1; acquiring the pool for Neighborhood House is described in "'Laddie" Trachtenberg," interview, pp. 14-15.

117. Council of Jewish Women, Board Meeting, 26 March 1913, JHSO: "Max Simon," interview, 7 March 1975, p. 5, JHSO.

118. David Solis Cohen, "Flag Day Speech at Neighborhood House" (undated).

119. Council of Jewish Women, Regular Meeting, 3 January, 6 November, and 18 December 1907; 1 March 1911; 7 February 1912; 4 November 1914, JHSO.

120. Data on Levin in the United States manuscript census, Multnomah County, Oregon, 1900, and in Portland city directories. In October 1933, the Ladies Auxiliary held a dinner honoring the 23rd year of the Hebrew School. See Minute Book Portland Hebrew School, 24 October 1933, JHSO.

121. Arthur A. Goren, *New York Jews and the Quest for Community: The Kehillah Experiment, 1908-1922* (New York: 1970), 110-33; Bert Treiger, "Principal's Report," *Observer* (Portland, 1921), no pagination.

122. See letterhead for the United Palestine Appeal in 1926, which lists men like Bert Treiger, J. Lauterstein, J. Sax, J. Shemanski, L. Bromberg, and D. Solis Cohen. See J. Rosenberg to D. Solis Cohen, 25 February 1926, D. Solis Cohen Papers.

123. Minute Book, Portland Hebrew School, 30 July and 17 August 1916; 12 October 1917; 16 July 1922, JHSO.

124. Ibid., 8 April 1917. By 1922 a few men like Moses Mosessohn had left Portland, but they were replaced on the new board by other rabbis in Portland. Men like Rosenstein, Nemerovsky, Director, and Brumberg remained. The talk of Joseph Shemansky is reprinted in *Observer* (Portland, 1931) p. 6 (copy in NYPL).

125. Minute Book, Portland Hebrew School, 8 March and 17 July 1926; 6 February and 21 May 1928; 13 January 1929.

126. Ibid., 13 November 1922; 21 June 1923; Robert McAfee to Rabbi Jonah Wise (n.d.), Minutes of Citizen's Committee Meeting, 21 June 1921, Jonah Wise Papers, AJA.

127. Minute Book, Portland Hebrew School, 26 September 1918; 28 April 1927; *Observer* (1933), p. 7; *Observer* (1936), p. 14; *Observer* (1937), p. 15; Council of Jewish Women, Minutes, 1 April 1925.

128. *Observer* (1933), p. 6.

129. Minutes, Portland Hebrew School, 8 April and 12 September 1917; Minutes, Jewish Education Association of Portland, 16 November 1933; Dorothy Fain Fisher to author, 4 October 1981; Fred Rosenbaum, *Architects of Reform, Congregational and Community Leadership, Emanu-El of San Francisco* (Berkeley: 1980) 147-74.

130. By the mid-1950s the Hebrew School represented a "vested interest," monopolizing instruction in Hebrew, which was resented particularly by the conservative synagogues. See Rabbi Joshua Stampfer, interview, 28 February 1980, JHSO.

4. The Immigrant District and the New Middle Class, 1900–1930

1. Victor Greene, *For God and Country: The Rise of Polish and Lithuanian Consciousness in America* (Madison: 1975), 34, 47-53; Edward R. Kantowicz, *Polish-American Politics in Chicago, 1888-1940* (Chicago: 1975), 15, 18-23; Caroline Golab, *Immigrant Destinations* (Philadelphia: 1977), 113-119. 130-31; Josef J. Barton, *Peasants and Strangers: Italians, Rumanians and Slovaks in an American City, 1890-1950* (Cambridge: 1975), 58, 90, 103, 120, 148-50.

2. John Bodnar, *Immigration and Industrialization: Ethnicity in an American Mill Town, 1870-1940* (Pittsburgh: 1977), 129, 131, 137.

3. Allan H. Spear, *Black Chicago: The Making of a Negro Ghetto, 1890-1920* (Chicago: 1967); Gilbert Osofsky, *Harlem: The Making of a Ghetto, Negro New York, 1890-1930* (New York, 1971); William Toll, *The Resurgence of Race: Black Social Theory from Reconstruction to the Pan-African Conferences* (Philadelphia: 1979), 195-220.

4. Barton, *Peasants and Strangers*, 54-55, 75, 86-88, 100, 128, 162; Humbert S. Nelli, *The Italians in Chicago, 1880-1930: A Study in Ethnic Mobility* (New York: 1970), 44-46, 116-17, 234-5, 242-44.

5. Jeffrey S. Gurock, *When Harlem Was Jewish, 1870-1930* (New York: 1979), 145; Lloyd P. Gartner, *History of the Jews of Cleveland* (Cleveland: 1978), 268-71, Deborah D. Moore, *At Home in America: Second Generation New York Jews* (New York: 1981), 76-80.

6. Stephan Thernstrom, *The Other Bostonians: Poverty and Progress in the American Metropolis, 1880-1970* (Cambridge: 1973), 112-44; Clyde and Sally Griffen, *Natives and Newcomers: The Ordering of Opportunity in Mid-Nineteenth Century Poughkeepsie* (Cambridge: 1978), 58, 76, 119-120; Bodnar, *Immigration and Industrialization*, viii–xix.

7. The major exception is Arthur A. Goren, *New York Jews and the Quest for Community: The Kehillah Experiment, 1908-1922* (New York: 1970). Goren, however, focuses on the activities of a handful of leaders of the Kehillah rather than contacts between ordinary business and professional people who may have belonged to particular lodges and benefit societies.

8. The Tualitin Country Club was founded in 1912 primarily as a golf club for some members of Beth Israel. Its 41 members are listed in *The Portland Blue Book* (Portland, 1930), 154.

9. *The American Jewish Yearbook 5668, September 9, 1907, to September, 1908* Philadelphia: 1907), 367 estimates Portland's Jewish population at 5,000. *American Jewish Yearbook 5685, September 29, 1924 to September 18, 1925* (Philadelphia: 1924), 580, estimates Jewish population of Portland for 1920 as 9,000. Population estimates for this date for Oregon, however, seem wildly out of proportion at 18,000 (p. 575). *American Jewish Yearbook 5701, October 3, 1940 to September 21, 1941* (Philadelphia: 1940), 236, lists a population for Portland of 10,700. United States Bureau of the Census, *Religious Bodies, 1926, vol. I, Summary and Detailed Tables* (Washington, 1930), 515, notes a Jewish population of about 12,000.

10. Gurock, *When Harlem Was Jewish*, 86, 125-33.

11. "Flora Steinberg Rubenstein," interview, 9 December 1973, 2, 5-7.

12. "Estelle Director Sholkoff", interview, 21 May 1975, 1, 5; Dorothy Fain Fisher to author, 4 October 1981.

13. On the Jewish "radicals," see "Dr. Max Simon," interview, 7 March 1975, 3-4, and Lloyd P. Gartner and Albert Vorspan, *History of the Jews of Los Angeles* (San Marino: 1970), 141-42; "Moses 'Scotty' Cohen," interview, 4 June 1975, 2.

14. "Dr. Max Simon," interview, pp. 2-5.

15. Manly A. Labby," interview, 7 January 1975; 3 and 9 February 1976, pp. 2-3.

16. "Hyman Morris Kirshner," interview, 23 June 1974, pp. 1-4.

17. "Miriam Rosenfeld," interview, 15 April 1975, p. 5; "Freda Gass Cohen," interview, 25 April 1975, pp. 4, 10.

18. Manly A. Labby," p. 1.

19. Information on the garment industry and unionization from the oral histories of Harold Hirsch, Hyman Kirshner, and Manly Labby. Information on support for strikes and Annette's cafe from Miriam Sandrow to author, 6 October 1981.

20. "Dr. Max Simon," p. 4; "Louis Albert," interview, 7 December 1973, pp. 3-4. On a similar absence of *landsleit* in Los Angeles, despite its much larger Jewish population in 1930, see Vorspan and Gartner, *History of the Jews of Los Angeles*, 164.

21. "Estelle Director Sholkoff," 3.

22. "Minutes," Council of Jewish Women, 26 October 1921, JHSO.

23. "Sadie Schwartz Horenstein," interview, 9 December 1975, p. 1.

24. Roy Lubove, *The Professional Altruist: The Emergence of Social Work as a Career, 1880-1930* (New York: 1969), 14-15. Caroline Golab, *Immigrant Destinations*, 112-13, distinguishes between the "neighborhood" as a geographic area and the "community" as a set of social networks, because most often more than one ethnic group occupied a geographic "neighborhood." Each was joined more through a network of associations than through mere physical proximity. In South Portland,

Eastern European Jews were the largest group, though Italians also occupied many of the smaller blocks. We use "neighborhood" here in the social sense, as an area with a general physical boundary where residents of a particular ethnic group are held together through their own voluntary associations.

25. "Leon Feldstein," interview, 30 November 1973, p. 1.

26. "Estelle Director Sholkoff," p. 4.

27. "Freda Gass Cohen," p. 4. Fred Gass, her sister Rose, and her brothers Oscar and David all graduated from the Portland Hebrew School in the late 1920s and early 1930s. They were among about 120 young people who must have spent most of their day, at least five days a week, in the company of close friends who also attended the same public and ethnic schools. Data on Portland Hebrew School graduates has been extracted from copies of *The Observer*, published annually by the graduating class.

28. Data on pupils at the Shattuck and Failing schools has been obtained from class lists supplied by the Administrative Department of the Portland Public Schools, and from Pupil Enrollment cards for the Portland public schools, on microfilm at the State of Oregon Archives, Salem, Oregon. Persons have been traced through Portland city directories.

29. "Gaulda Jermuloske Hahn," interview, 10 June 1980, pp. 2-3.

30. Miriam Sandrow to author, 17 December 1980.

31. "Harry Policar," interview, p. 5; "Estelle Director Sholkoff," interview, p. 5.

32. Minutes, Portland Hebrew School, 23 September 1925; 28 April 1927; 16 February 1928.

33. Minute Book, Jewish Shelter Home, 30 September and 7 October 1927. In this discussion all names have been omitted and privacy protected.

34. Ibid., 13 February 1924.

35. Ibid., 19 February 1924.

36. "Gaulda Jermuloske Hahn," interview, continuation, 17 December 1980, p. 2.

37. Steven Hertzberg, *Strangers within the Gate City, The Jews of Atlanta, 1845-1915* (Philadelphia: 1978), 120-21; Lloyd P. Gartner, *History of the Jews of Cleveland* (Cleveland: 1978), 58-60.

38. Minute Book, Jewish Shelter Home, 23 January, 28 February, and 17 April 1923.

39. The tragedy of this case is recreated from ibid., 2 June, 10 November, and 8 December 1925; 5 January, 4 May, and 22 November 1926. The father in late 1926 sued the mother, then in the state mental asylum in Salem, for divorce.

40. For the new importance of psychiatry in social work, see Lubove, *Professional Altruist*, ch. 5. See also "Gaulda Jermusoske Hahn," interview, continuation, p. 2.

41. "Max Simon," p. 5.

42. B'nai B'rith Building Association, Minute Book, 20 October 1910, pp. 4-12.

43. Ibid., p. 12. Data on place of birth from federal manuscript census, Multnomah County, Oregon, 1900.

44. B'nai B'rith Building Association, Minute Book, p. 7.

45. Ibid., 20 October 1910 (p. 13); 22 March 1913 (p. 39).

46. Ibid., 2 March 1914 (p. 67); 25 October 1914 (p. 75).

47. Ibid., 31 October 1915 (p. 90); 16 December 1915 (p. 106); 11 September 1916 (p. 131).

48. "Mrs. Mollie Blumenthal," interview, 17 March 1976, pp. 7-8.

49. Horace M . Kallen to Stephen Wise, 22 August 1915, Stephen Wise Papers, AJHS.

50. Marvin Lowenthal to Horace M. Kallen, 20 October 1916; Horace M. Kallen Papers, AJA.

51. *Scribe*, 9 January 1920.

52. *Scribe*, 7 April 1922.

53. Ibid., 26 September 1919; 9 and 23 January 1920; 7 April 1922; Ben Selling to Joseph Krauskopf, 6 February 1920, Joseph Krauskopf Papers; Jesse Bogen to Jonah Wise, 28 December 1920, Jonah Wise Papers, AJA.

54. J. I. Ascheim to Jonah Wise, 12 February 1921, J. Wise Papers; *Scribe*, 26 September 1919; Minutes, B'nai B'rith Lodge 65, 2 February and 1 March 1927, B'nai B'rith Papers, OC.

55. Ben W. Olcott to Jonah Wise, 21 August 1920; R. C. Clark to Wise, 17 May 1921; W. L. Hand to Wise, 24 March 1922; Joseph H. Hedges to Wise, 13 April 1923, J. Wise Papers.

56. Jonah Wise to Martin Mayer, 15 May 1922, J. Wise Papers.

57. *Scribe*, 12 and 19 May and 2 June 1922; Kenneth T. Jackson, *The Ku Klux Klan and the City, 1915-1930* (New York: 1967), 214; William Toll, "Progress and Piety: The Ku Klux Klan and Social Change in Tillamook, Oregon," *Pacific Northwest Quarterly*, 69 (April 1978), 75-85; Blaine Brownell, "A Symbol of Modernity: Attitudes toward the Automobile in Southern Cities in the 1920s," *American Quarterly*, XXIV (1972): 20-44.

58. Toll, "Progress and Piety," 84-85.

59. Ben Selling, Jonah Wise, Nathan Strauss to Louis Marshall, 20 October 1922; Marshall to Jesse Winburn, 21 October 1922; Marshall to Sellingt, 21 October 1922; Winburn to Marshall, 21 October 1922; Marshall to Selling, 23 October 1922, J. Wise Papers.

60. Earl Pomeroy, *The Pacific Slope: A History of California, Oregon, Washington, Idaho, Utah and Nevada* (Seattle: 1965), 227-28; Jackson, *Ku Klux Klan and City*, 214.

61. "David Finkelstein," interview, 23 April 1976, pp. 7-8; "Judge Gus Solomon," interview, 16 February and 23 June 1976, pp. 7-8; "Gilbert Sussman," interview (1976), pp. 8-9.

62. "Harold Hirsch," interview, pp. 28-29; "Judge Gus Solomon," interview, pp. 7-8; "Harry Policar," interview, p. 6.

63. *Portland '400' Directory, 1891* (Portland: 1891) lists 41 Jewish families out of 545 total families. *The Portland Blue Book and Social Register of Oregon, 1930* (Portland: 1930) lists 30 Jewish families out of 802 total families. With few exceptions, the same Jewish families were listed in both years. For San Francisco, see Peter Decker, *Fortunes and Failures: White Collar Mobility in Nineteenth Century San Franscisco* (Cambridge, Mass.: 1978), 238.

64. *Portland Blue Book, 1930*, 4.

65. Stephen G. Spottswood to Wayne Morse, 18 February 1949; Leslie S. Perry to Morse, 31 August 1949; "Protection for Civil Rights for Portlanders," by Mrs.

Betty Britton Sale, and "Answers to the Critics," by Edwin C. Berry (executive secretary, Portland Urban League), Wayne Morse to David Robinson, 2 September 1950; Robinson to Morse, 18 September 1950; Wayne Morse Papers, OC; "Dr. Max Simon," pp. 6-7; "Judge Gus Solomon," pp. 22-23.

66. Minutes, B'nai B'rith Lodge 65, 7 and 21 February and 16 October 1928; 10 September 1930; Minutes, Council of Jewish Women, 16 December 1916; John P. Roche, *The Quest for the Dream: The Development of Civil Rights and Human Relations in Modern America* (New York: 1963), 23; Jonah Wise to M. J. Finkelstein, 17 May 1923, J. Wise Papers.

67. Minutes, Board Meeting, Temple Ahavai Shalom, November 6 & 21 & 28, 1923, January 7, 1924, President's Report, November 2, 1924; Minutes, Board Meeting, Temple Beth Israel, December 31, 1923, January 10, February 7, May 13 & 21, September 11, 1924. (Plans for the new building fill the minutes for the rest of the decade.)

68. Pomeroy, *Pacific Slope*, 249.

69. *Scribe*, 26 September, 10 October 1919; Minutes, B'nai B'rith Lodge 65, 14 January, 15 March, and 6 September 1927, OC; B'nai B'rith Lodge 416, 3 and 17 October 1893; Minutes, North Pacific Lodge 314, July 1899 through September 1904, indicate amateur musicals for 416 and no special entertainment for 314.

70. "Harry Policar," interview.

71. Minutes, B'nai B'rith Lodge 65, 20 March and 2 October 1928; 2 January 1929; 14 May, 11 June, and 24 September 1930.

72. Otis L. Graham, Jr., *An Encore for Reform: The Old Progressives and the New Deal* (New York: 1967), 109-10, 206.

73. Council of Jewish Women, Minutes, 22 February 1922; 27 September 1926.

74. Ibid., 22 February 1922; 31 January, 3 October, 4 February, and 2 December 1925; 6 January 1932.

75. Ibid., 2 November and 28 December 1921; 14 May 1924, 4 February 1925.

76. Ibid., 23 February and 29 September 1927.

77. Ibid., 2 May 1923; 26 January 1924; 30 September 1925; 7 December 1927; 2 October 1929.

78. Ibid., 27 April 1921; 26 December 1923; 4 February 1925; 29 September 1927; 4 December 1929.

79. United States Bureau of the Census, *Census of Religious Bodies: 1926, vol. I*, 575; Papers Relating to the Portland, Oregon, Jewish Population Census, March 1947, Tables I & II, WJHS.

80. Minutes, B'nai B'rith Lodge 65, 11 September 1925; 13 November 1929; 8 January 1930, B'nai B'rith Papers, OC.

81. Minutes, Executive Committee, Lodge 65, 5 December 1929. Treasurer's reports for 1927 and 1928 show decline in membership from 760 to 681, in receipts from initiation fees from $454 to $200. Minutes, Lodge 65, 24 September and 8 and 22 October 1930; Chairman, Entertainment Committee, to Mr. Tonkon (and 24 other "leading members"), 3 October 1930, B'nai B'rith Papers, OC.

82. Minutes, Lodge 65, 24 September and 8 and 22 October 1930; Ralph Herzog to 12 members, asking them to telephone 15 members each asking for full attendance at the meeting that night (no date, circa late 1930), B'nai B'rith Papers, OC.

83. Minutes, Executive Committee, Lodge 65, 12 July 1928, B'nai B'rith Papers, OC.

84. Ralph Herzog to Ben S. Backman, 20 March, 1930, J. L. Asher to Harry Kenin, 20 May 1930, B'nai B'rith Papers, OC; B'nai B'rith Lodge 65, Minute Book, 3 January 1933, B'nai B'rith Papers, WJHS.

85. Minutes, B'nai B'rith Lodge 65, 1 February 1927, B'nai B'rith Papers, OC.

86. Hertzberg, *Strangers within the Gate City*, 39-42; Jonathan Mesinger, "The Jewish Community in Syracuse, 1850-1880: The Growth and Structure of an Urban Ethnic Region," Ph.D. dissertation, Syracuse Univ., New York, 1977; Marc Raphael, "The Utilization of Public Local and Federal Sources for Reconstructing American Jewish Local History: The Jews of Columbus, Ohio," *American Jewish Historical Quarterly*, LXV (September 1975), 13, 29-32; Mitchell Gelfand, "Jewish Economic and Residential Mobility in Early Los Angeles," *Western States Jewish Historical Quarterly*, XI (July 1979), 338; Vorspan and Gartner, *History of Jews of Los Angeles*, 128; Arcadus Kahan, "Economic Opportunities and Some Pilgrims' Progress: Jewish Immigrants from Eastern Europe in the United States, 1890-1914," *Journal of Economic History*, XXXVIII (March 1978): 237-51.

87. Sidney Goldstein and Calvin Goldscheider, *Jewish Americans: Three Generations in a Jewish Community* (Englewood Cliffs, NJ.: 1968), 49-60; Ernst Krausz, "The Edgware Survey: Occupation and Social Class," *JJS*, XI (June 1969): 86-98; Vorspan and Gartner, *Jews of Los Angeles*, 118, 203.

88. Because in this analysis we are interested in the impact of new leadership on social cohesiveness, mobility data for individuals will be subordinated to the changing profile of the lodge.

89. Hertzberg, *Strangers within the Gate City*, 100-1.

90. Griffen, *Natives and Newcomers*, 180-84.

91. Darrel J. Vorwaller, "Social Mobility and Membership in Voluntary Associations," *American Journal of Sociology*, LXXV (January 1970), 488; Harold Wilensky, "Orderly Careers and Social Participation: The Impact of Work History and Social Integration in the Middle Mass," *American Sociological Review*, XXVI (August 1961), 522.

92. *Thirteenth Census of the United States, 1910; IV. Population, Occupation Statistics* (Washington: 1913), 194 (Table III); *Fifteenth Census of the United States: 1930 Population; IV. Occupation by States* (Washington: 1933), 1358.

93. "J. Jerome Berg," interview, 6 March 1976, pp. 1-4.

94. Daniel D. Luria, "Wealth, Capital and Power: The Social Meaning of Home Ownership," *Journal of Interdisciplinary History*, VII (Autumn 1976), 268-70, for the argument that home ownership retards social mobility because it ties potential capital into an assest that does not control labor power. Most of Portland's Jews who acquired homes were small entrepreneurs and professionals seeking stability and security, not control over labor.

95. Howard Chudakoff, *Mobile American, Residential and Social Mobility in Omaha, 1880-1920* (New York: 1972), 159; Thernstrom, *Other Bostonians*, 98-101; Sam B. Warner, Jr., *Streetcar Suburbs: The Process of Growth in Boston, 1870-1900* (Cambridge, Mass.: 1962), 79-80, notes how the location of churches slowed the movement from adjacent blocks.

96. Charles F. Gould, "Portland Italians, 1880-1920," *Oregon Historical Quarterly*, LXXVII (September 1976): 247-53.

97. Ronald H. Bayor, *Neighbors in Conflict: The Irish, Germans, Jews and Italians of New York City, 1929-1941* (Baltimore: 1978), 152; Gartner, *Jews of Cleveland*, 268-70; Vorspan and Gartner, *Jews of Los Angeles*, 117-18, 203.

98. Ahavai Shalom membership list in minute book, 1919, traced through city directories.

99. Neveh Tzedek prominent members listed in *Scribe*, 18 December 1931.

100. Linath Hatzedek members listed in Linath Hatzdek Ledger, 1913-1926, WJHC.

101. Sephardic Jews listed in *Dedication Program, Congregation Ahavath Achim, Sunday, June 5, 1966* (Portland, 1966), WJHS.

102. Keneth Roseman, "American Jewish Community Institutions in Their Historical Context," *JJS*, XVI (June 1974): 25-38.

5. An Entrenched Middle Class and a Politicized Ethnicity, 1930-1945

1. Ronald H. Bayor, *Neighbors in Conflict: The Irish, Germans, Jews and Italians of New York City, 1929-1941* (Baltimore: 1978); St. Clair Drake and Horace R. Cayton, *Black Metropolis: A Study of Negro Life in a Northern City* (New York, 1962 ed.); H. Viscount Nelson, *The Philadelphia N.A.A.C.P.: Epitome of Middle Class Consciousness*, Afro-American Studies Professional Paper, 1972, Center for Afro-American Studies, UCLA.

2. Daniel D. Luria, "Wealth, Capital, and Power: The Social Meaning of Home Ownership," *Journal of Interdisciplinary History*, VII (Autumn 1976): 261-82, sees home ownership not as a means to acquire capital, but as a retreat to security. The tendencies described in this chapter generally verify his observation. Deborah D. Moore, *At Home in America, Second Generation New York Jews* (New York, 1981), strangely ignores the Depression and its effects even on the middle class.

3. "J. Jerome Berg," interview, 6 March 1976, 4, JHSO.

4. "Harold Hirsch," interview, 7 and 26 July, 10, 11 and 13 August, and 14 December 1977; 14 March 1978, p. 18, JHSO; Miriam Sandrow to author, 17 December 1980, letter in possession of author.

5. "Frieda Gass Cohen," interview, 25 April 1975, p. 5, JHSO. Information on the business reverses of Cohen and Goldstein, in the minutes of the board meetings of Beth Israel, 1 October 1931; 6 April 1932; 8 February 1934, Beth Israel Papers (microfilm), OHS.

6. "Judge Gus J. Solomon," interview, 16 February and 23 June 1976, pp. 9-10, JHSO.

7. "Gaulda Jermuloske Hahn," interview, 10 June 1980, 9; "Frieda Gass Cohen," 13.

8. Bayor, *Neighbors in Conflict*, 20.

9. Names of Jews were extracted from lists of those employed by the city in ledger books, stored in the basement of city hall. Changes in employment levels are noted in "Portland, Oregon, a Statistical Summary," unpaginated mimeographed

report, in Portland, Oregon, Chamber of Commerce Research Department, *Ten Studies and Surveys of Portland and Oregon, 1935,* OC.

10. "Report and Minutes of Meeting Unemployment Committee, January 23, 1930," Portland Chamber of Commerce Papers, OC.

11. Mrs. Miriam Sandrow to author, 26 May and 17 December 1980, letters in possession of author.

12. Stephen Thernstrom, *The Other Bostonians: Poverty and Progress in the American Metropolis, 1880-1970* (Cambridge, Mass.: 1974), 67 (Table 4.10), 73-74.

13. See Chapter 4, Table 27.

14. Papers relating to Portland, Oregon, Jewish Population Census, March 1947, manuscript summary of "Industrial Classification," WJHC.

15. Ben Selling to Uncle (Leo?), 29 April 1883; Selling to J. Fred Clarke & Company, 5 May 1883, Ben Selling Papers, OHS.

16. Stanley Buder, *Pullman: an Experiment in Industrial Order and Community Planning, 1880-1930* (New York: 1967), 103, 122, 214; Victor Greene, *For God and Country: The Rise of Polish and Lithuanian Consciousness in America* (Madison: 1975), 35, 39, 41-2.

17. The implications of many contemporary studies suggest that the separation of generations occurred after World War II. For example, Sidney Goldstein and Calvin Goldscheider, *Jewish Americans: Three Generations in a Jewish Community* (Englewood Cliffs, N.J.: 1968), 52 ff. indicates that large proportions of younger Jews moved to their suburban locations after World War II. While this is undoubtedly true, as Jeffrey Gurock has shown (*When Harlem Was Jewish, 1870-1930* (New York: 1979) 56), patterns of behavior often associated with one type of locale can take place elsewhere if social conditions are conducive. In the case of Portland, separation of the generations has occurred several times, in the 1890s for the Germans, and in the 1920s-1930s for the larger Eastern European groups. The move to areas beyond the city limits—which prevailed in Portland as in Providence during the 1950s and 1960s—extended but hardly initiated the more important social phenomenon of generational separation.

18. H. I. Chernichowsky, "Report," in *Observer* (1936), 15.

19. Average births for the years 1926-1930, 1931-1940, and 1941-1946 have been computed from "Papers relating to Portland, Oregon, Jewish Population Census, March, 1947," Table VIII; Portland's vital statistics are taken from "Portland, Oregon, a Statistical Summary," unpaginated. National data is taken from George Masnick and Mary Jo Bane, *The Nation's Families: 1960-1990* (Cambridge, Mass.: 1980), 41-48.

20. Enrollment data provided in Minutes, Congregation Ahavai Shalom, 15 October 1936; Congregation Neveh Shalom Archives; Beth Israel, Minutes, Board Meetings, 5 September 1935; 14 November 1934; H. I. Chernishowsky, "Report," *Observer* (1936): 15. The sex ratio of the graduates has been compiled from lists of graduates in *Observer* for the 1920s and 1930s.

21. Enrollment at the various branches of the Portland Hebrew School is noted in the annual reports of Principal H. I. Chernichowsky published in *Observer*. See also, Minutes, The Jewish Education Association of Portland, 23 May and 16 July 1929; 11 May 1933, and passim. In his report for 1939, Chernichowsky reported that

the East Side school could not collect a sufficient amount in tuition and donations to remain open.

22. Council of Jewish Women, Minutes, 30 April 1930; 29 April 1931; 30 April 1932.

23. Ibid., 5 November and 3 December 1930; 4 November and 30 December 1931.

24. Opportunity Bake Shop, "Minutes," 15 June 1937 (quotation); 1 November 1939; 31 January 1940.

25. "Report and Minutes of Meeting Unemployment Committee, January 23, 1930," Portland Chamber of Commerce Papers.

26. Opportunity Bake Shop, Minutes, 12 December 1935; 28 February 1940.

27. Ibid., 14 January 1937; 23 September 1936.

28. Ibid., 29 March 1939.

29. Ibid., 30 September 1935; 9 January and 13 February 1936.

30. Ibid., 28 September 1938.

31. Ibid., 26 January 1939.

32. Ibid., 28 May and 2 October 1941.

33. Ben Selling to David Bressler, 29 November 1907, Industrial Removal Office Papers, AJHS.

34. Ben Selling to Industrial Removal Office, 10 September 1917, IRO Papers. Data on employment located in *Portland City Directory, 1940* (Portland, 1940), 1502, and on home ownership, 2056. The reports on Mrs. Swerdlick, Mrs. Tinkleman, and the other women are filed on the last page of the Bake Shop Minute Book.

35. Note that Mrs. Marianne Kalisher, employed briefly at the Bake Shop, was an emigré from Germany. According to the social workers she had learned to be a machine operator and would no longer work at the shop. See Portland Committee on Emigres, Minute Book, 31 December 1939; 15 January 1940.

36. Beth Israel, Minute Book, 8 February, 8 March and 3 May 1923; 10 January 1924, 5 September and 2 October 1929; 6 November 1930.

37. Ahavai Shalom, Minute Book, 23 September 1920.

38. Ibid., 20 September 1921; 29 April 1922; 31 July 1924; 23 May 1926; 25 January 1928; Beth Israel, Minutes, 20 November 1920; 6 October 1924; 29 September 1927.

39. Alex E. Miller to the Officers and Members, Ahavai Shalom, 15 November 1925, in Minute Book, Ahavai Shalom.

40. Ahavai Shalom, Secretary's Report, 1925, showed receipts for the year of $9,526.25, and expenditures of $10,125.18. The same report, for 1928, showed receipts of $12,779.00 and expenditures of $12,969.75.

41. Ahavai Shalom, Minute Book, 21 and 25 November 1923; 7 January 1924; 2 November 1924.

42. Beth Israel, Minutes, 31 December 1923; 7 February, 27 May, 1 September, 15 October and 29 December 1924; 8 January 1925.

43. Ibid., 22 September 1926.

44. Report to the Congregation from the Building Committee, headed by Julius Meier and Max S. Hirsch, 13 May 1924, and speech of A. M. Eppstein, 22 September 1926, Beth Israel Minutes.

45. Ahvai Shalom, Minutes, 14 January and 2 May 1935; 14 April, 8 August, and 10 February 1938.

46. Beth Israel, Minutes, 24 October 1928.

47. Ibid., 22 December 1931; 3 March, and 6 October 1932; 4 January, 6 April, and 14 November 1934; 31 December 1939.

48. Ahavai Shalom, Minutes, 15 October 1936.

49. Mrs. Miriam Sandrow to author, 13 June 1980, letter in possession of author.

50. Beth Israel, Minutes, 3 November 1932; 4 January and 6 April 1934.

51. Ibid., 16 May 1935; 16 May 1938; 22 December 1931.

52. Ibid., 6 April and 11 and 26 May 1932.

53. Ibid., 11 January 1935.

54. Ibid., 18 October 1934; 11 January and 18 April 1935; 9 April and 7 and 21 October 1936; 7 January and 4 November 1937; 6 October 1938; 13 February 1939.

55. Ibid., 6 June 1938; B'nai B'rith Lodge 65, Minutes, 20 July 1938, WJHC.

56. Beth Israel, Minutes, 11 January, 5 September, and 7 November 1935; 6 February, 9 April, and 21 October 1936; 11 February and 4 November 1937; 8 December 1938.

57. Ibid., 6 May 1932; 8 May 1933; 14 November 1934; 13 January, 31 March, and 1 September 1938; 7 December 1939.

58. Ibid., 16 December 1937.

59. Ibid., 22 April 1937; 1 September 1938; 6 April 1939.

60. Editorial, *Scribe,* I (10 October 1919), p. 1.

61. Horace M. Kallen to Stephen Wise, 26 July 1933; Kallen to Wise, 15 October 1934; Kallen to Martin Weitz, 15 November 1934; Kallen to Stephen Wise, 19 October 1935; Horace M. Kallen Papers, YIVO Institute; Bayor, *Neighbors in Conflict,* 68.

62. B'nai B'rith Lodge 65, Minutes, 5 February and 10 March 1936; 23 February 1937.

63. Ibid., 25 April 1935; 22 January and 1 January 1939.

64. Ibid., 3 January 1933; 25 May 1937.

65. H. I. Chernichowsky, "Report," *Observer,* 1937, p. 15, and 1938, p. 17. In the former year Chernichowsky wrote, "In the concept of Jewish education, Palestine is occupying an increasingly greater part. The Palestine ideal is all-embracing. It claims the revitalization of the entire people, its language and culture on our historical soil. This ideal is being utilized to fire our youth with the enthusiasm of service for such a great cause." In 1938, he added, "The schools are the agencies that maintain Jewish culture and justify Jewish existence as an *ethnic group."*

66. William Toll, "Mobility, Fraternalism and Jewish Cultural Change: Portland, 1910-1930," *AJH,* LXVIII (June 1979), 465.

67. B'nai B'rith Lodge 65, Minutes, 7 and 28 March 1933; Mrs. Miriam Sandrow to author, 13 June 1980, letter in possession of author.

68. Mrs. Miriam Sandrow to author, 13 June 1980.

69. B'nai B'rith Lodge 65, Minutes, 10 May 1933.

70. Ibid., 12 August and 4 November 1935; 13 May and 24 June 1936.

71. Ibid., 12 October 1938; 22 October 1940; Richard Neuberger to Milton

Mayer, 5 October 1939; Neuberger to George R. Leighton, 15 November 1939; Neuberger to Mrs. Nathan Harris (President, Portland Woman's Peace Council), 11 May 1940; Neuberger to Robert S. Allen, 16 May 1940; Richard Neuberger Papers, OC.

72. B'nai B'rith Lodge 65, Minutes, 27 March and 9 October 1935; 23 September 1936; 10 May 1939; Beth Israel, Minutes, 13 February 1939. Conditions in New York are discussed in detail in Bayor, *Neighbors in Conflict*, 15, 26, 31, 84, 98, 155-57.

73. "Gus Solomon," interview, 9-10; "Harold Hirsch," interview, 28; "Max Simons," interview, 6-7.

74. Richard Neuberger to Bailey Stortz, 13 September 1941, and letters on the same day to John Robertson (secretary to Senator George Norris), Morris H. Rubin (editor, *Progressive*), Oswald Garrison Villard to Neuberger, 19 September 1941, Neuberger Papers. See also Miriam Sandrow to author, 30 January 1981.

75. B'nai B'rith Lodge 65, Minutes, 27 November 1935; 27 October 1937.

76. Kurt Schlesinger, interview, 16 June 1977, 5 (quotation), and story of his experiences under the Nazis, 36. More harrowing stories were brought to Portland by the survivors of the concentration camps. Two compelling accounts are those of "Diana Galanta Golden," interview, 21 September, 24 November, and 10 and 20 December 1975; and Lydia "Libbey" L. Brown and Bernard "Barry" Brown, interview, 26 November and 14 December 1975, JHSO.

77. Portland Committee on Emigres, Minute Book, 5 August 1936.

78. Ibid., 25 September 1937; 16 January and 27 March 1940.

79. Ibid., 28 March and 16 May 1939.

80. Ibid., 27 November 1939.

81. Ibid., 31 May and 31 October 1938; 16 May 1939; Schlesinger, interview, 11.

82. Portland Committee on Emigres, Minute Book, 25 September and 9 December 1937.

83. Schlesinger, interview, 17.

84. Portland Committee on Emigres, Minute Book, 28 March 1939.

85. Schlesinger, interview, 11. By 1940, the Schlesingers had moved to an apartment a block away at 2164 NW Hoyt Street. Those among the emigrés residing at the Cecelia in 1940 were Bruno and Louise Linde, Edmund and Marian Kalisher, Peter and Claire Opton, Arthur and Maria Pollack, and Harry and Herta Sichel.

86. Schlesinger, interview, 11.

87. John H. Miller, interview, 10 and 17 August 1976, 10-11; Portland Committee on Emigres, Minute Book, 16 January 1940.

88. Portland Committee on Emigres, Minute Book, 16 January 1940.

89. Ibid., 9 July 1940; Opportunity Bake Shop, Minute Book, 27 March 1940; B'nai B'rith Lodge 65, Minutes, 27 March 1940.

90. Ibid., 13 July, 8 September, and 29 November 1938; 23 January 1939; 27 January and 9 June 1941.

91. Nineteen emigres have been located in the 1940 city directory, of whom fourteen, including two widows, were still in Portland in 1950. In addition, three persons not located in the 1940 directory were found in the 1950 directory. Among

the seventeen individuals or couples, four were employees, one was an agent for the Mutual Benefit Life Insurance Company, six owned small markets, one was a physician, and one was a lawyer.

92. Portland Committee on Emigres, Minute Book, 27 September 1940.

93. The minutes of the Committee resume on 3 April 1947 and continue through December 1948.

94. B'nai B'rith Lodge 65, Minutes, 12 May 1937.

95. Richard Neuberger to E. Sheltin Hill, 24 October 1946, Neuberger Papers; David Robinson to Wayne Mores, 29 August 1950, Wayne Mores Papers, OC; Gus Solomon, interview, 17-20.

96. Lloyd P. Gartner, History of the Jews of Cleveland (Cleveland, 1978): 296; Goldstein and Goldscheider, Jewish Americans, 49-52; Ernest Krausz, "The Edgware Survey: Demographic Results," JJS, X (June 1968): 88-89.

Conclusion

1. Moses Rischin, "The Jews and Pluralism: Toward an American Freedom Symphony," (New York: Institute on Pluralism and Group Identity, 1980), 2, 6.

2. Martin Cohen, "Structuring American Jewish History," American Jewish Historical Quarterly, LVII (December 1967): 139-40.

3. Michael R. Marrus, The Politics of Assimilation: A Study of the French Jewish Community at the Time of the Dreyfus Affair (Oxford: 1971), 30-34; Fritz Stern, Gold and Iron: Bismark, Bleichroder and the Building of the German Empire (New York: 1977), 162; Judith L. Elkin, "Goodnight Sweet Gaucho: A Revisionist View of the Jewish Agricultural Experiment in Argentina," American Jewish Historical Quarterly, LXVII (March 1978): 210.

4. E. P. Thompson, The Making of the English Working Class (New York: 1964 ed.); Herbert Gutman, Work, Culture and Society in Industrializing America (New York: 1976), 3-78.

5. Sidney Goldstein and Calvin Goldscheider, Jewish Americans: Three Generations in a Jewish Community (Englewood Cliffs, N.J.: 1968), 1-6; Steven Hertzberg, Strangers within the Gate City: The Jews of Atlanta, 1845-1915 (Philadelphia: 1978), 4-6.

6. Deborah Dash Moore, At Home in America: Second Generation in New York Jews (New York: 1981).

7. Jeffrey Gurock, When Harlem Was Jewish, 1870-1930 (New York: 1979), 159-63.

8. Louis Wirth, The Ghetto (Chicago: 1928), 180, 188, 190-93, 195-264.

9. Gurock, When Harlem Was Jewish, 86-113.

10. Hertzberg, Strangers within the Gate City, 139-54; Marc Lee Raphael, Jews and Judaism in a Midwestern Community: Columbus, Ohio, 1840-1975 (Columbus, Ohio: 1979), 25-31, 109-37, 157-68.

11. Caroline Golab, Immigrant Destinations (Philadelphia: 1977), 132-34; Maxwell Whiteman. "Philadelphia's Jewish Neighborhoods," in Allen F. Davis and Mark

H. Haller, *The Peoples of Philadelphia: A History of Ethnic Groups and Lower-Class Life, 1790-1940* (Philadelphia: 1973), 232-36; Edward R. Kantowicz, *Polish-American Politics in Chicago, 1888-1940* (Chicago: 1975), 117; John Bodnar, *Immigration and Industrialization, Ethnicity in an American Mill Town, 1870-1940* (Pittsburgh: 1977), 102.

12. Moses Rischin, *The Promised City: New York's Jews, 1870-1914* (New York: 1964), 220-57.

Index